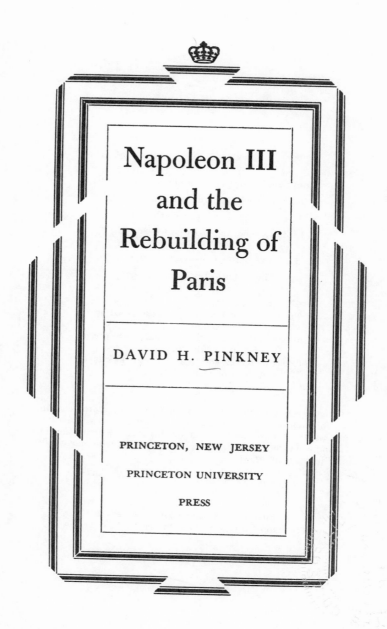

Napoleon III and the Rebuilding of Paris

DAVID H. PINKNEY

PRINCETON, NEW JERSEY

PRINCETON UNIVERSITY

PRESS

Copyright © 1958 by Princeton University Press

L.C. Card: 58-6108

ISBN 0-691-00768-3 (paperback edn.)

ISBN 0-691-05136-4 (hardcover edn.)

First PRINCETON PAPERBACK Edition, 1972

Third Hardcover Printing, 1972

Publication of this book has been aided by
the Ford Foundation program
to support publication, through university presses,
of works in the humanities
and social sciences, and by the Research Council
of the University of Missouri.

Printed in the United States of America
by Princeton University Press, Princeton, New Jersey

PREFACE

HE WHO ASPIRES TO WRITE THE HISTORY OF PARIS during the years of the Second Empire eventually meets with an obstacle left in his path by the Communards of 1871. When they withdrew across the city before the advancing troops of the national government they set fire to many buildings, among them the City Hall and the old and the new buildings of the Prefecture of Police. In those fires perished the municipal and departmental manuscript sources of the Paris of Napoleon III and Baron Haussmann. The loss is in a sense irreparable, but happily other sources still exist, and from them the story of these two momentous decades in Parisian history can be written. The archives of the national parliament, where Parisian affairs were often discussed, and of the national ministries concerned with Paris are now in the French National Archives. Printed reports and other papers of the municipal government survive in many collections as do contemporary memoirs, guides, newspapers and periodicals, and books.

For the means to use these scattered sources I am indebted to the Social Science Research Council and to the Research Council of the University of Missouri. I gratefully acknowledge travel and research grants from both councils that made possible two periods of research in Paris, a semester of leave from academic duties, the acquisition of sources in reproduction, and the employment of research assistants. The latter council and the Ford Foundation made generous grants toward the cost of publication.

A number of individuals, too, contributed to the completion of this book, and I am grateful to all of them, particularly to Donald McKay of the Department of History, Amherst College; Shepherd Clough of the Department of History, Columbia University; Donald Egbert of the Department of Art and Archaeology, Princeton University; my colleagues Noel Gist of the Department of Sociology and Charles Mullett of the Department of History, University of Missouri; and in France, Louis Chevalier, Professor of the History of Paris and the Parisian Region in the *Collège de France*; Michel Roussier, Librarian of the *Bibliothèque administrative de la Préfecture de la Seine*; Paul Leuilliot of the *Ecole pratique des Hautes Etudes*; and Louis Girard of the University of Paris. I here record my warm thanks to all of them and to the editors of the *Journal of Modern History*, published by the University of Chicago Press, and the *Journal of Economic History*, published by the New York University Press, for permission to use parts of my articles in those journals, to John F. Pinkney for his professional guidance on questions of engineering involved in my subject, to Helen Reisinger Pinkney, who read and listened to the manuscript in many shapes and forms, and to R. Miriam Brokaw of the Princeton University Press.

D.H.P.

Columbia, Missouri
April 1957

A NOTE ON PLANS OF PARIS

Readers interested in consulting more detailed city plans of Paris than can be included in this book are referred to Département de la Seine, *Les Grands Travaux de Paris, 1789-1889; Atlas* (Paris, 1889); Charles Merruau, *Souvenirs de l'Hôtel de Ville de Paris, 1848-1852* (Paris, 1875), plan facing page 496; and contemporary Galignani and Baedeker guidebooks to Paris.

CONTENTS

PREFACE vii

I PARIS IN 1850 3

II THE PLAN AND THE MEN 25

III FROM PLANS TO PAVEMENTS 49

IV BUILDINGS AND PARKS 75

V A BATTLE FOR WATER 105

VI PARIS UNDERGROUND 127

VII THE CITY GROWS 151

VIII MONEY AND POLITICS 174

IX PARIS IN 1870 AND AFTER 210

BIBLIOGRAPHY 223

INDEX 233

ix

ILLUSTRATIONS

List of Plates following page 116

1. A typical narrow street of old Paris
2. The Boulevard Richard Lenoir
3. Cross section of a Parisian house about 1850
4. Water pumping station on the Pont Nôtre-Dame, 1852
5. The cartoonist Cham comments on the towers erected for the triangulation of Paris
6. "But this is where I live—and I don't even find my wife."
7. "Good! There's another house being pulled down. I'm going to raise all my tenants' rents two hundred francs."
8. Demolitions for the Rue de Rennes
9. Demolitions for the Avenue de l'Opéra
10. The principal façade of the new Opera House
11. The architects' sketch of the Central Markets
12. Clearing of the area between the Louvre and the Tuileries, 1852
13. Ground plan of the Louvre and the Tuileries palaces
14. The Louvre and the Tuileries as completed by Napoleon III
15. The Ile de la Cité seen from the Right Bank, 1867
16. Typical Parisian apartment house erected during the Second Empire
17. Plan of the Bois de Boulogne after its transformation in the 1850's
18. Bird's eye view of the Park of the Buttes-Chaumont
19. Cholera protests to Haussmann that demolition of old houses in Paris has left him homeless
20. Construction workers mourn the dismissal of Haussmann

MAPS AND PLANS

Principal new streets in Paris built between 1850 and 1870, page 73
Principal public parks of Paris, 1870, page 103
Seine River Basin and the aqueducts built by Haussmann
and Belgrand, page 125
Collector sewers of Paris, 1870, page 149

NAPOLEON III
AND THE REBUILDING OF PARIS

"I WANT TO BE A SECOND AUGUSTUS," wrote Louis Napoleon Bonaparte in 1842 from his prison in the fortress of Ham, "because Augustus . . . made Rome a city of marble."[1] This nephew of the Emperor Napoleon, sentenced to life imprisonment for an attempt to overthrow the monarchy two years earlier, was hoping to revive the Empire, and he was also dreaming of rebuilding Paris as a city of marble befitting the new imperial France. In 1846 he escaped from prison, and in 1848 he returned to Paris to become the President of the Second Republic. A few years later he did restore the Empire, styling himself Napoleon III, and in the two decades after 1850 he rebuilt much of Paris.

The political edifice proved fragile, and in 1870 it collapsed beyond all hope of reconstruction, but the Paris he built remained. In the broad new boulevards and avenues, the public buildings, the parks and squares, the networks of water mains and sewers, he left a permanent impression on the city. By 1870 his public works had given Paris its present appearance. The white domes of Sacré-Coeur did not yet top the hill of Montmartre nor did the Eiffel Tower break the low line of buildings on the Left Bank. Horses had not yet surrendered the streets to automobiles nor gas street lights given way to electric lights, but the tree-lined boulevards, the broad avenues, the many public parks and squares, the monumental buildings terminating long vistas were all there in 1870; and together with public markets, aqueducts and reservoirs, and great collector sewers created at the same time they have continued to serve Paris to this day.

Far beyond Paris, too, Napoleon III and his Prefect of the

[1] A. des Cilleuls, *Histoire de l'administration parisienne au XIXe siècle* (Paris, 1900), II, 208.

Seine, Georges Haussmann, left an indelible mark. For half a century and more their work profoundly influenced the city planning and civic architecture of the European world. During the Second Empire and immediately after other French cities copied their construction of broad thoroughfares across old and crowded quarters. Lyon, Marseille, Toulouse, Rouen, Avignon, and Montpellier still bear in one or more wide and straight avenues the imprint of the capital's example. Brussels underwent a transformation in the 1860's and 1870's that gave the city new tree-lined boulevards, classical perspectives, and even a *bois* with a spacious avenue leading to it like the Avenue de l'Impératrice to the Bois de Boulogne in Paris. Rome, Stockholm, Barcelona, Madrid, all felt the influence of Napoleon's and Haussmann's work in the half century after 1870. The Emperor Maximilian carried their ideas across the Atlantic and in the Paseo de la Reforma in Mexico City gave the New World the first of its many copies of Parisian boulevards.

In the United States the boldness and magnitude of their conceptions had a special appeal during the confident decades following the Civil War. The city planners of the late nineteenth and early twentieth centuries, notably Daniel Burnham, Charles McKim, Frederick Law Olmsted, and others associated with the City Beautiful movement owed much to Louis Napoleon and Haussmann. Today one may see the influence of Second Empire Paris in contemporary Washington, replanned by Burnham and McKim, in Philadelphia's Benjamin Franklin Parkway, in Burnham's "Plan for Chicago" (out of which came the present lake front and Michigan Boulevard), and, to go no further, in Cleveland's Mall.

The rebuilding of Paris was an immense and complicated operation, and its history is not a simple narrative of plans, demolitions, and building but a complex story of architecture and engineering, slum clearance and sanitation, emigration and urban growth, legal problems of expropriation and human problems of high rents and evictions, public finance and high politics, dedicated men and profiteers. It involved planning on an unprecedented scale—parts of cities, even entire new cities like Versailles, Karlsruhe, or Saint-Petersburg, had been

planned and built, but no one before had attempted to re-
fashion an entire old city. It posed technical problems for
which there were no ready solutions—no accurate map of Paris
existed in 1850 and one had to be made, starting with triangulation of the whole city; no one knew how to measure underground sources of water supply; no one knew how to cut a
trench through sandy soil big enough for a sewer that was a
virtual underground river. The whole operation was constantly
complicated by a growing population (the city's inhabitants
nearly doubled in numbers in the 1850's and 1860's) that
intensified difficulties of housing, provisioning, and sanitation.
Costs were enormous. In 1869 Haussmann estimated the expenditure on rebuilding the city since 1850 at 2,500,000,000
francs, about forty-four times the city's outlay on all expenses
of government in 1851. An equivalent expenditure in New
York City today, forty-four times the expenditures in the
budget of 1956-57, would be $84,000,000,000. The city sought
to raise the money from existing taxes (it levied no new ones),
the resale of condemned property, subsidies from the national
government (which always involved a struggle with the provincial majority in the Legislative Body), and public loans,
but these means proved to be inadequate, and Haussmann re-
sorted to less orthodox methods of financing that opened to
political opponents of the Empire an avenue of attack upon the
whole imperial regime and brought the rebuilding of Paris
into national politics. In a democratic regime it would have
become a political issue much earlier. The transformation of
the city within two short decades probably would not have
been accomplished in a state less authoritarian than the Second
Empire.

The great rebuilding operation inevitably aroused opposition, and Haussmann, an aggressive and impatient man, did
little to allay it. Provincial interests objected to lavish expenditures on the capital, and timid souls in Paris and out, recalling
the Revolution of 1848, feared the growing proletarian population that public works attracted to the city. Conservative
banking houses objected to spending they regarded as inflationary. Residents in particular quarters protested against real

or fancied neglect of their neighborhoods. Condemnation of property for new boulevards and streets that cut across built-up areas disturbed established property rights and emotional attachments. Proprietors usually received generous indemnities, but thousands of tenants were forced by demolitions and rising rents to leave familiar quarters in the old city and live in peripheral areas. For the hundreds who were dissatisfied, however, there were thousands who profited directly from the expenditures of the city (almost 20 per cent of the Parisian labor force was employed in the building trades at the height of the construction boom in the middle sixties) and thousands more who recognized the civic value of new streets, parks, sewers, and water supply. Orleanist and Republican opposition tried to exploit the discontent but without notable success until the latter 1860's, when they learned of Haussmann's unorthodox financial methods. Then the opposition drummed on "the fantastic accounts of Haussmann" as proof of the imperial regime's extravagance, incompetence, and irresponsibility, and momentarily they enjoyed success, forcing Haussmann from office in 1870 and slowing public works almost to a stop.

But the magnitude of Napoleon's and Haussmann's accomplishment in rebuilding the old city into a model for the world to admire and copy was not long obscured. No one who recalled the Paris of 1850 and contrasted it with the Paris of 1870 could lightly dismiss their work. Napoleon III's Paris of 1870 would be familiar to anyone who knows Paris of the 1950's, but the Paris of 1850, in which Napoleon III began his work of reconstruction, was more akin to the half medieval city of the eighteenth century. When Charles Dickens described a poor quarter of Paris before the Revolution in *A Tale of Two Cities*, published in 1859, he had only to recall the slums he had known there in the late forties and early fifties.

This Paris of 1850 betrayed centuries of existence behind a ring of fortified walls. The first fortifications, built by Philip Augustus at the end of the twelfth century, enclosed only about 600 acres immediately opposite the islands on both sides of the river. In the next four centuries the walls on the Right Bank were twice moved outward, but by 1650 they were still only on the line of the present Rue Royale and the inner boulevards (the boulevards des Capucines, des Italiens, and the others that extend the line eastward to the Place de la Bastille), and enclosed but 1400 acres. Louis XIV, more secure than his predecessors, demolished much of the fortified wall, but a century later the government raised a new ring around the capital, this one *not* to protect the citizens of Paris against foreign enemies but to protect tax farmers against the Parisians. The farmers had contracted to collect the *octroi*, a levy on goods entering the city, and even in the eighteenth century Parisians were skillful at tax evasion. This "Wall of the Fermiers-généraux," broken by sixty gates, encircled Paris on the present second ring of boulevards, and in 1850 with but one minor change it still marked the legal limits of the city. In the 1840's a timid government fearful of the renewal of the anti-Napoleonic coalition against France threw a new ring of fortifications around the capital, but lying generally about a mile beyond the tax wall it was not yet confining in 1850.

The royal governments discouraged construction of buildings outside the city's walls, and as the population waxed, the city instead of expanding outward had grown by crowding ever more people into the central quarters. Houses were raised story above story. Gardens and open spaces were built over, courtyards omitted, little more than wagon tracks left for streets. By 1850 the area within the inner ring of boulevards on the Right Bank, the seventeenth century line of fortifications, was an almost impenetrable hive of tenements and shops. Here in an area not twice the size of New York City's Central Park, piled one above another in rooms or tiny apartments, lived more than one-third of the city's one million inhabitants. The density of the population was higher than on the lower East Side of New York in the 1930's.[2]

This concentration of Parisians was more oppressive than one familiar only with twentieth century Paris might assume, for in 1850 few parks and open spaces relieved the overcrowding. In prosperous quarters private gardens, more common

[2] David H. Pinkney, "Napoleon III's Transformation of Paris: The Origins and Development of the Idea," *Journal of Modern History*, XXVII (1955), 128.

then than at present, offered some relief to the well-to-do, but there were no municipal parks except the dusty Champs Elysées and the Place des Vosges. A few nationally owned gardens were ordinarily open to the public: the south bank of the river had the Luxembourg Garden and the Jardin des Plantes, but on the Right Bank only the Tuileries Garden broke the built-up area, and it was on the edge of the heavily populated districts. The center and east end of Paris were without adequate public parks. The garden of the Palais Royal and the tree-lined boulevards provided touches of greenery in the city, but in 1850 many of the trees were gone, cut down in 1848 for barricades. The forty-eighters' subsequent ventures in tree planting, some one hundred "trees of liberty" scattered haphazardly about the city, were never a real replacement, and most of them had died before the spring of 1849.[3]

In the crowded areas enclosed by the inner boulevards of the Right Bank lay some of the city's worst slums. Late in the Empire the republicans blamed Napoleon III and his Prefect of the Seine, Baron Haussmann, for having created the slums of eastern Paris. Demolition of old houses in the central and western quarters had, they claimed, expelled the poor from these sections and concentrated them in the neglected eastern quarters and suburbs. Mixing memory with fancy they depicted Paris of the good old days before Napoleon III as a city where all social classes lived happily side by side in all parts of the city. Distinctions in wealth were reflected in the floors on which tenants lived, the poorer tenants occupying the lower-rent rooms on the top floors, the wealthy the large apartments on the second floor, and the moderately well-off the intermediate levels. A sense of solidarity united all the residents, and in times of distress the more prosperous tenants cared for the poorer.[4] It was a pretty picture with a small measure of truth in it. The social differences between quarters had been less marked in Paris than in London and perhaps other large cities, but the

---

[3] *Journal officiel de l'Empire français*, Supplément, May 1869, p. 7 (hereafter cited as *J.O.*); Charles Merruau, *Souvenirs de l'Hôtel de Ville de Paris, 1848-1852* (Paris, 1875), pp. 287-88, 356-57.

[4] *J.O.*, Mar. 6, 1869.

mixture of classes and fortunes was breaking down well before Napoleon III's time. An American resident observed in 1850 that in the high apartment buildings the tenants never knew their neighbors, and the English novelist, Edward Bulwer Lytton, had the same experience. Certainly the supposed mutual understanding had not prevented the bitter class warfare of June 1848.[5]

Class quarters did exist in Paris at mid-century, and the poorest of them were dismal slums. In the crowded center of the city eastward from the Church of Sainte-Eustache and the Rue Montmartre rose a mass of ancient and decaying tenements, ordinarily five or more stories high, without courtyards, and with frontages of only some twenty feet. The streets were narrow and winding. Many had no sidewalks, and they were usually wet from the open sewers that ran in the gutters. The sunlight seemed never to penetrate these dark caverns, and by night peaceful citizens avoided them. Here, especially in the streets near the Rue Saint-Denis, in miserable furnished rooms rented by the night lived the outcasts and the disinherited of Paris, men and women without fixed abode or occupation, living by theft and prostitution. Yet this same section of Paris was a part of the city's principal industrial district, which extended eastward beyond the boulevards into the old faubourgs. From thousands of tiny shops and the dark rooms of piece-workers poured forth a stream of clothing, jewelry, artificial flowers, bronze and gold work famous throughout the fashionable world.[6]

But while these crowded quarters produced wealth they also bred disease and social unrest. The death rates here and in the slums of the southeast were the highest in the city. Here the epidemics of cholera that plagued Paris in the nineteenth century usually had their beginnings and their heaviest inci-

[5] Merruau, *Souvenirs*, pp. 330, 353-55; Catherine Gore, *Paris in 1841* (London, 1842), pp. 244-45; J. J. Jarves, *Parisian Sights and French Principles* (N.Y., 1852), pp. 8-12; Edward Bulwer Lytton, *Night and Morning* (Philadelphia, 1879).

[6] Pinkney, "Napoleon III's Transformation of Paris," pp. 128-29; Paris, Chambre de Commerce, *Statistique de l'industrie à Paris . . . pour les années 1847-1848* (Paris, 1851), Part I, pp. 82-190; *Moniteur universel*, Jan. 2-3, 1851.

dence, and here were the strongholds of revolutionary resistance in 1830, in 1834, in 1839, and again in 1848.[7]

The entire east end of Paris was a working class district, and within this half of Paris the slums were not confined to the area enclosed by the inner boulevards. The peripheral sixth and eighth arrondissements had sections of extreme poverty comparable to those around the Rue Saint-Denis, and the center of the Ile de la Cité between the Palace of Justice and the cathedral was another blemish on the city's face, a maze of dark and twisting streets. "The mud colored houses," wrote Eugène Sue, "broken by a few worm-eaten window frames, almost touched at the eaves, so narrow were the streets. Black, filthy alleys led to steps even blacker and more filthy and so steep that one could climb them only with the help of a rope attached to the damp wall by iron brackets."[8] Fourteen thousand people lived within the narrow confines of the island, and, Sue recorded, it swarmed with "released convicts, thieves, murderers. When a crime is committed the police cast a net into these depths and almost always drag out the guilty persons."[9] In the years of the cholera, 1832 and 1849, the death rate on this little island was exceeded in only two other quarters among the forty-eight into which Paris was divided.[10]

The fashionable residential districts were already in the western half of the city: in the neighborhood of the Rue de la Paix and the Rue de la Chaussée d'Antin and along the Rue Saint-Honoré on the Right Bank and in the Faubourg Saint-Germain across the river. Even these wealthy districts frequently adjoined surprising islands of slums. One lay between the Rue de Richelieu and the present Avenue de l'Opéra, and just to the west of the present Gare Saint-Lazare around the Place de Laborde was a center of vagrants as bad as anything in the east end. Another slum had risen in the most unlikely spot of all—in the space between the Louvre and the courtyard

7 Département de la Seine, *Recherches statistiques sur la ville de Paris et le département de la Seine* (Paris, 1826-60), VI, 457, 677; Merruau, *Souvenirs*, pp. 184-88, 198-99.
8 Eugène Sue, *Les Mystères de Paris* (New edit., Paris, [n.d.]) I, 1-2.
9 *Ibid.*, I, 1.
10 Seine, *Recherches statistiques*, VI, 457.

of the Tuileries Palace.[11] Balzac spoke of it as "one of those protests against common sense that Frenchmen love to make." Clearing of the area was started in 1849, but in 1850 most of it remained untouched. Balzac described the appearance of a part of it during the July Monarchy:

Beyond the little gate that leads from the Carrousel bridge to the Rue du Musée, anyone visiting Paris . . . is bound to notice a dozen houses with dilapidated façades, whose discouraged landlords have not troubled to repair them. . . .

· · · · · ·

In passing this dead wedge and happening to notice the Impasse du Doyenne, one experiences a chilling of the soul, and wonders who could possibly live in such a place, and what goes on there at night, when the alley becomes an ambush, and where the vices of Paris, wrapped in the mantle of the night, are given full scope.[12]

"Our grandsons will refuse to believe," he added, "that such a piece of barbarism existed for thirty-six years in the heart of Paris. . . ."

In sharp contrast with crowded quarters of the center was the present west end of Paris. Beyond the Rond Point des Champs Elysées and the Place de Laborde only the lines of houses along the principal streets, such as the Avenue des Champs Elysées and the Rue du Faubourg Saint-Honoré, and a few scattered structures marred the open fields and woods. North of the Gare Saint-Lazare the Quartier de l'Europe, laid out in lots in the 1820's, remained deserted a quarter of a century later, and the Park of Monceau was "returning to virgin forest," its environs almost uninhabited. To the south, Passy, part of the present fashionable Sixteenth Arrondissement, was only a rural retreat for Parisians seeking relief from the heat of summer in the city, and a guidebook described Auteuil, now in the same arrondissement, as "a charming village, a league to the west of Paris."[13]

On the south bank of the Seine lay a second maze of medieval

[11] Pinkney, "Napoleon III's Transformation of Paris," p. 129.
[12] Honoré de Balzac, "La Cousine Bette" in *Oeuvres complètes de Honoré de Balzac* (Paris, 1912-14), XVII, 61-62.
[13] Merruau, *Souvenirs*, p. 356; *Moniteur*, April 16, 1852, Feb. 19, 1853; Galignani, *New Paris Guide for 1851* (Paris, [1851]), p. 514.

streets like the labyrinth within the inner boulevards on the Right Bank. Vestiges of this old Left Bank still exist, and one familiar with the area between the Place Saint-Michel and the Rue Dauphine can imagine the appearance of much of the Left Bank a century ago. The fortifications had perhaps been even more confining on this side of the river than on the other, for Philip Augustus' wall had remained unchanged for nearly five centuries, and in 1850 a narrow belt extending less than a mile back from the river included nearly half the inhabitants of the Left Bank. Beyond it one came upon lightly settled streets and wide stretches of open fields still within the city's legal boundaries.[14]

At the eastern end of the Left Bank the Bièvre River, now covered over in its course through the city and almost unknown, had attracted a variety of industrial plants that required water for their operations, and from its entrance into the city at the present Boulevard Auguste Blanqui to its confluence with the Seine above the Pont d'Austerlitz, the stream was bordered by a succession of tanneries, launderies, and chemical works. Adjoining this industrial district on the north, between the Jardin des Plantes and the Rue Saint-Jacques, lay another conspicuously blighted area. In the eighteenth century the residents of this benighted district were scarcely thought of as Parisians, and the taunt of having learned one's manners in the Place Maubert was a French, eighteenth century equivalent of having been born in a barn. When Victor Hugo, in *Les Misérables*, wanted to emphasize the extremity to which Marius had sunk after his grandfather cut him off he placed him here in a lodging house on the Boulevard de l'Hôpital. Like the slums of the Right Bank the district was made up of narrow streets lined with rented lodgings in which misery found a refuge and crime a breeding ground. In the cholera epidemic of 1832 the two quarters that included this slum area were among the half

14 Départment de la Seine, *Résultats statistiques du dénombrement de 1896 pour la ville de Paris et le département de la Seine* (Paris, 1899), p. 438; Galignani, *Guide for 1851*, p. 46; Jarves, *Parisian Sights*, p. 63; *Siècle* (Paris), Aug. 26, Dec. 20, 1847, June 7, 8, 1858; *Moniteur*, Nov. 30, 1857.

dozen quarters with the highest death rates, and in the epidemic of 1849 one of them again stood equally high among the quarters most seriously affected.[15]

Scarcely a fourth of the population of Paris lived on the Left Bank, and this part of the city had grown less rapidly than the Right Bank in the first half of the century. Property owners protested that the national and the city governments had neglected their side of the river while lavishing expenditures on the opposite bank, attracting residents away from the Left Bank and depreciating property values. Until 1848 toll bridges owned and operated by private concessionaires hampered free movement between the two banks. Of the sixteen bridges across the Seine within Paris in 1848 only six were free, and four of these served only the old city opposite the islands. If a man wished to cross the river below the islands, he had the choice of the public Pont Royal by the Louvre, the Pont de la Concorde, or one of the toll bridges, but if he were above the islands he must pay a toll or go out of his way to the nearest free bridge, across the Ile Saint-Louis. The toll bridges were not popular, and in February, 1848, rioters destroyed the collection booths, and neither the owners nor the government dared reinstitute the tolls. In the succeeding two years the city bought back the concessions and thereafter maintained the bridges as part of the public way.[16]

Even with the tolls gone two of the bridges retained startling survivals of earlier centuries. The Pont Nôtre-Dame was disfigured by a water pumping station erected during the seventeenth century on wooden piles in mid-stream adjoining the bridge. Two rows of shops lined the sidewalks of the Pont Neuf. Louis XIV had originally authorized their establishment on condition that they be removed each night, but they soon became permanent fixtures and overran the sidewalks. Suppressed at one time in the eighteenth century, they were shortly reestab-

[15] *Moniteur*, Nov. 25, 1851; *Siècle*, June 8, 1858; Chambre de Commerce, *Statistique . . . 1847-1848*, Part I, pp. 82, 138, 143, 151, Part III, pp. 977, 981-83; Seine, *Recherches statistiques*, VI, 457; Léon Lesage, *Les Expropriations de Paris (1866-1890); 1er série, 1866-1870* (Paris, 1913), pp. 29-30.

[16] Merruau, *Souvenirs*, pp. 141-42; *Moniteur*, Aug. 19, 1851, Mar. 3, 1852.

lished and continued there until the city rebuilt the bridge in the 1850's.[17]

The toll bridges had handicapped free movement between the two banks, but they were minor obstacles to traffic compared with the medieval street system. Evolved in a city of a few tens of thousands, for pedestrians, sedan chairs, and horsemen, it was ill-suited for the carriages and wagons of a city of one million inhabitants. Except on the boulevards or along the quais, which offered only circuitous routes to most traffic, one could not on the Right Bank travel directly across the city from east to west. The Louvre, the Palais Royal, and the Bibliothèque Nationale lay like a long barricade athwart the western end of the inner city, and the maze of ancient streets and houses just to the east formed a second and broader barrier. Only two passages pierced the first. One, between the Louvre and the Palais Royal, was used by the Rue Saint-Honoré, the principal street from the western limits of the city, but once past this point it narrowed to the width of an alleyway and then ended in an impasse less than half a mile east of the Palais Royal. The Rue de Rivoli was to pass through the same break, but in 1850 this broad avenue, projected by the first Napoleon to cut across the entire city, ran only from the Place de la Concorde to a point about at the end of the present Avenue de l'Opéra. A quarter of a mile to the north the Rue des Petits-Champs led from the boulevards and the Rue de la Paix through the gap between the Palais Royal and the Bibliothèque Nationale, but ended at the central barrier just short of the Place des Victoires. The Rue Rambuteau, the principal contribution of Louis Philippe's regime to the solution of Paris' traffic problems, provided the only direct passage through the central labyrinth, but over most of its length it was only thirty feet wide (compared with the Rue de Rivoli's seventy-two feet and the boulevards' one hundred or more feet). Moreover, on the west it never got past the Church of Sainte-Eustache, and the narrow streets that continued it ran into the barrier of the Palais Royal.[18]

[17] *Moniteur*, Sept. 9, 1852; Eugène Belgrand, *Les Travaux souterrains de Paris* (Paris, 1873-77), III, 256-57, 290, 293.

[18] Galignani, *Guide for 1851*, attached street plan; Merruau, *Souvenirs*, pp. 343, 350-52; *Moniteur*, Dec. 11, 1867.

On the east of the city was a third barricade—the Canal Saint-Martin. Except at the quais and the Place de la Bastille and two other points the passages across it were only narrow bridges. In 1850 the area to the east was but thinly settled except near the river and traffic across the canal light, but should traffic increase serious bottlenecks would certainly develop.[19]

Movement from north to south on the Right Bank was almost as difficult as movement from east to west. Between the Place de la Concorde and the Place de la Bastille no wide street led from the boulevards to the quais. The Tuileries Garden, the Louvre (its courtyard still uncleared), and the labyrinthine streets of the center formed a rampart defending the approaches to the river. The Rue Saint-Denis and the Rue Saint-Martin, two ancient streets that continued royal highways from the north, penetrated this rampart and led to bridges across the Seine, but in their final courses they narrowed to a width of a few yards. The parallel Rue du Temple, another main thoroughfare, was the scene of frequent traffic jams, and it reached the Place de l'Hôtel de Ville and the Pont d'Arcole only through a bottleneck of two tiny passageways. One need only walk along the Rue du Temple or the Rue Saint-Denis today to be astonished and incredulous that these streets, wider now than in 1850, could ever have been main arteries through a city of a million inhabitants.[20]

On the Left Bank traffic was no better served. From L'Institut de France to the Pont d'Austerlitz no adequately broad thoroughfare cut southward through the heavily settled belt along the river. The Luxembourg Garden, the hill of Sainte-Geneviève, and the Jardin des Plantes were obstacles to traffic, and the streets that ran through the gaps were in some places scarcely wide enough to permit the passage of two wagons side by side. Other streets in the Latin Quarter were little better than *culs de sac*, at best like the Rue Dauphine, which carried traffic south from the Pont Neuf only to deposit it in the Carrefour de Buci, which lacked adequate outlet for the traffic that four converging streets poured into it, or like the Rue de

[19] Département de la Seine, *Les Travaux de Paris, 1789-1889; atlas* (Paris, 1889), Pl. XI; Galignani, *Guide for 1851*, p. 278.
[20] Galignani, *Guide for 1851*, street plan; Merruau, *Souvenirs*, pp. 350-52; *Moniteur*, June 23, 1851.

Tournon and the Rue de Seine, which, opposite the entrance to the Luxembourg Palace, started purposefully toward the Seine and ended ignominiously behind the Institute, one hundred yards short of the river.[21]

The Luxembourg Garden and Palace together with the Place de l'Odéon and its enclosing buildings formed a barrier to east-west movement. The Rue de Vaugirard, one of the ancient streets of Paris, led across the city from the southwest and passed between the palace and the Odéon Theater but ended abruptly not two hundred yards beyond. Between the Odéon and the river no major street connected the Latin Quarter on the east with the Faubourg Saint-Germain on the west, and the narrow streets that did wind across this section failed to connect conveniently with the more adequate thoroughfares of the Faubourg Saint-Germain.

The confused street pattern made even a short trip across the city a complex journey. Baron Haussmann, who as Prefect of the Seine later carried out Napoleon III's transformation of Paris, described the tortuous route he followed in his student days in the 1830's from his home on the Right Bank to the School of Law in the Latin Quarter:

Setting out at seven o'clock in the morning from the quarter of the Chaussée d'Antin, where I lived with my family, I reached first, after many detours, the Rue Montmartre and the Pointe Sainte-Eustache; I crossed the square of the Halles, then open to the sky, among the great red umbrellas of the fish dealers; then the rues des Lavandières, Saint-Honoré and Saint-Denis; . . . I crossed the old Pont au Change, which I was later to rebuild, lower, widen; I next walked along the ancient Palais de Justice, having on my left the filthy mass of pot-houses that not long ago disfigured the Cité. . . . Continuing my route by the Pont Saint-Michel, I had to cross the poor little square [Place Saint-Michel]. . . . Finally I entered into the meanders of the Rue de la Harpe to ascend the Montagne Sainte-Geneviève and to arrive by the passage de l'Hôtel d'Harcourt, the Rue des Maçons-Sorbonne, the Place Richelieu, the Rue de Cluny and the Rue des Grès, on the Place du Panthéon at the corner of the School of Law.[22]

[21] Galignani, *Guide for 1851*, street plan; Merruau, *Souvenirs*, pp. 352-53; *Moniteur*, Jan. 8, 1853.

[22] G. E. Haussmann, *Mémoires* (Paris, 1890-93), III, 535-36.

Haussmann might be suspected of exaggerating to emphasize the value of his subsequent work, but one will search a contemporary street plan in vain for a more direct route between the two terminal points.

Haussmann's long daily trek from home to work was, however, unusual in the Paris of his youth and even later. Parisians of a century ago ordinarily lived, worked, and found their pleasures within the confines of a few blocks, having yet to acquire that "dizzying idea" that Jules Romains noted among Parisians of the twentieth century that "they could move about just as they liked and that distance was the last thing that counted." Balzac's Jules and Sylvia Rogron living in Paris in the 1820's knew nothing of the city beyond their own street, and even a substantial citizen like César Birotteau in the normal routine of his life as businessman, deputy mayor, and judge never went beyond the inner boulevards and only rarely crossed the river. The next thirty years brought no change in common habits. Gervaise Macquart, the heroine of Zola's *L'Assommoir*, who came to Paris in 1850, lived first on the Boulevard de la Chapelle. After her marriage she moved to a lesser street nearby, later opened her laundry shop a few doors away, and when she had to give it up she took a room in the same building and lived there until her death in 1859. On only a few occasions did she leave the neighborhood. Following her marriage in the local mayor's office a member of the wedding party proposed a visit to the Louvre, and although they were all residents of Paris only one of the twelve in the party had ever been there, and their behavior on the walk to the Louvre and back betrayed that the center of Paris was strange to them.

Neither the wedding party nor Haussmann apparently ever considered taking a bus, although Paris had been served by public buses since 1828, and in 1850 had thirty lines (with fascinating names like Gazelles, Doves, and Reunited Women) and more than 300 buses. They were equipped, moreover, with cushioned seats, and every passenger was assured of one, for once all the places were filled no more riders were taken. But old habits were not likely to be broken down while the fare remained at 30 centimes, about one-tenth of an ordinary worker's daily wage in 1850, and while fashionable Parisians would not be seen on the public buses. In 1856, the first year for which information is recorded, the average number of fares paid by each of the city's residents during the entire year was only thirty-nine.[23]

This localized existence, contrasting so oddly with urban life today, appears less strange when considered against the pattern of Paris' streets in 1850. Continued toleration of such a system of streets reflected perhaps a distaste for movement, but the streets themselves discouraged mobility. And it was not only their dimensions and their aimlessness that dismayed the traveler. They were paved with nine inch cubes of sandstone whose edges quickly crumbled under constant wear and produced a surface that was jolting and noisy and offered an uncertain footing for pedestrians and horses alike. The slightest rain turned the dirt from the paving sand into black mud. Although the administration under the July Monarchy had built sidewalks along most streets, the pedestrian on the narrow ways often had to depend on the hospitality of shop doors to avoid being run down or splattered with mud and the filthy water that flowed in the gutters. In the winter when this water froze, ice was an added hazard. By night the streets were little inviting either to carriages or to pedestrians. During six months of the year some 12,000 gas lamps and 1,600 surviving oil lanterns were lighted nightly along the streets. During the remainder of the year only a fraction of them was used and for only part of the night. The permanently fixed gas lights installed during the July Monarchy were an improvement over the oil lamps that swayed like ships' lanterns on ropes hung across the streets, but even they cast little light on the streets.[24]

Certainly an inconvenient city, Paris of 1850 was also a smelly city. Perfumery was not a major business for no reason. The crowding together of tenements with factories and shops produced a concentration of industrial and domestic odors in areas

23 Galignani, *Guide for 1851*, p. 8; Alfred Martin, *Etudes historiques et statistiques sur les moyens de transport dans Paris* (Paris, 1894), pp. 86-87.

24 Haussmann, *Mémoires*, III, 137-38, 145, 152-54; Galignani, *Guide for 1851*, pp. 38-39; *Moniteur*, Dec. 12, 1861, Dec. 4, 1862; *Revue générale de l'architecture et des travaux publics* (Paris), XII (1854), 257-58.

where air could not easily penetrate to disperse them. The droppings of the city's 37,000 horses, removed only once a day, and the garbage nightly piled on the street for collection added to the city's odors, but the principal assault upon the Parisian's nostrils must have come from the sewers, the gutters that substituted for them on many streets, and the cesspools and carts used in the disposal of human excrement.[25]

The city had built its sewers over the course of centuries, adding to them bit by bit to satisfy the immediate needs of the time. In the course of the first half of the nineteenth century successive administrations made many improvements: they extended the total length of the system more than five-fold and nearly completed the centuries-old project of enclosing the principal sewers, but in 1850 the system was still shockingly inadequate for a growing city of one million inhabitants. The three principal collector-sewers were still those used in the Middle Ages: the Seine River itself, the Bièvre River on the Left Bank, and the ancient stream of Ménilmontant (called the Ceinture Sewer), running eastward from Ménilmontant between the inner boulevards and the *octroi* wall to the Seine at Chaillot. The latter two were enclosed, but, of course, the Seine, which received the discharge of the other two collectors and of a number of smaller sewers as well, lay open both to sight and to smell. A manual system of removing toilet sewage spared the river the city's human excreta, but pollution came from the wastes of households and shops, and the seepage of cesspools and cemeteries. Ordinarily the flow of the river assured self-purification quickly enough to avoid serious offense and to prevent any menace to health as long as the river was not used for water supply.[26] Nevertheless, a speaker in the Legislative Body near the end of the Empire recalled with distaste "the black torrents" that two decades earlier poured into the river from sewers under the Pont Neuf, the Pont Royal, and the Pont de la Concorde.[27] Zola watching the river near the Pont Royal in those days saw "the surface . . . covered

[25] Marc Caussidière, *Mémoires* (3d edit.; Paris, 1849), II, 168; *Builder* (London), VIII (1850), 50-51, XIII (1855), 481, 514; *Moniteur*, Dec. 7, 1854.
[26] *Moniteur*, Dec. 7, 1854; Belgrand, *Travaux*, V, 30-31.
[27] *J.O.*, Feb. 28, 1869.

with greasy matter, old corks and vegetable parings, heaps of filth. . . ."[28]

The Seine was not the only sewer disguising under a different name. Two-thirds of the city's streets ran with the waste water of the adjacent shops and houses, for despite the extension of the sewer system since the Revolution, Paris had in 1851 only eighty-two miles of underground sewers to serve more than 250 miles of streets.[29] Most streets still depended on streams in the gutters to carry rain and waste water to the nearest underground sewer. At best these waters were unsightly and gave off a slight odor. When allowed to stand for twenty-four hours, as they might if caught in a depression of a gutter, or when they included liquid excreta, which were permitted in the gutters after 1850, they emitted a nauseating odor.[30] In the covered sewers the excreta hastened fermentation, making worse the noxious smell issuing from the openings, despite twice weekly cleanings. Rains caused the gutters to overflow, spilling their contents into cellars, courtyards, and vestibules of neighboring buildings. The underground sewers, too, had been built without any thought of the amount of water they might be required to carry during a heavy rain. Every downpour brought a torrent of water from the slopes of Montmartre and Belleville into northeast Paris. It overflowed the sewers and flooded sections of the outer boulevards and neighboring streets and penetrated into cellars of adjoining buildings.[31]

The method of removing human excrement seemingly might have been designed to spread bad odors. Each proprietor provided a cesspool in the form of a masonry ditch or some less satisfactory receptacle in which his tenants deposited this sewage, and each night some 200 carts overran the sleeping city to collect the contents of filled ditches. When the carts were loaded to overflowing they made their dripping way to La Villette, where a pump, supplemented by canal boats, awaited to move the vile smelling mass on to a disposal plant in the

28 Emile Zola, L'Assommoir (N.Y., 1924), p. 77.
29 Moniteur, Oct. 1, 1851; Belgrand, Travaux, v, 145-46.
30 Belgrand, Travaux, v, 266.
31 Moniteur, Jan. 22, 1853, Dec. 7, 1854, Feb. 9, 1859; Galignani, Guide for 1851, p. 51.

Forest of Bondy, six miles to the east of Paris. Not until 1849 was disinfection of the household ditches made obligatory, and even then the process used failed to neutralize the bad odors, nor did covers confine them. They spread through streets and houses, and at night the heavy wheels of the carts bumping over the cobblestones awakened Parisians so that they might not miss the revolting smell broadcast by the leaking wagons.[32]

Sewage disposal and water supply are ever closely related problems, and in Paris a century ago there was one shockingly direct connection. The city drew part of its water supply from that main collector sewer, the Seine, and pumped it largely at points downstream from the mouths of sewers emptying into the river. Most of the remainder of the city's water supply came from sources little more inviting.

The water system of Paris, like the sewers, was a haphazard creation of centuries, expanded from time to time to meet immediate needs. Before the first Napoleon the city had depended on the Seine and on springs or wells for its water. Napoleon added 21,000,000 gallons daily of waters of the Ourcq River, which he brought to Paris by a canal also used for navigation. Succeeding regimes made a few lesser additions, and by the middle of the century the city had at its disposal an average of twenty-six gallons daily for each inhabitant, far below New York City's present average of about 150 gallons though near the thirty to thirty-five gallons then accepted as adequate for large cities. But the antiquated distribution system permitted use of only about half the available supply, and most of it was of such poor quality as to inspire wonder that consumers took even that much.[33]

Only one house in five had water piped to it, and in all Paris fewer than 150 houses had running water above the first floor. This niggardly equipment was not owing alone to the stinginess of Parisian landlords. A quarter of the city's streets had no water conduits, and where water was available the uncertainty of supply must have repelled customers. In the summer when

[32] Belgrand, *Travaux*, v, 250-52, 268-69.
[33] Haussmann, *Mémoires*, III, 274-83; *Moniteur*, Dec. 5, 1854; *J.O.*, Supplément, May 1864, p. 7.

demand was heavy the customer could frequently get only a trickle from his water tap, because most of the secondary distribution pipes were so small that they emptied more quickly than they could be refilled, even though the reservoirs were full. In the winter flow was frequently cut off by freezing of water in pipes laid too close to the surface.[34]

Large sections of the city, owing to their elevation, could not get water above ground level. The Ourcq Canal provided more than two-thirds of the water supply, but a fifth of the city lay above the level at which it could be distributed, and in another two-fifths it could not be delivered higher than the ground floor of buildings. In the first Napoleon's time no one expected to have water except in hydrants and fountains at street level, and the Ourcq system with a few supplemental sources for high districts had sufficed. By 1850, however, it was thought essential to distribute water to every house, as in London and other English cities, and then the Ourcq was a practical source of supply for only two-fifths of the city's area and half its population. The water available from springs and artesian wells could furnish but a tiny fraction of the remaining demand, and the aging pumps on the Pont Nôtre-Dame, those installed before the Revolution at Chaillot and near the Invalides, and a newer machine above the Pont d'Austerlitz lacked the capacity to pump Seine water in adequate quantity to three-fifths of the city.[35]

With water taps still a rarity Parisians ordinarily obtained their water from individual wells, from public fountains, or from water sellers. Most houses had their own wells, but the water from them, infected by infiltration, was at best suitable only for washing and cleaning. For drinking and cooking water Parisians went to the 1700 public fountains that lined the streets and there obtained water for only the trouble of carrying it home. More well-to-do citizens bought their water from dealers who, like the milkmen in our time, delivered a standing order to the customer's door each day. The smaller dealers supplied themselves without cost at public fountains,

---

[34] Haussmann, *Mémoires*, III, 237; *Moniteur*, Dec. 5, 7, 1854.
[35] Haussmann, *Mémoires*, III, 281-85; *Moniteur*, Dec. 5, 1854.

but the more substantial merchants equipped with tanks drawn by horses or large casks hung over the carrier's shoulders, bought filtered water at commercial fountains maintained by the city.[36]

According to the best standards of the time water distributed in a city should be soft, agreeable to taste, limpid, and at an even temperature in all seasons. None of the water of Paris met the requirements. All of it contained chemical impurities that made it at least moderately hard. The waters of the Seine and the Ourcq were warm in the summer and excessively cold in the winter. They arrived in Paris turgid from clay in suspension and infected with organic matter, and the Seine picked up much more organic matter as it passed through the city. Except at the merchant fountains the city made no provision for filtering and, indeed, made no effort to purify the water. It was simply distributed as it arrived.[37]

In the first half of the nineteenth century Paris had suffered two fearful epidemics. Cholera, a pestilence unknown or un-identified in the West before the 1830's, had moved westward out of India in the preceding decade and descended on Europe in 1831. In Paris it attacked 39,000 persons and killed 18,400 of them, including the Prime Minister himself. It struck again across Europe in 1848-49, and this time 19,000 Parisians died. Among medical men a great controversy had raged between the contagionists and the anti-contagionists over the means of transfer of this and other epidemic diseases, but by the time of the second epidemic the anti-contagionist view was generally accepted in France and in Britain and Germany as well. Although subsequently proved erroneous, its influence was salutary, for the anti-contagionists believed that cholera arose from local causes: accumulations of filth, over-crowding, lack of air and light, faulty drainage, infected sewers, polluted water, unwholesome food; and this belief tended to turn attention away from usually fruitless quarantines at frontiers, to efforts to remedy the evil within. The two great epidemics aroused popular and official alarm, and the anti-contagionist theory

[36] *Moniteur,* Dec. 5, 1854; Feb. 7, 1859; *Builder,* XVII (1859), 13; Belgrand, *Travaux,* IV, 430, 438-47.

[37] *Annuaire des eaux de la France pour 1851* (Paris, 1851), pp. 13-14; *Moniteur,* Dec. 5, 1854; Belgrand, *Travaux,* I, 457-58.

directed it toward problems of public hygiene. In the teeming slums of Paris and in the sewers and water supply it found abuses crying for reform.[38]

Americans forever puzzling over why Frenchmen behave so oddly like Frenchmen can find in Paris of a century ago another paradox wanting explanation. Here were the highly civilized and reputedly luxury-loving Parisians tolerating the inconveniences and hazards of an overgrown medieval city: alley-like streets without issue, slums without light and air, houses without water, boulevards without trees, crowding unrelieved by parks, and sewers spreading noxious odors. The needs of the city were apparent, and the daily congestion of traffic, the death rate (the highest in France), the two great cholera epidemics proclaimed them for all to see. Successive administrations had made efforts to meet them—a new street there, a passageway widened here, new sidewalks, more sewers, a few thousand gallons added to the city's water supply, but their efforts had been fragmentary. They had lacked the courage, the imagination, and the temerity to attack the staggering problem of virtually rebuilding the city, and if Paris were to support a growing population without peril to public order and public health, nothing less would suffice.

[38] Pinkney, "Napoleon III's Transformation of Paris," pp. 129-30.

II · THE PLAN AND THE MEN

LOUIS NAPOLEON fancied himself something of an architect. An English visitor calling at the Bibliothèque Nationale in the early 1850's for a copy of Hittorf's *L'Architecture polychrome chez les Grecs* was told that it had been sent to the Elysée Palace for the President of the Republic, who only a few days earlier had asked for it together with several other books on architecture.[1] While in exile in Britain he had laid out a portion of the grounds of Brodick Castle in Scotland, an estate of his friend, the Duke of Hamilton.[2] During his early years back in Paris after 1848 his visitors often found him surrounded by sketches of landscaping in the Bois de Boulogne or, pencil in hand, working over a street plan of Paris.[3] When Georges Haussmann, the Prefect of the Seine who later directed the transformation of Paris, labored as a little-known provincial prefect in the Department of the Yonne, Louis Napoleon already had on paper his ideas for rebuilding the city and had begun urging them on a reluctant prefect and municipal council.[4] On the day when Haussmann took the oath of office as the Prefect of the Seine, Napoleon handed to him a map of Paris on which he had drawn in four contrasting colors (the colors indicating the relative urgency he attached to each project) the streets that he proposed to build.[5] This map, the work of Louis Napoleon alone, became the basic plan for the transformation of the city in the two following decades.

[1] *Builder* (London), x (1852), 380.

[2] Thomas W. Evans, *Memoirs* (N.Y., 1905), p. 35.

[3] E. F. de Beaumont-Vassy, *Histoire intime du Second Empire* (Paris, 1874), pp. 189-90; Charles Merruau, *Souvenirs de l'Hôtel de Ville de Paris, 1848-1852* (Paris, 1875), p. 364.

[4] Merruau, *Souvenirs*, pp. 365-66; Adolphe de Granier de Cassagnac, *Souvenirs du Second Empire* (Paris, 1879-82), II, 223; G. E. Haussmann, *Mémoires* (Paris, 1890-93), III, iv; Fialin Persigny, *Mémoires* (Paris, 1896), p. 259.

[5] Haussmann, *Mémoires*, II, 53; Merruau, *Souvenirs*, p. 366.

Very briefly a planning commission was involved in the project. Napoleon told Haussmann at their first meeting that he had created the commission, including the prefect, to assist him in developing his proposals into a definitive plan for remaking the city's street system. The commission met once, and Haussmann then suggested to the Emperor that its business would be expedited if the number of members in addition to the Emperor and the prefect were reduced to a minimum. "You mean," replied Napoleon, "that if there were none that would be best." Haussmann affirmed this unvarnished summation of his wishes. The commission never met again, and Napoleon and Haussmann together developed the Emperor's original sketches into the master plan for the transformation of Paris.[6]

The map of Paris on which Napoleon drew his original projects did not survive the Empire. The Emperor gave it to Haussmann as a guide, and like many other sources of the history of Paris, it was presumably destroyed in the burning of the City Hall in 1871. In the latter 1860's Haussmann on the Emperor's request had three or four copies made from it, but all save one were lost along with the original. At the time of the Exposition of 1867, however, Napoleon had presented one copy to King William of Prussia, who carried it back to Berlin, where many decades later a French historian, André Morizet, found it in the *Schlossbibliothek*. This fortunate remnant is not an entirely accurate rendering of the original plan. It fails to distinguish between streets proposed by Napoleon himself and those initiated by Haussmann. It included some streets that were not part of his original plan (all the Boulevard Saint-Germain, for example) and, presumably because they were completed before the establishment of the Empire, it excluded some that Napoleon did propose (portions of the Rue de Rivoli and the Rue de Rennes, for example).[7]

More revealing of Napoleon's own ideas is a plan in his own hand drawn up in the last year of his life on the request of the

6 Haussmann, *Mémoires*, III, 53-58.

7 Merruau, *Souvenirs*, p. 366; André Morizet, *Du vieux Paris au Paris moderne* (Paris, [c.1932]), pp. 129-31, city plan in back cover.

former Secretary-General of the Prefecture of the Seine, Charles Merruau. On it Napoleon colored in red those streets built on his express order and in green those he proposed but which were not built during his reign.[8] An old man's memory can have many lapses, and an attempt to reconstruct the plans of twenty years earlier could become more an expression of regrets than an honest record of intentions, yet Napoleon's coloring of this map does generally agree with the written records left by his contemporaries.

Among the Emperor's proposals the most important for the city's immediate needs were the completion of the Rue de Rivoli from east to west across the city and the construction of a comparable major way through the center of the city from north to south. The idea of a magistral avenue from Vincennes in the east to the Bois de Boulogne in the west dates from at least as early as the reign of Louis XIV. Napoleon I began to build it, and the government of the July Monarchy and the provisional government of 1848 had taken some halting steps toward continuing it. Louis Napoleon proposed to complete the street from the Rue de Rohan to a point beyond the City Hall whence the Rue Saint-Antoine could carry it to the Place de la Bastille. The problem of north-south traffic through the city, Napoleon I had neglected, but Louis Napoleon proposed to break through the central labyrinth of streets on the Right Bank with a boulevard running from the station of the Strasbourg Railway (the present Gare de l'Est) to the Pont au Change. The plan shows that he intended to extend the boulevard southward across the river and through the Latin Quarter to the Boulevard du Montparnasse, but Haussmann claimed that he suggested to the Emperor the continuation of this so-called Boulevard du Centre on the island and the Left Bank.[9] The northern and southern sectors together now form the line of the boulevards de Strasbourg, de Sébastopol, du Palais, and Saint-Michel, and with the Rue de Rivoli at right angles to them they constitute "the great crossing" of Paris.

A number of other proposed streets on the plan cut through

8 Merruau, *Souvenirs*, pp. 366-67, city plan in back cover.
9 Haussmann, *Mémoires*, III, 47-48.

the crowded central quarters. On the Right Bank were the Rue du Pont Neuf and the Rue de Turbigo leading to the Central Markets, and the Avenue Napoléon, now the Avenue de l'Opéra. On the Left Bank he planned the Rue des Ecoles, the Rue de Rennes, and a diagonal street running northward from the Rue de Rennes slightly west of the line of the present Boulevard Raspail. The last was never built, but it perhaps inspired the Boulevard Raspail, proposed by Haussmann and constructed during the Third Republic. For the Rue des Ecoles the Emperor claimed no credit, possibly because Haussmann persuaded him that it was a mistake, but the initiative for it did in fact come from him.[10] The Rue de Rennes he proposed to continue from the Church of Saint-Germain des Prés to the Quai de Conti, opening a through way from the Gare Montparnasse to the river, and a municipal street plan of the 1860's showed a proposed bridge from the Quai de Conti across the tip of the Cité to join the Rue du Louvre on the Right Bank.[11] The bridge was never built nor was the extension of the Rue de Rennes beyond Saint-Germain des Prés (as every passenger on a Rue de Rennes bus has been reminded as the vehicle went careening down the narrow Rue Bonaparte to reach the quais).

On the Right Bank Napoleon planned to complement the inner boulevards with new boulevards extending them to the eastern and western extremities of the city. Starting from the Place du Chateau d'Eau (now the Place de la République), he drew southwestward a long, straight avenue (the Boulevard Voltaire of the Republic) to the Place du Trône, and on the west the Boulevard Montmartre was to be extended to the Place de l'Etoile by way of the future Boulevard Haussmann and the Avenue de Friedland. Napoleon's plan also shows that he proposed to complete the ring of inner boulevards by extending it to the Left Bank with the construction of the Boulevard Saint-Germain, cutting through the crowded quarters just south of the river from the Pont de la Concorde on the west to the Quai Saint-Bernard on the east. Haussmann recorded in his

10 Merruau, *Souvenirs*, pp. 375-90; Haussmann, *Mémoires*, III, 48.

11 Archives nationales (Paris), C 1134, Corps législatif, Session 1869, Dossier No. 140.

28

memoirs, however, that the Boulevard Saint-Germain was not part of the Emperor's plan and that only with difficulty did he convince Napoleon of its importance.[12] The two men frankly differed, moreover, on the bridge to carry this boulevard across the river at its eastern extremity. Haussmann wanted the bridge placed in line with the projected Boulevard Henri IV, with which it was to connect on the Right Bank. He had carefully located this boulevard on the axis of the column in the Place de la Bastille and the dome of the Panthéon, and, a determined classicist in his city-planning, he did not want the straight line broken nor the vistas lost. The bridge would then be diagonal to the line of the river, and all other bridges were at right angles. The Emperor regarded this deviation as both esthetically and structurally unsound, and he put his absolute veto on Haussmann's proposal. When Haussmann prepared the copy of Napoleon's map that eventually went to Berlin, he had the bridge sketched in as he himself wanted it. The exiled Emperor drawing up the plan for Merruau took care to show it as he wished it—at right angles to the river. When it was eventually built under the Third Republic (as the Pont Sully), the builders followed Haussmann's proposal.[13]

Not shown on either of Napoleon's maps were two major parts of his program. One was the construction of a central market ample in size and readily accessible to all Paris, and the other was the development of the Bois de Boulogne into a spacious public park for the citizens of the capital. For the former Napoleon revived and extended a project originally instituted by his uncle and taken up again by the municipal administration in the 1840's, but the latter was his own project, perhaps inspired by his experience in London.

Where did Napoleon acquire the idea of rebuilding Paris? The question interested his contemporaries, and it has continued to fascinate historians in succeeding generations. According to one contemporary, Arsène Houssaye, Louis Napoleon himself attributed the conception of the idea to a chance meeting with a young man in New York City in the latter

[12] Haussmann, *Mémoires*, III, 48-49.
[13] *Ibid.*, II, 522-23.

1830's. This man showed him a plan for a model city that he proposed to build entirely anew in a single operation and not "as in Europe, one house at a time." Napoleon was intrigued and later declared, "That day I promised myself on my return to Paris . . . to rebuild the capital of capitals. . . ."[14] The story seems a bit ingenuous. One might with equal plausibility maintain that he acquired the germ of his plans from the works of the utopian reformers Fourier and Cabet in which they described model communities intended, among other objects, to remedy the evils of over-crowding and disorder that they had observed in cities of their time.

Possibly Napoleon picked up the idea from that group of French social reformers called the Saint-Simonians. They were not concerned with the ideal city but with practical improvements in Paris. In 1832, moved by the frightening toll of cholera in Paris, the Saint-Simonian journal, the *Globe*, proposed a specific program of slum clearance and building in the city.[15] Its heroic scale, as well as some of its details, suggests an affinity with Louis Napoleon's later plans. Like Napoleon the *Globe* proposed to extend the Rue de Rivoli eastward from the Louvre to the Place de la Bastille, both to provide a traffic artery across the city and to bring light and air to crowded quarters where cholera had claimed so many victims. Scores of acres of slums in the center and east were to be completely razed and replaced by new, uncrowded structures, and the Ile de la Cité, cleared of most of its buildings, was to become a wooded public park.

Some aspects of Louis Napoleon's plans were almost certainly inspired by his observations while in exile in London. Driving across the Bois de Boulogne not long after his return from England he remarked to his companions, "We must have a river here, as in Hyde Park, to give life to this arid promenade,"[16] and later he did build there a lake reminiscent of the Serpentine, and he transformed the Bois into a park in the informal style he had known in England. He was in London at

14 Arsène Houssaye, *Les Confessions* (Paris, 1885), IV, 88, 93-94.
15 *Globe* (Paris), April 2, 11, 16, 1832.
16 Merruau, *Souvenirs*, p. 367.

a time when that city and others throughout Britain were awakening to appreciation of grave problems of public health and traffic congestion brought on by rapidly growing populations. He saw the completion of public works intended to render the center of London more accessible, and, having many English friends active in public life, he surely heard discussions of the problems of increasing traffic and public health. He must, moreover, have been an interested observer of that violent storm, centering about the person of Edwin Chadwick, over enforcement of sanitary standards in British cities.

Fascinating as such speculations and inferences may be for amateurs of Louis Napoleon, they are ultimately quite futile. The idea of the transformation of Paris was not original with Louis Napoleon, and he might have picked it up from one or many of half a hundred sources. Embellishment of imperial capitals had been a common practice among ambitious rulers since Augustus undertook to make Rome a city of marble, and the Renaissance idea of building a city or a part of it according to an overall plan found many practitioners among the absolute rulers of early modern Europe, who perhaps saw in it a dramatic way of proclaiming their political power. The Bourbons of France carried on both these traditions. Louis XIV not only left the world a prime example of a planned city in Versailles; he also embellished Paris by constructing the "great boulevards" of the Right Bank. Henry IV built the Place des Vosges, Louis XV, the Place de la Concorde; and each of them gave the city a number of decorative buildings.

At least as early as the middle of eighteenth century, however, discerning men saw that Paris required something more than occasional monumental and decorative works. In 1739 Voltaire confided to Prince Frederick of Prussia his dismay at the waste of money on fireworks in Paris when the city cried for parks and fountains and markets.[17] A decade later he wrote an essay on "Des Embellissements de Paris," deploring the lack of open space, "the center of the city dark, confined, frightful," "the public markets established in narrow streets, parading

[17] Voltaire, *Oeuvres complètes* (Paris, 1876-78), x, 127.

31

squalor, spreading infection, and causing continual disorder."[18] Paris must have, he insisted, larger markets, spacious squares, fountains that actually ran; narrow streets must be widened, hidden monuments uncovered.

In 1765 an architect named Pierre Patte published a book, *Monumens érigés à la gloire de Louis XV*, in which he urged the preparation of a single, comprehensive plan for the transformation of Paris, the plan to be aimed primarily at achieving easy communications between quarters and unhampered movement of traffic from the center of the city to the periphery. In this book and in other writings he also advocated increases in the city's water supply, establishment of cemeteries beyond the walls, and the improvement of street lighting. In these suggestions and in his reflections on the evils of cities he might easily be taken for a nineteenth century urban reformer or city planner, but when he came to recommendations of specific improvements in the city's streets he remained a man of his age. His principal project, the clearing of the crowded Ile de la Cité and the Ile Saint-Louis, had as its purpose the creation of a monumental site for a new cathedral in the western end of the Cité. It was a work of embellishment; the needs of communication were forgotten. Napoleon and Haussmann largely achieved the clearing of the Cité of its old houses, as Patte had urged, but for a different purpose, and happily his proposal for a new cathedral in the academic classic style of his time found no echo in the Second Empire.

During the Revolution, when the government's holding of large parcels of confiscated land offered an opportunity for reconstruction of the city, an official commission called the Commission of Artists drew up a comprehensive plan for the embellishment and sanitation of the city.[19] The so-called "Plan of the Artists" included the future Rue de Rivoli in two sections, the first running from the Place de la Concorde to the northeast corner of the Louvre and the second from the center of the Perrault front of the Louvre straight east to the Place

18 *Ibid.*, v, 390-95.
19 "Plan des Artistes" in Département de la Seine, *Les Travaux de Paris, 1789-1889; atlas* (Paris, 1889), Pl. x.

de la Bastille. It also included public markets on the site of the future Central Markets. On the Left Bank the plan proposed a portion of the future Boulevard Saint-Michel, a broad avenue cutting south from the Place Maubert across the Montagne Sainte-Geneviève on the axis of the Panthéon, and another at right angles to it running from the Luxembourg Garden to the Panthéon (the future Rue Soufflot) and from the Panthéon to the Jardin des Plantes. Some few of the commission's proposed streets were built in the revolutionary decade of the 1790's, but it was left to the first Napoleon to go much beyond pleading and planning and make the first considerable effort at transforming the old city.

Napoleon III may well have acquired his idea of rebuilding Paris from the example of his uncle. Their ambitions for Paris were similar, and although the third Napoleon actually achieved much more in Paris, the accomplishments of the two men were closely akin. In 1798 the young General Bonaparte had declared, "If I were master of France, I would want to make Paris not only the most beautiful city that had ever existed, but also the most beautiful that *could* exist."[20] When he was "master of France" he began the Rue de Rivoli and completed it from the Place de la Concorde almost to the Palais Royal; opened two other famous streets, the Rue de la Paix and the Rue de Castiglione, and numerous lesser streets. He rebuilt and extended the quais along the Seine; erected four new bridges; and built many public buildings and monuments; and brought waters of the Ourcq River to Paris as the city's principal water supply. Like Louis Napoleon and Haussmann, he combined street building with slum clearance by cutting new streets through heavily settled districts (with complete disregard, critics said, of historical monuments) to force demolition and replacement of old and decaying buildings. These accomplishments impressed the aspiring Louis Napoleon, and in his first published defense of the Napoleonic record, *Des Idées napoléoniennes* (1839), he called attention to the Emperor's generous expenditures on public works and admiringly listed in detail

[20] Antoine Arnault, *Souveniers d'un sexagénaire* (Paris, 1833), IV, 102.

the many works executed in Paris.[21] He subsequently rode to his initial political triumphs on the reputation of the first Napoleon. He frankly sought to imitate him, and the transformation of Paris may originally have sprung from the ambitious nephew's desire to copy the successes of his uncle.

But even had Louis Napoleon not been the nephew of Napoleon Bonaparte and had he returned to Paris in 1848 completely innocent of any thought of rebuilding the city, he could very quickly have acquired the idea there. The needs of the city were so glaring that they could scarcely be overlooked, and the thought of major public works to satisfy them was very much in the air in 1848. Only the year before on the initiative of the Prefect of the Seine, Count de Rambuteau, the Municipal Council had approved expenditure of 50 million francs on a six-year program of construction, a program including the enlargement of the central markets, the construction of the Rue de Lyon, the widening of portions of a number of critical streets, and the extension of the Rue Lafayette.[22] The program was interrupted by the Revolution of February 1848, the funds diverted to other uses. The Provisional Government decreed the continuation of the Rue de Rivoli and the completion of the north wing of the Louvre parallel to that street but actually accomplished nothing. Throughout 1848, however, public demand was insistent for a revival of the program, and any ruler or aspiring ruler looking for a project that was popular and useful and a source of employment for a restless population would certainly be attracted to a major program of public works in Paris.[23]

Louis Napoleon did not, however, simply adopt as his own the earlier programs of the Municipal Council or the provisional government. He incorporated their projects in his plans, but he went far beyond them. His predecessors, when not occupied with purely decorative works, undertook piecemeal alterations that might enable the city to get along a few more years with

[21] Louis Napoléon Bonaparte, *Oeuvres* (Paris, 1848), I, 246-47, 373-77.

[22] *Moniteur universel*, Mar. 1, 1847: Claude Rambuteau, *Memoirs* (N.Y., 1908), p. 228; Merruau, *Souvenirs*, pp. 109-10.

[23] Merruau, *Souvenirs*, pp. 75-76, 115-18, 149-50, 380; Persigny, *Mémoires*, p. 242; *Moniteur*, Oct. 5, 1849, Aug. 4, 1851.

its antiquated streets, congested markets, and flooded sewers. Napoleon proposed many entirely new streets that would facilitate the increasing flow of traffic for decades, bring light and air to crowded slums, and at the same time embellish the city. His predecessors had been dismayed by the expense of even their modest programs. Napoleon was prepared to match the audacity of his building with boldness in finance. His planning had many faults and many gaps now readily apparent, but in its time it was enlightened and advanced. Not since the Commission of Artists drew up its plan for the reconstruction of the city's streets in the 1790's had anyone in authority proposed so comprehensive a plan, and never before had one been proposed by a head of state who was determined to see it through to completion.

Napoleon's purpose in undertaking the audacious task of transforming Paris is, a century later, still controversial. Much of the history of the Second Empire has been polemical—written either by apologetic imperialists or by censorious monarchists and republicans. The latter sought out the vulnerable points in the Napoleonic record, and when they came to the transformation of Paris they commonly emphasized the strategic purposes of Louis Napoleon and neglected other aims likely to be more popular. Napoleon ordered the building of long, straight boulevards, they said, the better to shoot down his enemies with artillery fire; he made them wide to forestall the building of barricades; and he cut them through the crowded working class quarters of the east end in order to break up and, if necessary, to facilitate the military encirclement of the usual centers of resistance. The evidence usually offered in proof of these sinister intentions is isolated statements from Haussmann's memoirs and the assumption that because such and such a street *could* serve a strategic purpose it must have been built for that purpose alone.[24]

Strategic considerations did certainly have a place in Louis

[24] David H. Pinkney, "Napoleon III's Transformation of Paris: The Origins and Development of the Idea," *Journal of Modern History*, xxvii (1955), 132. Georges Pillement in his *Destruction de Paris* (Paris, [c. 1941]), published during the German occupation, condemned Empire and Republic alike for their "imbecilic demolitions" in Paris during the preceding hundred years.

Napoleon's plans as they did in the plans of preceding governments. Eight times between 1827 and 1849 barricades had been thrown up in the streets of Paris, always in the crowded eastern half of the city, and on three occasions they had been the prelude to revolution. It had occurred to Napoleon's predecessors that new streets might contribute to breaking up centers of insurrection. A speaker in the National Assembly in 1851 declared that after the Society of Seasons' abortive revolt in 1839 demand for "anti-riot streets" was widespread in Paris, and he accused Louis Philippe's minister, Thiers, of doing nothing for the poor quarters except to build such streets.[25] The assembly's reporter on the proposal to extend the Rue de Rivoli in 1851 defended it on the grounds that it would cut across "a fortress of sedition."[26] Haussmann frankly avowed that Napoleon, as well as he himself, had similar intentions in some instances, and the location of certain streets and of permanent barracks affirmed it.[27] The Rue de Turbigo, for example, cut through the nub of resistance around the Conservatoire des Arts et Métiers. The boulevards Voltaire and Mazas made possible the encirclement of the Faubourg Saint-Antoine, and the Rue Monge and the rues Gay-Lussac and Claude Bernard similarly neutralized the Montagne Sainte-Geneviève on the Left Bank. Barracks for the permanent quartering of security troops and police arose at key points about the east end—behind the City Hall, on the Place de la République, near the Place de la Bastille, and on the Rue Mouffetard. But to facilitate the enforcement of public security was only one of Napoleon's purposes and probably not the most important to him. Persigny, one of Napoleon's earliest followers, enumerating in his memoirs the guiding principles of the planned transformation of Paris when he was Minister of the Interior in 1852, included no mention of strategic considerations, and Persigny least of all men would dissimulate the government's intent to use force in maintaining order.[28]

[25] *Moniteur*, Aug. 5, 1851.

[26] *Moniteur*, July 27, 1851, Dec. 7, 1854; Eugène Belgrand, *Les Travaux souterrains de Paris* (Paris, 1873-77), v, 252-63, 268-69.

[27] Haussmann, *Mémoires*, II, 318, III, 21, 54-55; *Moniteur*, Mar. 28, 1855, May 2, 1861, Dec. 11, 1867.

[28] Persigny, *Mémoires*, pp. xx, 239-40.

But even though Napoleon was anxious to maintain order, his public works in Paris were not intended solely for the negative purpose of suppressing disorder. He meant also to attach the populace of Paris so securely to his regime that they would not want to revolt or even resort to violent protest. A popular saying in the city ran, "When building flourishes, everything flourishes in Paris."[29] After the Revolution of 1848 the building industry languished. Funds appropriated for public works were not spent for that purpose, and private builders were reluctant to risk building in the uncertain times. Martin Nadaud, a deputy in the National Assembly and himself a former construction worker, declared in 1851 that in the preceding three or four years not forty houses had been built in Paris and that most building workers had been unemployed since 1847.[30] Parisians had seen in the June Days of 1848 terrifying consequences of economic distress among the workers of the capital, and in the succeeding years there was a very lively apprehension of a renewed insurrection. It even inspired serious demands that the government be moved out of Paris.[31] Napoleon, however, believed he had a way to dissipate the spectre of revolt. In November, 1851, he told the National Assembly that the best means to forestall the "demagogic" revolution threatening France was to satisfy the legitimate interests of the public by, among other things, assuring steady employment through public works. There was, of course, nothing novel in this. It had long been a policy of the royal governments to provide work relief, but Louis Napoleon had a more sophisticated purpose in mind. His Saint-Simonian advisers told him that the prolonged depression, which was a source of revolutionary discontent, could be ended by generous government spending to stimulate the lagging economy into full activity, and to achieve that end he proposed to spend on a much larger scale than any preceding government.

[29] Paris, Chambre de Commerce, *Statistique de l'industrie à Paris . . . pour les années 1847-1848*, Part I, p. 89.
[30] Merruau, *Souvenirs*, pp. 116-17, 480, 484; Rambuteau, *Memoirs*, p. 293; *Moniteur*, Oct. 4, 7, 1849, Aug. 3, 1851.
[31] Merruau, *Souvenirs*, p. 355; *Moniteur*, Nov. 28, 1850; Lucien Davesiès, *Paris tuera la France: necessité de déplacer le siège du gouvernement* (Paris, 1850), pp. 25-43, 47-70.

He underlined his faith in the practical political value of public works when he fixed the original date for his seizure of personal power for September 17, 1851, to follow by two days his laying of the cornerstone of the first pavilion of the new Central Markets in Paris.[32] This ceremony, a symbolic demonstration of his concern for the city's needs and his determination to provide employment, would, he was apparently convinced, strengthen his position in the critical moment of displacing the legal government. The subsequent postponement of the *coup* did not result from any revision of that conviction. After he did seize power in December, 1851, he could override much of the opposition to his plans, and with the fate of his regime hanging in the balance he ordered a rapid speeding up of public building in Paris and elsewhere. Not until the last year of the Empire was building allowed to slow down, and a cynical opponent of the regime observed that it was *"condamné à travaux forcés à perpetuité."* "A week's interruption of the building trade," he said, "would terrify the Government."[33] Near the end of the Empire, nevertheless, one of Napoleon's ministers could boast to the Legislative Body of seventeen years without street riots in Paris, and to many who could recall 1848 and 1849 that was strong recommendation of the regime.

The political and strategic purposes of Louis Napoleon in Paris were indeed very real. Vanity, too, played a role, urging him, like his predecessors, to undertake works of embellishment, but these works had also the political object of adding to the prestige of the regime. But to conclude that he was solely or even primarily preoccupied with these purposes in his planning for Paris is to misunderstand both Louis Napoleon and the time in which he lived. While in exile Louis declared his conviction that "A government is not . . . a necessary ulcer; . . . it is rather the beneficent motive force of every social organism."[34] The state should use its power directly to relieve distress and to promote the welfare of all its citizens. In transforming Paris he was thinking both of providing employment and of making

[32] Merruau, *Souvenirs*, pp. 442-43.

[33] N. W. Senior, *Conversations with Distinguished Persons during the Second Empire from 1850-1863* (London, 1880), I, 193.

[34] Bonaparte, *Oeuvres*, I, 189.

Paris a more healthy and livable city than he had found it in 1848. He intended that new streets cutting across slum areas and the clearing for public buildings should force the demolition of old and dilapidated houses and bring light and air and sun into the poorest quarters. He planned parks and public gardens and planted squares that would relieve the city's vast expanse of stone and pavement, and in the Bois de Boulogne he would make easily accessible to all Parisians the broad open space formerly found only in the more distant state forests.[35]

He was also intent on rendering the city more livable by facilitating the movement of traffic. Important parts of the city were to be joined directly together by straight avenues covering the shortest possible distance such as Wren had proposed for London after the Great Fire of 1666. He was concerned with the growing traffic to and from the railway stations, "the new gates of Paris." The only approach to the Strasbourg Railway station, the narrow Rue Neuve de Chabrol, could ill accommodate the 12,000 vehicles that used it daily, and not a day passed without an accident. Napoleon proposed to build a broad avenue, the future Boulevard de Strasbourg, from this station straight to the inner ring of boulevards, and the Boulevard de Magenta to connect the new avenue with the station of the Belgian Railway, the present Gare du Nord. His suggested Rue de Rennes led from the railway station on the Boulevard du Montparnasse to the Church of Saint-Germain des Prés and on to the Seine. Other streets he planned to provide access to the new central markets and to major public buildings.[36] One of Napoleon's few known criticisms of Haussmann was that the Prefect in fixing the lines of streets gave more thought to appearance than to traffic. "In London," the Emperor said reproachfully, "they are concerned only with giving the best possible satisfaction to the needs of traffic."[37]

This aspect of Napoleon's plans concerned with public health,

[35] *Moniteur*, Dec. 11, 1850; Persigny, *Mémoires*, pp. 239-40; Merruau, *Souvenirs*, pp. 365, 367-74; Haussmann, *Mémoires*, II, 271-72, III, 172; Granier de Cassagnac, *Souvenirs*, II, 222.

[36] Persigny, *Mémoires*, pp. 236-40; Merruau, *Souvenirs*, pp. 364-65; *Moniteur*, July 27, 1851.

[37] Haussmann, *Mémoires*, III, 523.

slum clearance, and traffic fits readily into the pattern of the
urban reform and public health movements of the 1830's,
forties, and fifties in Britain, Germany, and France. For this
part of his career he may properly be placed in the respectable
company of Edwin Chadwick, Lord Shaftesbury, and the
founders of the Health of Towns Association in England, and
with Jacob Riis and Robert Moses, who in later generations
wrestled with similar problems in New York City.

Plans, however good, were but a first step toward filling the
city's needs, and for the following steps it was men, not plans,
that were primarily important. Long before Napoleon's time
Voltaire had concluded his pamphlet on the rebuilding of
Paris with the prayer, "May God find some man zealous enough
to undertake such projects, with a soul firm enough to follow
them through, with a mind enlightened enough to plan them,
and may he have standing enough to make them succeed."[38]
A century later Voltaire's wish was fulfilled not by one man but
by two: Napoleon III and Haussmann. Napoleon had a mind
sufficiently enlightened to envisage the broad plan for transforming Paris and the standing to give it virtually unassailable
political backing. Haussmann had the firmness and zeal to see
the plan through to reality.

The map Napoleon presented to Haussmann in 1853 was
only a preliminary sketch. It had to be developed into working
plans and then transformed into stone and mortar over the
almost insuperable obstacles of expense, vested property interests, the inertia of municipal authorities, and political hostility.
The Emperor had neither the time nor the abilities for these
heavy tasks. They fell upon the chief administrative officer of
the city, the Prefect of the Department of the Seine, and without a prefect who was both sympathetic and audacious the
Emperor's plans would have remained but another pipe-dream
like his project for a Nicaraguan canal or his agricultural communities for the extinction of poverty. From the preceding
regime Napoleon had inherited a timid and unsympathetic
prefect named Berger. He tried to win him over, but by 1853
the Emperor realized that his plans would be frustrated as long

[38] Voltaire, *Oeuvres*, v, 595.

as Berger remained in office, and he sought a replacement who had the interest, determination, and temerity the job and the occasion required.[39] His choice fell upon Georges Haussmann, a career prefect who had served the Bonapartist cause well in three critical posts since 1848.

Haussmann, a French Protestant of Alsatian extraction, was descended from soldiers of the first emperor. His father had been a young officer in the Napoleonic armies, and his maternal grandfather, a Baron Dentzel, was an imperial general who held a number of important posts, including the military governorship of Vienna. At the time of the marriage of his daughter to the young officer Haussmann in 1806 General Dentzel had been on the staff of Prince Eugène de Beauharnais, the Emperor's step-son and Louis Napoleon's uncle, and when the first son was born of the marriage the Prince consented to be his godfather. The child was christened Georges Eugène, the middle name after the prince, a Bonapartist connection that Georges did not fail to exploit in the 1850's.[40]

Educated at the Collège Henri IV, the Collège Bourbon, and the School of Law in Paris, Georges Haussmann entered the public service in 1831 as a supporter of the new Orleanist monarchy. His first post was secretary-general of the Prefecture of the Vienne, but he was soon appointed a sub-prefect, and in the succeeding fifteen years he served in various sub-prefectures throughout France. The February Revolution of 1848 found him as sub-prefect of Blaye on the Gironde estuary below Bordeaux. Replaced as sub-prefect by a political appointee he stayed on in the Gironde in a lesser post and nominally rallied to the new republic, but discerning the direction of political winds he soon began working for the election of Louis Napoleon as president of the republic. In the elections in December Napoleon won 78 per cent of the votes in the Gironde, and Haussmann was rewarded with a prefecture. Napoleon sent him to the Var, a department where the republicans were threateningly active and where the frontier with Italy required close vigilance. From here he was moved the following year to an-

[39] Persigny, *Mémoires*, pp. 240-45; Haussmann, *Mémoires*, II, 32-33.
[40] Haussmann, *Mémoires*, I, 3-14.

other trouble spot, the Department of the Yonne, and late in November, 1851, he was appointed Prefect of the Gironde and "Commissioner extraordinary of the Government" to assure the adherence of the monarchist city of Bordeaux to the new regime shortly to be established by Napoleon's *Coup d'Etat* of December 2, 1851. Here as in his preceding posts Haussmann carried out his mission with vigor and intelligence, and in October, 1852, Napoleon chose a great celebration staged by Haussmann on the President's visit to Bordeaux as the occasion to announce the reestablishment of the Empire.[41]

The following year when the Emperor and Persigny, the Minister of the Interior, decided to replace the hostile Berger, Persigny interviewed several of the principal prefects of provincial departments. He was especially impressed by Haussmann; less, he said by his remarkable intelligence than by the defects in his character, which, Persigny thought, especially qualified him for the Prefecture of the Seine at that time.[42]

I had before me [wrote Persigny] one of the most extraordinary types of our time. Big, strong, vigorous, energetic, at the same time, sly, crafty, with a resourceful mind, this daring man was not afraid to show openly what he was. . . . He revealed to me the principal facts of his administrative career apologizing for nothing; he would have talked for six hours without stopping, provided it was on his favorite subject—himself. . . . while this absorbing personality showed off before me with a kind of brutal cynicism, I could not contain my lively satisfaction. 'To fight,' I said to myself, 'the ideas, the prejudices of a whole school of economics, the artful, sceptical men . . . from the corridors of the Bourse or the law courts here is the man ready made. There . . . this vigorous athlete, with a strong backbone, with a thick neck, full of audacity and cunning, capable of opposing expedients with expedients, snares with snares, will certainly succeed.' I enjoyed the prospect of throwing this lion in the middle of the pack of foxes and wolves excited against all the generous plans of the Empire.[43]

The final choice was made by the Emperor. According to Haussmann, who probably got his information from his friend, Frémy, General-Director of Administration in the Ministry of

41 Haussmann, *Mémoires*, I, 26-581; Morizet, *Du vieux Paris*, pp. 157-72.
42 Persigny, *Mémoires*, pp. 250-53.
43 *Ibid.*, pp. 253-55.

the Interior, Persigny submitted to the Emperor a list of candidates for the post of prefect. In the presence of the Minister and Frémy Napoleon scanned it quickly and, stopping by the name of Haussmann, whom he knew not only as his strong supporter in the Var, in the Yonne, and at Bordeaux, but also as the godson of Prince Eugène, declared, "Useless to go farther; there's the man I need."[44]

Called hastily from Bordeaux, Haussmann took the oath of office as Prefect of the Seine on June 29, 1853. In this post he had an authority unique among the prefects of the Empire, and, despite the fact that he was a career man and his predecessors for years had been political appointees, he enjoyed a prestige that no other prefect of the Seine had possessed. Imperial Paris, like Washington, D.C., was governed not by its citizens but by the central government. As prefect, Haussmann had in his authority not only the usual prefectoral duties of assuring the execution of national laws in his department but also all the functions of municipal government ordinarily held by an elected council and a mayor. As the Emperor's delegate in the administration of the capital he had no superior but the Emperor himself. During his long term of office he saw the Emperor personally almost every day. After 1860 he sat in the Council of State and, when Parisian affairs were being considered, in the cabinet itself as the equal of ministers in fact, and he came very close to equality in name when he nearly persuaded the Emperor to create a Ministry of Paris with himself at its head. The Municipal and Departmental Councils were appointed by the Emperor and offered no insurmountable opposition to Hausmann's authority, and Napoleon raised him to the Senate and gave him the title of Baron so that no one in the Municipal Council might pretend to superior prestige. Haussmann remained in this office for seventeen years, until his dismissal early in 1870, after certain of his financial operations had made him a political liability to the Emperor in the new parliamentary empire.[45]

[44] Haussmann, *Mémoires*, II, 10-11.
[45] *Ibid.*, I, 3-4; II, 72-74, 209, 217-18, 223; A. des Cilleuls, *Histoire de l'administration parisienne au XIXe siècle* (Paris, 1900), II, 17-18, 154-55, 237-38.

Haussmann's great contribution to the transformation of Paris was the resolute accomplishment of the Emperor's plans. "It was the Emperor who marked out all this," he declared, "I have been only his collaborator."[46] But that summation alone does him less than justice, and Haussmann, rarely a modest man, in other statements claimed a larger role. Certainly he was a creative collaborator. He not only elaborated Napoleon's plans; he made numerous and important additions to them. He added new streets, parks, and public buildings, and he made two original contributions of primary importance: the supplying of Paris with abundant spring water and the construction of a system of collector sewers that ended the contamination of the Seine within the city. For the conception of these less conspicuous and, Haussmann complained, less appreciated aspects of the transformation of Paris the Prefect claimed and deserved primary credit.

In his own time Haussmann was a controversial figure accused of many faults, ranging from puerile artistic taste and extravagance to graft and dangerous political ambitions. Probably no one in his position could have been popular even had he tried, for the accomplishment of the Emperor's assignment required that he be a disturber of long established habits and associations, and Haussmann did not try to be popular. Baroche, one of Napoleon's ministers, complained in 1862 that his urgent request to Haussmann for information he needed to defend the municipal administration on the floor of the Legislative Body went unanswered for a week.[47] At times he was an impatient and petulant superior. When the director of one of the municipal offices ventured to note that his department did not understand a certain decision of the administration, Haussmann wrote on the margin of his report, "It's of little importance that your department should understand, still less that it should approve." Opposite a mildly critical observation from another subordinate he wrote, "I don't like observations, especially when they are fallacious!"[48] These incidents, like Persigny's

46 Evans, *Memoirs*, p. 144.
47 Jean Maurain, *Baroche, Ministre de Napoléon III* (Paris, 1936), p. 232.
48 A. des Cilleuls, *Histoire de l'administration parisienne*, I, 540.

characterization, help to explain both why Haussmann was able to accomplish so much and why at the same time he made so many enemies.

Yet Persigny's statement is a caricature, exaggerating the coarse and cynical aspects of the man's character. There was nothing cynical about his devotion to the Empire. In his personal dealings he held the loyalty of his subordinates, and he was capable of winning over opponents by rational persuasion and personal charm. An opponent, trying to explain away an influential doctor's support of Haussmann on the location of a new hospital, told the Legislative Body that the doctor has been "Haussmannized," converted by the Prefect's personal fascination over him. His apparent coarseness did not exclude artistic interests. As a young man he used his spare time to study music at the Paris Conservatory, and as prefect he devoted much thought (too much, the Emperor believed) to improving the appearance of Paris.

The roles of Napoleon and Haussmann in the transformation of Paris are clear. The contributions of the lower ranks of participants in the great undertaking are less clear, and in most cases will probably never be indisputably established. Persigny, for example, claimed as his own the proposal to finance the great public works in the city, without increases in tax rates, by long-term loans to be redeemed out of rising tax receipts and by profits from the re-sale of condemned property. Haussmann, on the other hand, reported the idea as his own. On the work of his subordinates Haussmann's memoirs are the principal source, and one of his closest associates, Alphand, observed that Haussmann had an amazing faculty for assimilation and "often took for his own, with the greatest good faith, the ideas he had once adopted" from others.[49]

Among the engineers and architects who did contribute to the rebuilding of Paris three still stand out. Their memory has survived because of the key posts they held, because Haussmann chose to single them out in his memoirs, and in two cases because the men themselves wrote accounts of their own work.

Two of them, Adolphe Alphand and Eugène Belgrand, were

[49] Haussmann, *Mémoires*, III, v.

government engineers, members of the *Corps des Ponts et Chaussées*, who had first attracted Haussmann's attention when he was a prefect in the provinces. Belgrand, holding the minor rank of "ordinary engineer," was assigned to one of the arrondissements of the Department of the Yonne when the Prefect Haussmann noted his success in bringing to the town of Avallon an abundant supply of fresh spring water. Haussmann's questioning revealed that Belgrand since his student days had been interested in water problems. By independent study and research he had become well versed in geology and hydrology, and he had already published the first of a series of learned articles. Haussmann, an amateur of those fields, was attracted by Belgrand and had him transferred to the chief town of the department to improve that city's water supply. In 1854 when Haussmann decided to explore the possibilities of furnishing Paris with spring water, he asked Belgrand, who was then stationed at Rouen, for a report on springs in the Paris Basin capable of supplying the city. Later he brought Belgrand to Paris and placed him at the head of the municipal Water and Sewer Service. In that post throughout Haussmann's term of office and beyond he built the city's famous system of collector-sewers and brought to Paris the spring water of the valleys of the Dhuis and the Vanne. Haussmann regretted Belgrand's inability to delegate authority ("He always," Haussmann complained, "remained an *Ingénieur ordinaire*") and his cavalier attitude toward expense once a project was begun. He practiced every economy in planning but thought nothing of making expensive changes once work was in progress. But few construction engineers since the building of the pyramids have escaped the latter complaint, an almost universal protest of administrator against engineer. Throughout his career in Paris Haussmann found him not only an able engineer but a "loyal and sure friend." Belgrand saw to his own place in history by starting five large volumes on his work in Paris, *Les Travaux souterrains de Paris*, and his friends completed them after his death.[50]

Another close collaborator in Paris, Adolphe Alphand, was

[50] *Ibid.*, III, 106-07, 111-19; Belgrand, *Travaux*, I, ii-iv, 70.

supervising work on the port of Bordeaux when Haussmann was Prefect of the Gironde. Although an engineer by profession he first attracted Haussmann's serious attention by his planning and execution of the impressive decorations of the banquet and assembly rooms for Louis Napoleon's visit to Bordeaux in October, 1852. Later when Haussmann needed an engineer with the talents of an artist to take over the landscaping of the Bois de Boulogne, he recalled Alphand and his work in Bordeaux. Brought to Paris he was placed in charge of the Bois and subsequently became chief of the Park Service. By the end of the Empire he was Director of Streets and Parks and also had under his authority the municipal Lighting Service. During his career in Paris he was responsible not only for the completion of the Bois de Boulogne but also for the planning and construction of the other great parks and the many public squares and for the landscaping of the principal streets. He survived both the fall of Haussmann and the fall of the Empire, and under the Republic he came closer than any other man to being Haussmann's successor. Although not prefect in name, he was the executive officer in charge of most branches of the municipal administration, and it was he who succeeded to Haussmann's seat in the Academy of Fine Arts. He, too, like Belgrand, published an account of his work, *Les Promenades de Paris*.[51]

The third of the principal collaborators, Deschamps, Haussmann found in Paris when he became Prefect of the Seine. This man, whom Haussmann's memoirs alone saved from the anonymity he apparently cherished, held in 1853 the imposing title of Keeper of the Plan of Paris, but like the Master of the Rolls in England, who has no Rolls, Deschamps had no "Plan of Paris." His function was merely to keep the individual alignment plans of the various city streets. An architect trained in the *Ecole des Beaux Arts*, he retained the typical *Beaux Arts* student's disdain for the conventions of dress and manners, and in his personal relationships he was, in Haussmann's judgment, difficult and even disagreeable, but these apparently unfavorable characteristics combined with his professional competence recommended him to Haussmann. In order to assure coherence

51 Haussmann, *Mémoires*, ii, 570-72, iii, ii, 125-32.

in the whole building program for Paris and to maintain standards in specifications the Prefect created the Service of the Plan of Paris. One of its branches prepared the plans for new streets and determined what property would have to be condemned, what buildings demolished. Another branch appraised the property to be taken, and the appraisals were used by the Municipal Council in fixing the indemnities to be offered to owners and tenants and the prices to be asked buyers of materials from demolished buildings. The Service was fairly infested with opportunities for graft and fraud, and Haussmann wanted at the head of it a man who was not only technically competent but also inaccessible to outside influences and a stern example of integrity for his subordinates. The misanthropic Deschamps filled the place admirably and died a poor man.[52]

[52] *Ibid.*, III, 2-9.

III · FROM PLANS TO PAVEMENTS

AT LEAST AS EARLY AS 1851 Louis Napoleon urged the municipal administration to undertake the most essential parts of his
plan for Paris. Among half a dozen projects to which he attached
particular importance, he gave primary urgency to two: the
completion of the Rue de Rivoli and the construction of the
new Central Markets. Work on the latter, initiated by Napoleon
I, had been resumed in 1847, and in the succeeding years the
expropriation and clearing of the site in the heart of the city
had gone slowly forward, but by the beginning of 1851 not one
of the eight proposed pavilions had been started. In 1849 the
National Assembly had approved continuation of the Rue de
Rivoli beyond the point reached by Napoleon I, but the project was only incidental to the clearing of the area around the
Louvre and involved but three hundred yards of pavement.

Louis Napoleon rebelled at this slow pace. In 1851 he sum-
moned the Prefect of the Seine, Berger, to a cabinet meeting
at the Elysée Palace, and there pressed him to begin at once
both the extension of the Rue de Rivoli 1,000 yards through
the densely populated quarters between the eastern end of the
Louvre and the City Hall and the construction of the pavilions
of the Central Markets.[1]

Berger demurred. The city, he believed, could ill afford the
expense of these operations in the uncertain times. Only two
years earlier it had borrowed 25,000,000 francs for public works,
a loan that would not be retired until 1858, and it had since
then acquired the additional burden of buying out the owners
of the toll bridges across the Seine. Municipal revenues had
exceeded preliminary estimates by 5,000,000 francs in 1850, but
Berger believed this no measure of future income. He attrib-

[1] Charles Merruau, *Souvenirs de l'Hôtel de Ville de Paris, 1848-1852* (Paris,
1874), pp. 375-76; Fialin Persigny, *Mémoires* (Paris, 1896), p. 237.

uted the excess to an extraordinary yield from the *octroi* resulting largely from Parisians' replenishment of stocks depleted during the troubled years of 1848 and 1849. The commitment of the city to large additional expenditures on the promise of what would probably prove a mere windfall was a risk that the prudent Berger did not care to take.[2]

Napoleon could not wait. The year of crisis, 1852, when his own term as President and the life of the National Assembly would expire, was at hand, and he was not eligible for reelection. If he were to change the constitution or, failing that, were he to stay in power in violation of the constitution, he would have to consolidate the public favor he had won in 1848. He owed his overwhelming victory in the presidential election of 1848 to popular dissatisfaction with preceding regimes and to the magic of his name. The Rue de Rivoli and the Central Markets were projects of the first Napoleon; they were popular; and they had been long delayed by the temporizing of monarchist and republican governments. A decade earlier in exile Louis Napoleon had written a successful campaign pamphlet, *Des Idées napoléoniennes*, contrasting the inaction of the monarchy with the accomplishments of the Empire, and now by undertaking two conspicuously Napoleonic projects he could proclaim that contrast anew and at the same time establish himself as the man who could continue the Napoleonic record of accomplishment.

Had Berger persisted in his opposition he probably would have lost his post two years earlier than he actually did. The warning of two of his associates that continued resistance was equivalent to resignation apparently moved him. He shortly made another call upon the President and told him that he would undertake the two projects.[3]

The program met with opposition in the Municipal Council. The projected work was all on the Right Bank, and delegates from the Left Bank wanted some of the money spent on their side of the river, particularly on the construction of the Rue

[2] Merruau, *Souvenirs*, pp. 165, 377; *Moniteur universel*, Jan. 20, Apr. 27, 1849, Aug. 4, 1851.

[3] Merruau, *Souvenirs*, p. 378.

des Ecoles in the crowded and neglected Twelfth Arrondissement. But the plans for this street were far from complete, and
Napoleon had ruled out any further delay. The representatives
of the Left Bank could not enforce their wishes, for the councillors from the opposite bank outnumbered them four to one.[4]

Financing was the major problem. Berger estimated the total
cost at 58,000,000 francs, and if the city were to depend solely
on its own resources the work would have to be spread over
eight or ten years. Pressed by Louis Napoleon, the Municipal
Council proposed to complete it in less than half that time. The
city asked the central government for a subsidy, but the request
was turned down (on the grounds that funds available for
public works should be spent on completing the main railway
lines). The municipal authorities then petitioned the National
Assembly for authority to borrow 50,000,000 francs. On August
4, 1851, the Assembly gave its consent and authorized new taxa-
tion to retire the loan by 1870. To private builders it granted
an indirect subsidy in the form of a twenty-year exemption
from property taxes and doors and windows taxes on all buildings erected on the new section of the Rue de Rivoli.[5]

Berger did not float the loan until the spring of 1852, but
with 20,000,000 francs advanced by the Bank of France against
anticipated proceeds of the loan he began work at once. The
first expropriations of land and buildings in the line of the Rue
de Rivoli were made in mid-October, and within a year
wreckers had cut a broad path straight through the crowded
central quarters. For the first time Parisians could stand in the
Place de l'Oratoire on the north side of the Louvre and see
across the old city to the City Hall. The construction of the
Central Markets made even more startling progress. Two weeks
after the passage on August 4 of the bill authorizing the 50,-
000,000 franc loan Berger posted the plans of the market site
for public inspection as required by law, and on September 15
Napoleon laid the cornerstone of the first new market pavilion.[6]

Following the overthrow of the Republican government in

[4] *Ibid.*, pp. 423-24.

[5] *Moniteur*, July 16, 25, 27, Aug. 4, 5, 1851; Archives nationales (Paris), C 993,
Assemblée nationale, Session 1851, Dossiers No. 701-02.

[6] *Moniteur*, Aug. 19, Sept. 16, Oct. 16, 20, 1851, Sept. 8, 1852.

December, 1851, Louis Napoleon accelerated the pace of demolition and building. He ordered all previously authorized work pushed forward rapidly, and having no longer to contend with a refractory national assembly he authorized by simple decree a succession of new projects. Just ten days after the *Coup d'Etat* he opened a new credit for the final clearing of the area between the Louvre and the Tuileries, and in March, 1852, appropriated 26,000,000 francs for the enlargement of the Louvre and its junction with the Tuileries Palace on the Rue de Rivoli side. In the same month the Municipal Council approved the construction of the first section of Louis Napoleon's great north-south counterpart of the Rue de Rivoli, the one hundred-foot-wide Boulevard de Strasbourg from the station of the Strasbourg Railway to the Boulevard Saint-Denis, and Napoleon granted a state subsidy of more than a million and a half francs toward its construction. A fortnight later came a decree authorizing the building of a Parisian "Crystal Palace," the Palace of Industry, between the Avenue des Champs Elysées and the Cours la Reine. The decision in July, 1852, to build the Rue des Ecoles, along the north slope of the Montagne Sainte-Geneviève, and the Rue de Rennes running northward from the Montparnasse railway station to the Rue de Vaugirard rescued the Left Bank from neglect. In the same summer the Prince President initiated one of his favorite projects—the conversion of the Bois de Boulogne, the state forest beyond the fortifications on the west of Paris, into a great city park such as he had admired in the West End of London.[7]

In this same period Napoleon used his new authority to remedy shortcomings in earlier projects initiated when his influence had been limited to persuasion. The extension of the Rue de Rivoli planned in 1851 had two serious defects. No provision had been made for building a section running for two hundred feet along the north side of the old Louvre. Here the street crossed the elongated Place de l'Oratoire, but this square and the buildings left standing on its northern side were out of

[7] Merruau, *Souvenirs*, pp. 484, 486-90; *Moniteur*, Oct. 4, 1852. In the months following the Coup d'Etat almost every issue of the *Moniteur* carried at least one announcement of public hearings on new construction projects, expropriations, or demolitions.

line with the rest of the street and were both an obstacle to traffic and a violation of a classic principle of city design. In December, 1852, Napoleon ordered the completion of this gap in the Rue de Rivoli and the continuation there of the uniform façades and sidewalk arcades already built along the adjoining western section of the street.[8]

Nearer the opposite end of the Rue de Rivoli the builders encountered much graver difficulties, unforeseen because the planners had worked without any accurate guide to the elevation of the ground in the area through which they projected the street. Adherence to the proposed plane of the thoroughfare, the builders found, would require a cut several yards deep through the hillock of Saint-Jacques la Boucherie. Then if the new avenue were to be accessible from transverse streets and if adjoining buildings were not to be left perched high in the air, the entire quarter had to be leveled down to the elevation of the new street. That was a major undertaking, involving the demolition of scores of buildings, the reconstruction of numerous streets, the lowering of the quais along the Seine, and the rebuilding of two bridges. It eventually cost more than 11,000,-000 francs. The Law of August 4, 1851, on the 50,000,000 franc loan had made no provision for this immense operation. In July, 1852, Louis Napoleon signed a decree authorizing the additional work and providing a subsidy of 1,500,000 francs to cover part of the expense.[9]

In his *Memoirs* Haussmann gave the impression that before he became Prefect of the Seine in June, 1853, the Emperor had been able to accomplish very little in Paris. The transformation of the city was, in fact, already well started when Haussmann took office, but it is true that after Napoleon's first success in initiating and then accelerating the work in 1851 and 1852, he encountered from Berger and some members of the Municipal Council increasing hostility to continuation of the quickening pace. Berger might have summed up his views on municipal finance by changing the word "kingdom" to "city" in Adam Smith's famous pronouncement on national finance, "What is

[8] Merruau, *Souvenirs*, pp. 489-90; *Moniteur*, June 9, 1852, Jan. 5, 1853.
[9] G. E. Haussmann, *Mémoires* (Paris, 1890-93), III, 16-19.

prudence in the conduct of every private family can scarce be folly in that of a great kingdom." He viewed the city's finances much as he did his own family budget—not only should expenditures be covered by assured income but they should be kept below income so as to permit savings. The 50,000,000 franc loan for the Rue de Rivoli and the Central Markets was the last retreat from familial prudence that he could conscientiously make, but after nearly a year of heavy pressure from the Minister of the Interior Persigny, he did propose to spend the 4,000,000 franc surplus in the budget of 1853 on public works. To him this was an important concession. To Louis Napoleon and Persigny, thinking of projects whose costs rose in the next seventeen years to more than 2,000,000,000 francs, a proposal to spend 4,000,000 only proved that Berger could not remain as prefect. In replacing him Napoleon removed the major obstacle to his program and at the same time proclaimed the great importance he attached to his plans for Paris. Berger was a sort of municipal Talleyrand, an Orleanist who came to his office under the Republic, survived the fall of the Republic, and then accommodated himself to the Second Empire. Napoleon tolerated such a dubious political background even in high place, but obstruction of his plans for Paris he would not have.[10]

The grand program that had shocked Berger appealed to the audacious Haussmann. He accepted the idea of spending in anticipation of increased revenues that the spending itself would help to produce. Long term loans held no terrors for him. Napoleon feared continued opposition from Berger's partisans in the Municipal Council and at his initial meeting with Haussmann advised him to find thirty-six loyal imperialists to replace the incumbent municipal councillors. He agreed, however, to Haussmann's suggestion to delay action until the council should make itself unpopular by obstructing the Emperor's program. Haussmann's first meeting with the council began inauspiciously when President Delangle declared coldly that all the councillors regretted Berger's premature retirement and had "complete confidence in the wisdom of his adminis-

10 Persigny, *Mémoires*, pp. 243-50; Merruau, *Souvenirs*, p. 165; Haussmann, *Mémoires*, II, 32-33.

tration." Haussmann held his peace and gave a soft answer that turned away even some of Delangle's wrath, and in talking with individual councillors he felt that they were not ill-disposed toward him. He left the meeting convinced that Delangle exaggerated Berger's strength in the council. To the Emperor he reported that he was confident he could win over a majority of the members to his views on the transformation of Paris. The others he could maneuver into resignation. Napoleon agreed to let him try, and in the end all but five were "Haussmannized," and the five die-hards resigned.[11]

This success did not free the new Prefect of all serious opposition. His career in Paris was a long battle against some few personal enemies, against many genuine opponents of the transformation of Paris (some even within the government), and against the political enemies of the Empire who, not daring to strike directly at the Emperor, found Haussmann a convenient target for their attacks. In these battles Haussmann fulfilled Persigny's expectations. Until 1869, when the political circumstances of the Liberal Empire forced Napoleon to sacrifice him, Haussmann contrived to better his enemies and critics in all but a very few encounters, and they were not vital to his purposes. Through persuasion and cajolery but chiefly through the exercise of authority given him by the Emperor he had his way. He undercut most of the opposition by astutely posing as merely the Emperor's agent in all that he did. He saw the Emperor almost daily and obtained the imperial approval of every new project before he presented it to the Municipal Council or to the council of ministers, and then he made clear that it represented the Emperor's wishes.[12]

Haussmann's primary assignment was to initiate the still untouched projects on Napoleon's plan of Paris. Yet nearly a year elapsed before he started any significant new streets. Work on those already begun by Berger was pushed forward, but the first year, 1853-1854, was primarily a year of preparation, preparation both for individual projects and for the whole transformation of Paris. Haussmann was convinced that the

[11] Haussmann, *Mémoires*, II, 35-36, 52-53, 140-45, 162, 240-42, 244.
[12] *Ibid.*, II, 223; Persigny, *Mémoires*, pp. 259-60.

municipal administration and private builders needed much more accurate plans of the city than any that existed in 1853, and he ordered his chief surveyor, Deschamps, to prepare a detailed map. During the next year Parisians saw erected on many street corners about the city scaffolding towers, each bearing a platform higher than the surrounding rooftops from which surveyors triangulated the entire city within the *octroi* wall. Emerging from this work was a large master plan of Paris, a copy on a scale of 1 to 5000 that Haussmann kept mounted in his own office, and many working copies on smaller scales. After the annexation of the suburbs in 1860 the annexed zone was similarly mapped. The experience with the Rue de Rivoli and the hill of Saint-Jacques la Boucherie demonstrated the need also of an accurate relief map of the city, and Haussmann had it prepared simultaneously with the detailed plan.[13]

In the first weeks of 1854 warm weather permitted an early beginning of the building season. Work on old projects and on private construction along the Rue de Rivoli and around the Central Markets resumed in January, and in the following months Haussmann, his preparations made, set in motion the machinery for the construction of a number of streets on the Emperor's plan. In June imperial decrees declared the public utility of two streets connecting the Central Markets with the quais and a third joining the enlarged Place de l'Hôtel de Ville with the Place du Chatelet. The Rue du Pont Neuf, sixty-five feet wide, led from the center of the markets to the Pont Neuf, and the Rue des Halles opened a diagonal route from the same point in the markets to the Place du Chatelet. The completion of these two streets was delayed until the following decade, but the third, from the Place du Chatelet to the City Hall, was nearly finished in 1855 when Queen Victoria visited Paris, and she permitted Haussmann to give her name to the new avenue. At the end of September, 1854, the Emperor authorized the construction of the last section of the Rue de Rivoli—at its eastern extremity from the City Hall to the Church of Saint-

13 Haussmann, *Mémoires*, III, 13-16, 29; *Builder* (London), XIX (1861), 17; Louis Lacour, *Annuaire général du Département de la Seine pour l'année 1860* (Paris, 1860), p. 718.

Paul on the Rue Saint-Antoine. When it was completed the following year Napoleon I's dream of a broad, straight thoroughfare across the city was realized, and the central barrier of
ancient buildings and narrow streets was at last broken.[14]

On the same day in September, 1854, that he sanctioned this
portion of the Rue de Rivoli Napoleon gave his approval to
the final plans for an additional section of the north-south axial
street in "the Great Crossing" of Paris, the Boulevard du
Centre (now the Boulevard de Sébastopol) extending the recently completed Boulevard de Strasbourg from the Porte Saint-
Denis to the river at the Place du Chatelet. It was one hundred
feet wide, and Haussmann, the *urbaniste-démolisseur*, cut it
through a densely built-up area. A major north-south street
might have been more simply built, critics said, by widening
the parallel Rue Saint-Denis, but Haussmann claimed that the
indemnities to owners and tenants of shops along that busy
street would raise the costs of such an operation above the costs
of an entirely new street through an area of lower property
values. The same decree authorized the building of four transverse streets and the extension or widening of a number of
accessory ways. This was the largest single street project yet
undertaken in Paris. It involved opening a broad path nearly
a mile long through the heart of the old city, and it required
four years for completion.[15]

Work had scarcely begun on the Boulevard de Sébastopol
when Haussmann in 1855 obtained approval of his proposal to
extend the boulevard to the Left Bank by the construction of
the future Boulevard Saint-Michel from the river southward
to the Rue Soufflot. A few years later an old street running
across the Ile de la Cité was widened to become the Boulevard
du Palais, linking together the northern and southern sections
of the central boulevard, and another existing street, lowered
and widened, became the extension of the "Boul Miche" to its
present southern limit at the Avenue de l'Observatoire. The
city and state together rebuilt the connecting bridges, the Pont
au Change and the Pont Saint-Michel, and in 1862 with the

14 *Moniteur*, Jan. 29, 1854; Haussmann, *Mémoires*, III, 21-24.
15 Haussmann, *Mémoires*, III, 50-54; *Moniteur*, Mar. 28, 1855.

termination of the last section on the Left Bank "the Great Crossing" was complete. It provided direct thoroughfares through the center of the city. Its construction had cleared out disgraceful slums on both banks and on the Cité, and on the Right Bank it broke through a major center of insurrection around the Conservatoire des Arts et Métiers.[16]

Haussmann with his liking for monumental vistas found one defect in the finished job, and it particularly irked him because it could have been so easily avoided. If the Boulevard de Strasbourg, whose line determined the direction of the Boulevard de Sébastopol and which was begun before he came to Paris, had been deflected only slightly to the east, he noted regretfully, the dome of the chapel of the Sorbonne would have formed a monumental terminus for the view southward along the new boulevard, balancing the façade of the Eastern Railway Station at the opposite extremity. When he built the Tribunal de Commerce on the Cité in the 1860's, Haussmann remedied this error to his own satisfaction by having the architect place the structure's northern façade and its dome in the line of the Boulevard de Sébastopol. On the opposite bank the façade of the Lycée Saint-Louis determined the direction of the Boulevard Saint-Michel, and had it been followed all the way to the river the northern end of the boulevard would have been without a monumental terminus. At the Rue des Ecoles Haussmann deflected the boulevard westward so that the vista from there northward was closed by the graceful spire of the Sainte-Chapelle.[17]

All the streets built during his administration Haussmann classified into three groups: the First, Second, and Third Networks. The distinctions among the three networks were, Haussmann insisted, purely financial. In the First Network he placed those streets, like the Rue de Rivoli, the Boulevard de Sébastopol, and the Boulevard Saint-Michel, authorized before 1858 and built with financial aid from the state, and the streets accessory to these whether subsidized or not. The Second Network included only those streets specifically listed in the agree-

16 Haussmann, *Mémoires*, III, 61-62, 80; *Moniteur*, July 28, 1857, Mar. 4, 1858.
17 Haussmann, *Mémoires*, III, 60, 523-24, 530-31.

ment of March 18, 1858, between city and state and whose costs were shared by city and state. In the Third Network were all other streets, built by the city alone without subsidy from the national government.[18]

Despite the Prefect's disclaimer of any but financial significance in this classification, the components of the First and Second networks did, in fact, have some coherence other than their financial affinity. The First Network was largely in the old city within the inner boulevards. It broke through the central barrier to traffic and opened much of the crowded inner quarters to light and air. The streets of the Second Network lay in the area between the inner boulevards and the *octroi* walls, and they made possible easy movement between the center of the city and the outlying districts that the administration wished to develop. Most of them had more than local importance. Some were extensions within the city of Imperial highways. Others connected stations of the national railway systems, and still others by joining the centers of public authority contributed to the maintenance of order in the capital city. The Third Network was more of a miscellany, being composed of major avenues that Haussmann had not managed to include in the agreement on the Second Network, short additions to streets already largely built, and numerous secondary and accessory streets.

The Second Network when originally defined by the contract of March 18, 1858, between city and state was supposed to include only those streets and boulevards that met the most pressing needs of the city. It was composed of twenty-three miles of streets divided into nine groups, each in a particular area of the capital. The contract committed the city to complete them within ten years, and the state agreed to bear one-third the estimated expense of 180,000,000 francs, but the Legislative Body subsequently limited the government's share to 50,000,000 francs.[19]

[18] *Ibid.*, II, 303-04, III, 55-56, 59-63.
[19] Arch. nat., C 1058, Corps législatif, Session 1858, Dossier No. 169. The streets of the Second Network are listed in the text of the contract of March 18, 1858 (reprinted in *Moniteur*, Sept. 18, 1858), and they are shown, together with those of the Third Network, with completion dates of each in Département de la Seine, *Les Travaux de Paris, 1789-1889; atlas* (Paris, 1889), Pl. XII.

One group of streets stood in the heart of what has become fashionable Paris around the Opera House. From a point on the Boulevard des Capucines now familiar to every habitué of the Café de la Paix the city built two diverging streets—one, the present Rue Auber, running northwestward, and the other, the Rue Halévy running to the northeast. The purpose of the first was to open a direct route from the terminus of the Western Railway on the Rue Saint-Lazare to the boulevards. The Rue Halévy appeared at the time to serve no particular need, but it had an important place in Haussmann's plans. He intended to move the Opera from its old location on the Rue Le Peletier to the area between the two new streets. The narrow approaches to the old opera house had been the scene of a bloody attempt on the life of the Emperor, and Haussmann intended that the new site should be safely accessible by commodious streets. The mere suggestion of a new opera house alarmed the economy-minded committee of the Legislative Body that examined the project of the Second Network, and it obtained from the President of the Council of State the assurance that a new building was not being seriously considered.[20] The text of the agreement of March 18, 1858, on the Second Network, moreover, carefully avoided any mention of the opera house or of the other streets that formed part of Haussmann's plans for it. But the Prefect was not deflected from his purpose. With city funds alone he built the three streets named for French composers—Scribe, Gluck, and Meyerbeer, that with the rues Auber and Halévy, bounded the site he had selected, and he began the Avenue Napoléon to provide both an approach from the southeast and a striking view (although the avenue was too narrow) of the new building's principal façade.[21] In 1860 the Emperor authorized the building of a new opera house on Haussmann's site. Unfinished when the Empire fell, both the Opera House and Avenue Napoléon were completed under the Republic, the latter with its present name, the Avenue de l'Opéra.

As part of the plans to improve the approaches to the Western Railway station the agreement of 1858 provided for the

20 *Moniteur*, Sept. 18, 1858.
21 Haussmann, *Mémoires*, III, 70, 87-88.

construction of the Rue de Rome from the station to the *octroi* wall. Using city funds alone Haussmann extended it southward to the Rue Auber and northward across the area annexed to the city in 1860. It then became a major link in a thoroughfare from the boulevards to the annexed districts of Neuilly and Les Batignolles, an area in which Haussmann built an extraordinarily large number of streets in the 1860's.

Another component of the Second Network, the Boulevard Malesherbes, led into this same area. Preceding administrations had long considered building a street northwestward from the Madeleine, symmetrical with the Boulevard de la Madeleine to the northeast, and had actually built portions of it on a straight line between the Barrière du Monceau and the southern end of the Madeleine. Napoleon III's street plan included a broad boulevard on this line, but the estimated cost of acquiring land for widening the existing sections and for filling the gaps was prohibitive.[22] Haussmann, consequently, turned the street slightly westward at a point about midway between the Madeleine and the city limits and directed it across the corner of the Park of Monceau to the *octroi* barrier, avoiding built-up areas. On the initiative of one of their number, Emile Pereire, the owners of the Plain of Monceau beyond the barrier donated land for the continuation of the boulevard to the fortifications, for two other avenues crossing it (the Avenue de Wagram and the Avenue de Villiers), and for the Place des Malesherbes at the junction of the new boulevard and the Avenue de Villiers. They asked no indemnity but took their generous reward in the increased value of their property that these streets opened to settlement. Their example helped Haussmann to acquire the land for about half of the same boulevard within the city limits in the same way.[23] The practical utility of the Boulevard Malesherbes connecting the center of the city with unsettled peripheral areas was clear, although one purblind deputy in the Legislative Body thought construction should be postponed until the area it served was more heavily populated. Haussmann, characteristically not satisfied

[22] *Moniteur*, Aug. 31, 1853.
[23] Haussmann, *Mémoires*, II, 499-501.

61

with utility alone, sought to compound utility with art. At the bend he had made in the new boulevard he built the Church of Saint-Augustin to terminate the vista along the street's southern section. Its dome, rising 160 feet above the street, he also placed in the line of the western section of the Boulevard de Beaujon, another street in the Second Network, but on that axis intervening buildings now block the view of all but the cupola atop the dome.[24]

The Boulevard de Beaujon, now the Avenue de Friedland and a part of the Boulevard Haussmann, was intended to relieve heavy traffic on the Avenue des Champs Elysées and to open up the area north of that avenue. It ran eastward from the Place de l'Etoile to the Boulevard Malesherbes, and Haussmann subsequently continued it, as the Boulevard Haussmann, to a point beyond the rising opera house, creating a street familiar to thousands of tourists, who each summer throng the Galeries Lafayette, Au Printemps, and the big hotels that now line it. Haussmann intended to extend this boulevard to the Boulevard Montmartre, but work was stopped in 1870, and those final three hundred yards remained unbuilt until 1927, the last of Haussmann's projects to be completed.

The Boulevard de Beaujon was also part of Haussmann's plan to make the Arch of Triumph of the Etoile the center of a series of broad radial avenues. In 1856 he had completed the spacious Avenue de l'Impératrice (now the Avenue Foch) leading from the Etoile to the Bois de Boulogne, and the Boulevard de Beaujon continued the line of that avenue on the opposite side of the Etoile. South of the Arch he rebuilt part of the roadway adjoining the old city wall, demolished in 1860, to form the present Avenue Kléber, and the same roadway together with a considerable extension of it (all renamed the Avenue de Wagram) carried the same line northward. The program of the Second Network provided for no other changes at the Etoile, but Haussmann added five more radiating avenues, bringing the total to twelve.

The city's work on one of the older avenues on the south side, the present Avenue Victor Hugo, produced a minor storm

24 *Ibid.*, III, 73; *Moniteur*, May 10, 1858.

typical of several that occurred when local property owners believed themselves neglected by the municipal administration. In 1863 the city began to lower the level of the street but completed the job on only one side, leaving the street divided and the buildings on one side perched twenty feet above the new street level. A "temporary" retaining wall was erected in what should have been the middle of the street and wooden stairways built at intervals along the wall. The proprietors protested vehemently, demanding either completion of the project or indemnification for losses in property values resulting from the splitting of the street, but at the Empire's fall the avenue remained split into two levels.[25]

To assure the symmetry of the Place de l'Etoile the Prefect located the radiating streets so that uniformly shaped building lots remained between every pair of streets. Eight of the lots were identical in size, and the four on the opposite sides of the Avenue Kléber and the Avenue de Wagram were double size. An imperial decree required that the buildings on these lots have uniform stone façades set off by lawns and that the lawns be separated from the street by decorative iron fences, identical before all the buildings. To provide access to these houses, whose monumental fronts must not be marred by entrances, Haussmann built a circular street around the back of the lots. The Prefect was proud of his development of the Place de l'Etoile and considered it one of the most successful undertakings of his administration.[26]

In the same section of the west end the approximate triangle bounded by the Avenue Kléber, the Avenue des Champs Elysées, and the river included the heaviest concentration of new streets in all Paris. In addition to two avenues radiating from the Place de l'Etoile, Haussmann here built the present Avenue George V and the Avenue de l'Empereur, both part of the Second Network, and a large number of secondary streets included in the Third Network. The Avenue George V led from the Avenue des Champs Elysées to the new Pont de l'Alma,

[25] Arch. nat., C 1147, Corps législatif, Session 1870, Dossier No. 259-60.
[26] Haussmann, *Mémoires*, III, 74-76; Adolphe Joanne, *Paris illustré en 1870 et 1877* (3d edit., Paris, [n.d.]), p. 132.

completed in 1855, and the bridge connected it with two new avenues, also part of the Second Network, on the Left Bank leading to the Champs de Mars and to the Ecole Militaire. The Avenue de l'Empereur began at the Place de l'Alma, adjacent to the bridge of that name, and led westward to the present Place du Trocadéro. After the annexation of the suburban zone in 1860 Haussmann continued it westward to provide another route to the Bois de Boulogne. The republicans could not tolerate an Avenue de l'Empereur, however useful it might be, and on its western section they substituted the name of an innocuous republican historian, Henri Martin (part of it is now the Avenue Georges Mandel). The eastern portion became the Avenue du Trocadéro until, after the War of 1914-1918, President Wilson here succeeded to the Emperor's place.

The eastern arrondissements of Paris complained of neglect in the city's street building program, and on the Right Bank Haussmann's street building was more heavily concentrated in the west. The Second Network included, however, two very large projects in the eastern half of the Right Bank. The Avenue Daumesnil, whose first section from the Place de la Bastille to the *octroi* wall was in the Second Network, served the same purpose in the east as the Avenue de l'Impératrice in the west. When extended to the Porte de Picpus in the fortifications it provided a direct route to eastern Paris' equivalent of the Bois de Boulogne, the Bois de Vincennes. It was the longest single street built during Haussmann's administration, stretching more than two miles across the eastern quarters of the city.

The second project in the east end was even more extensive, involving the construction of three major streets: the present boulevards de Magenta and Voltaire and the Rue de Turbigo, all radiating from the Place du Chateau d'Eau (now the Place de la République). The Rue de Turbigo had been projected when the plans of the Boulevard de Sébastopol were drawn, and the short sections on opposite sides of the boulevard were built as part of the Boulevard de Sébastopol project. The agreement on the Second Network called for its completion from the Central Markets to the Place du Chateau d'Eau. When finished in 1867 it helped to relieve traffic congestion on the streets leading to the markets, and it brought sun and air into the city's crowded central quarters. It also completed the destruction of the old hotbed of insurrection around the Conservatoire des Arts et Métiers and removed from the map of Paris an unhappily famous street, the Rue Transnonain, the scene of a massacre of republicans in 1834 immortalized in one of Daumier's most trenchant lithographs.

The Boulevard de Magenta was one of the thoroughfares that served "the new gates of Paris." Running north-eastward from the Place du Chateau d'Eau it passed before the Eastern and Northern Railway stations. The Boulevard de Strasbourg connected it with the entrance to the first, and Haussmann built the short Boulevard Denain to join it to the second. Following the annexation of the suburbs in 1860 Haussmann continued it as the Boulevard Ornano northward around the east side of the hill of Montmartre to the city limits at the Porte de Clignancourt.

The Boulevard du Prince Eugène, which later became republican as the Boulevard Voltaire, started at the Place du Chateau d'Eau and extended a mile and three-quarters without a curve to the Place du Trône (now the Place de la Nation). It was an important thoroughfare across the east end of Paris from the inner boulevards to the city limits, and it helped to embellish and develop one of the city's poor and neglected districts. The building of this boulevard involved the difficult problem of crossing the Canal Saint-Martin without creating an obstacle either to navigation in the canal or to traffic on the street. A fixed bridge would have had to be very high and its roadway excessively steep. A moveable bridge would alternately halt barges on the canal and block wagons on the street. The problem was ingeniously solved by lowering the water level of the canal twenty feet and vaulting over a section more than a mile long between the Place de la Bastille and the present Avenue de la République. The area above the canal became the Boulevard Richard Lenoir with two roadways on opposite sides of a center strip one hundred feet wide, embellished with lawns, trees, and fountains. Few projects directly served so many of Napoleon's purposes as did this solution, which opened the way for the Boulevard du Prince Eugène and removed one of the three great barriers to east-west movement across the city. It provided a new thoroughfare across a busy commercial district, gave the neighborhood a veritable park in its front yard in place of the dirty waters of the Canal Saint-Martin, and substituted for the defensive position the canal had offered to insurrectionaries a strategic way from which one could, Haussmann pointed out, "take from behind all the Faubourg Saint-Antoine." One may easily believe the Prefect's report that the Emperor was unreservedly enthusiastic. Under the Republic a section of the boulevard was ironically renamed after Haussmann's most notorious adversary, the author of the famous *Fantastic Accounts of Haussmann*—the section between the Avenue de la République and the Rue du Faubourg du Temple became the Boulevard Jules Ferry.[27]

Haussmann tried in vain to include in the Second Network another avenue radiating from the Place du Chateau d'Eau, the Avenue des Amandiers, joining the square with the Cemetery of the Père Lachaise and the second ring of boulevards. He subsequently built a short stretch of it as part of the Third Network, but it was left to a republican administration to complete it and rename it the Avenue de la République. Haussmann also had to relegate to the Third Network his rebuilding of the Place du Chateau d'Eau into the spacious rectangular Place de la République. He was proud of "the happy symmetry" of this square, but a generally sympathetic guidebook of 1870 complained that it was ill-proportioned and excessively large, dusty in the summer, a swamp in the winter, and dangerous for pedestrians at all times, and concluded that it would be "difficult to assemble on so vast an area more regrettable conditions."[28]

On the Left Bank the Second Network included a number of streets that favored the neglected and poverty stricken Twelfth Arrondissement on the southeast corner of the city. The new

27 Haussmann, *Mémoires*, II, 317-18; *Moniteur*, Jan. 16, 1858, Sept. 26, 1859, Aug. 7, 1861.
28 Joanne, *Paris*, p. 118.

boulevards Saint-Marcel and de Port Royal filled in the final gap in the second ring of boulevards on the Left Bank, and the new Boulevard Arago joined these two new boulevards with the imperial highway southward to Orléans. Haussmann wanted to extend the Boulevard d'Enfer, which ran north-westward from the Orléans highway, to the new Boulevard Saint-Germain near the river, but he failed to get it in the Second Network. In the Third Network he built only a short section of it at the crossing of the Rue de Rennes. A later administration completed it with the republican name of Raspail.

In addition to the new boulevards on the Left Bank the Second Network involved the widening of the Rue Mouffetard for about two-thirds of a mile north from the Barrière d'Italie. This street, renamed the Avenue des Gobelins, cleared a broad path through the crowded and unsavory district around the Gobelins factory, and with the Avenue d'Italie it was a commodious entry into the city from the southeast, with the dome of the Panthéon lying directly in its line. Continuation of the thoroughfare northward posed the problem of passing the obstacle of the Montagne Sainte-Geneviève. The Emperor had proposed to widen the Rue Mouffetard and the Rue Descartes over the hill and on to the Rue des Ecoles. Haussmann persuaded him to substitute two almost entirely new streets running around opposite flanks of the hill: the Rue Monge on the eastern side and the rues Claude Bernard and Gay-Lussac on the west.[29] These streets minimized the Montagne Sainte-Geneviève as a barrier to traffic, and they made it possible for troops to outflank this traditional center of insurrection.

The final paragraph in the agreement of March 18, 1858, provided for the completion of the Boulevard du Centre. It authorized the construction of the section on the island and the southern section from the Rue Soufflot to the Avenue de l'Observatoire. Although the latter part followed the line of an existing street its construction was no small operation, for it required the lowering of the street level to eliminate the

[29] Haussmann, *Mémoires*, III, 78-79.

steep hill in front of Ecole des Mines and the demolition of buildings bordering the street.

Included in the final paragraph along with the Boulevard du Centre was an accessory thoroughfare, the Rue de Médici, which aroused more controversy than any other street in the entire Second Network. The need for such a street connecting the quarter of the Odéon with the southern quarters of the city had been recognized at least a decade earlier, but in 1858 the proposal to build it across the corner of the Luxembourg Garden from the Odéon Theater to the Rue Soufflot created a small tempest. The Luxembourg Garden was legally the property of the Senate, and at the hearing on the project one of the officers of the Senate and the Senate architect protested against the street but failed to alter the city's plans. When work was about to begin in 1860 the Senate received a petition, signed by a dozen or so residents of the district, objecting to the proposed street. Haussmann out of deference to the Senate, of which he himself was a member, held up the project while a committee spent weeks considering the petition. It finally came to the floor of the Senate, and that high body devoted an entire day's session debating the merits and faults of these 270 yards of street. In the end the Senate sustained Haussmann's defense of the city's project, and the street was built as planned. Haussmann claimed that the entire storm was the petty creation of the Marquis d'Hautpoul, Grand Referendary of the Senate, and the Senate architect, who were outraged because the new street would require the demolition of the former's stables and the latter's residence.[30]

While the Second Network was still under construction, Haussmann built a few additional major thoroughfares that were part of the Third Network. They were streets that he had not succeeded in including in the Second Network or whose necessity became evident after the planning of the Second Network. On the Left Bank were the western extremity of the Boulevard Saint-Germain, from the Pont de la Concorde to the Rue Saint-Dominique, and the Rue de Rennes from the Rue de Vaugirard to the Church of Saint-Germain des Prés. On the

[30] Haussmann, *Mémoires*, III, 81-85; *Moniteur*, May 2, 1861.

opposite bank Haussmann using municipal funds alone built the long Rue des Pyrénées near the eastern limits of the city from Bercy to the Buttes-Chaumont and extended the Rue Lafayette from the Rue du Faubourg Poissonnière to a junction with the Boulevard Haussmann behind the new opera house. The former joined together the newly annexed quarters on the east side, and the latter carried an imperial highway from the east into the heart of Paris and provided the most direct route between the west end and the Northern and the Eastern railway stations.

North of the hill of Montmartre a populous quarter was growing up during the Empire. The new Boulevard Ornano provided access to it from the east side of Paris, and Haussmann was anxious to connect it conveniently with the western half of the city, too. Heavy wagons could not use the steep roads over the hill but had to take a circuitous route that doubled the distance. Various solutions to the problem were suggested, ranging from tunnelling through the hill to clearing it completely away. Haussmann proposed to build the Rue Caulain-court from the Boulevard de Clichy around the western and northern flanks of the hill. A bridge was to carry the street over the Montmartre Cemetery, and holders of lots in the area under the bridge were offered their choice of any of the lots remaining in the cemetery. The city assumed all expenses of moving bodies and monuments. Holders of lots in the corner cut off by the bridge were given the same privileges even though their lots were not directly touched by the project. When the land needed for the bridge piles had been cleared and Haussmann was about to begin construction, two sons of Admiral Baudin, who was buried in the corner of the cemetery cut off by the bridge, petitioned the Senate to annul the decree authorizing the project because it altered property rights granted them by the city and, therefore, violated the right of private property guaranteed by the Constitution. Their legal position, Haussmann maintained, was indefensible since a perpetual concession in a cemetery was not a sale of property and conferred no property rights, but the petitioners found a strong supporter in Senator LeRoy de Saint-Arnaud, who had been one of the aspirants to replace Berger as Prefect of the Seine and who welcomed this chance to harass his successful rival. After long debate the Senate sustained the legality of the decree but only by a narrow margin of votes, and Haussmann admitted that he was unable to destroy the sympathy of the Senate for the complainants. The Senate's attitude together with repeated demands for new studies of the project constrained Haussmann to postpone the construction of the bridge, and both it and the Rue Caulaincourt remained unbuilt at the end of the Empire.[81]

The Rue Caulaincourt was not the only project of Louis Napoleon and Haussmann unfinished when the Empire fell. In the last years of the Empire the heavy attack on Haussmann, his fall from favor, and his dismissal in January, 1870, slowed the building program, and when the Emperor surrendered at Sedan nine months later a number of projects remained incomplete, among them the Avenue de l'Opéra, the Avenue de la République, the Boulevard Saint-Germain, and the Boulevard Raspail. In the two preceding decades, however, the city had built some eighty-five miles of new streets, and private interests had completed another five miles. Thirty-three miles of old streets had been eliminated or incorporated into the newly built ways so the net gain in streets was around fifty-seven miles, an increase of about 12 per cent in the length of the city's street system. But by themselves these figures are misleadingly small. The new streets were much wider than the old. The average width of streets suppressed did not exceed twenty-four feet, and the new streets generally ranged between sixty-five and one hundred feet. Haussmann estimated that the average width of all streets in the old city in 1869, including the old as well as the new, was double what it had been in 1852. The pedestrian, who had fared so badly on many of the city's streets, could by 1869 walk safely on more than 700 miles of sidewalks, and he could enjoy the shade of nearly twice as many trees as in 1852, planted along the boulevards and principal avenues.[32]

Neither Haussmann's work on streets nor his difficulties with

[81] Haussmann, *Mémoires*, III, 93-100; *Times* (London), Jan. 16, 1868; *Journal officiel de l'Empire français*, Mar. 11, 1869.
[82] Haussmann, *Mémoires*, II, 513; *J.O.*, Supplément, May 1869, p. 7.

them ended with their original construction. One vexing problem was the discovery of street surfaces that would stand the wear of the rapidly mounting traffic. The number of carriages and wagons on the streets nearly doubled between 1853 and 1859 and continued to increase in the next decade. Traffic counts showed 9,000 horses daily on the Boulevard des Capucines in 1850, 23,000 in 1868; 4,000 on the Rue de Rivoli in 1850, 15,000 in 1868.[33] Sandstone blocks, the usual paving material in 1850, deteriorated quickly under such heavy use, and when the edges became worn they made a very rough and noisy surface. Before Haussmann's time the city substituted macadam on some streets, and its smoothness appealed to owners of carriages, its quiet, to residents on busy streets, and the Emperor, thinking chiefly of a firm footing for horses, insisted that all main streets be macadamized. Unfortunately, macadam surface was dusty in the dry months of summer, and muddy in wet weather, and required Parisians either "to keep a carriage or walk on stilts." Macadam, moreover, required expensive maintenance (four times as expensive as cobblestone streets, Haussmann claimed), and gravel washed from it by rains clogged the sewers and had to be removed at additional expense.[34]

On some streets Haussmann struck a compromise by installing a center of macadam bordered by strips paved with stones, but the costs and inconveniences of macadam bothered him, and he experimented with various substitutes: blocks of certain hard stones, wooden blocks, concrete, and asphalt. He favored small blocks of porphyry, a very hard stone, laid with tight joints to make a surface that was smooth and highly resistant to heavy wear. Constant use made it so slippery, however, that it was impractical on sloping streets. Wooden block paving was expensive to install and insufficiently resistant to the wear of heavy vehicles. Asphalt, which had long been used for sidewalks and street crossings, had the same faults and failed to offer much traction to horses' hooves, and some thought it far too quiet for the safety of pedestrians accustomed to using only

[33] *Moniteur*, Dec. 5, 1860; *J.O.*, Feb. 25, 1869.
[34] *Moniteur*, Dec. 5, 1860; *Builder*, VIII (1850), 188-89, XX (1862), 584; Haussmann, *Mémoires*, III, 137-38, 141-42; *Revue générale de l'architecture et des travaux publics* (Paris), XII (1854), 257-60.

the third of the three precautions, "Stop, Look, and Listen." But it had the advantage of being unsuitable for building barricades, and the problem of slipperiness could be solved by mixing sand with the asphalt. In the later years of the Empire it was being increasingly used on the streets in the center of the city. In 1867 the city began to repave with asphalt all the streets in the busy area from the Rue de Rivoli north to the inner boulevards and between the Rue Royale on the west and the Rue Croix des Petits-Champs near the old Louvre on the east.[35]

Lighting was another problem, for imperial Paris had inherited streets that were ill-lighted and often dangerous for travel by night. Through most of the decade of the fifties the street lamps were a responsibility of the Prefect of Police, and his Lighting Service brightened the streets of Paris with some 3,000 new gas lamps and substituted all-night lighting the year around for the seasonal and intermittent lighting of the forties. In the autumn of 1859 the Emperor transferred this service to the Prefecture of the Seine, and in the next decade the new service added 15,000 lamps, doubling the number in use. The area annexed to the city in 1860 received most of the new installations, but the old city benefited from the adoption of improved reflectors and new lamp fixtures that cast a minimum shadow and from the reduction of the height of the lamps above the street so that more light reached the pavement.[36] Experiments were made with electric lights, and some found practical application for night work on construction projects, but Haussmann spurned them for street-lighting, holding that they were injurious to the eyes.[37] Shortly before Haussmann became Prefect of the Seine a Parisian architectural journal carried an announcement that an experiment would be made in lighting the entire Rue de Rivoli with an electric floodlight to be in-

35 *Moniteur*, Sept. 30, 1858, Dec. 5, 1860, Feb. 19, 1861, Mar. 6, 1864, Dec. 11, 1867; *Builder*, xxiv (1866), 937, xxv (1867), 832, xxvi (1868), 120; Haussmann, *Mémoires*, iii, 139-44; *Revue de l'architecture*, xii (1854), 260.

36 Haussmann, *Mémoires*, iii, 156-57; *Moniteur*, July 5, 1851, Oct. 27, 1858, June 12, Dec. 12, 1861, July 18, 1862, Dec. 6, 1863; *J.O.*, Supplément, May 1869, p. 7; *Builder*, xx (1862), 571.

37 *Moniteur*, Aug. 26, 1853, May 9, 1854, Feb. 17, 1861; *Builder*, xxiv (1866), 611.

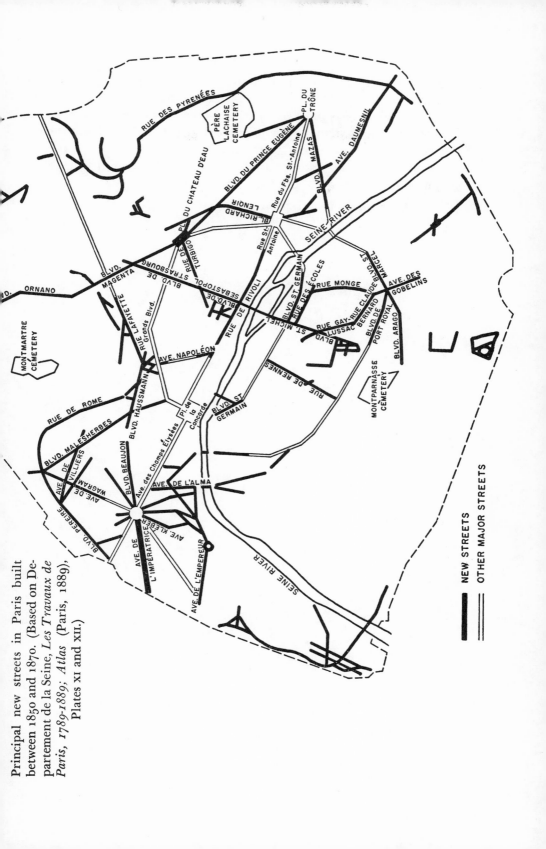

Principal new streets in Paris built between 1850 and 1870. (Based on Departement de la Seine, *Les Travaux de Paris, 1789-1889; Atlas* (Paris, 1889), Plates XI and XII.)

NEW STREETS

OTHER MAJOR STREETS

stalled like a lighthouse beacon at the street's eastern extremity near the City Hall.[38] There is no evidence that it was ever tried, and perhaps it was blocked by Haussmann. Although ordinarily a perspicacious man he made a reckless prediction about the electric light; ". . . apart from its inventor, its promoters, and its manufacturers," he declared, "no one will favor it after a time but oculists and opticians."[39]

[38] *Revue d l'architecture,* XI (1853), 79.
[39] Haussmann, *Mémoires,* III, 164.

IV · BUILDINGS AND PARKS

NAPOLEON III AND HAUSSMANN did not transform Paris with boulevards and avenues alone. New buildings and public parks did as much as streets to change the appearance and life of the city. Among the public buildings the well-known structures: the Central Markets, the final portions of the Louvre, the new Opera House, the *Salle du Travail* of the Bibliothèque Nationale, the Hôtel Dieu, were but a small part of a list that included more than seventy schools in the annexed area alone, fifteen churches and synagogues, two large hospitals, nine barracks, seven markets. Many other buildings were enlarged or rebuilt, and private building raised the total of new construction even higher.

Napoleon's career as a builder of monumental buildings began simultaneously with his career as a builder of streets. The Central Markets ranked with the Rue de Rivoli as one of the two most urgent projects he forced the reluctant Prefect of the Seine, Berger, to undertake in the summer of 1851, and when he accelerated public works following the *Coup d'Etat* in December, 1851, the completion of the Louvre stood side by side with the Boulevard de Strasbourg and the Rue des Ecoles among the newly instituted works.

The construction of the Central Markets was an immense project, long contemplated and often postponed. Napoleon I, struck by the congestion in the ancient market district east of the Halle aux Blés, had ordered the building of spacious new markets on this site, but the expropriation and clearing of a portion of the land were the only accomplishments before the Empire fell. In the 1840's the municipal authorities took up Napoleon's proposals once again, but they moved slowly—discussions began in 1842, the site was fixed and architects appointed in 1845, and preliminary plans drawn up in 1847.[1] Nothing had been built when Louis Napoleon became President of the Republic late in 1848, but he did find a project for which much of the spadework was already done, and it had a special appeal to him: it was Napoleonic in origin, and its completion would contrast Napoleonic accomplishment with Orleanist procrastination. Along with that other Napoleonic project, the Rue de Rivoli, he gave it first priority in his building program.

In reviving plans for the Central Markets Louis Napoleon also revived an old dispute over their location. The first Napoleon had personally selected a large rectangular area lying between the Halle aux Blés and the Rue Saint-Denis. In 1845 the Municipal Council rejected a rival position on the river front and retained Napoleon's site, but five years later the pressure of a group of promoters induced the Council to reconsider the location. This group, headed by an architect named Horeau, proposed to build three immense market pavilions in an elongated plot extending from the river where the Chatelet Theater now stands to the Market of the Innocents on the present site of Goujon's Fountain of the Innocents, and they conducted a vigorous campaign to get the plan accepted. They hired a well-known lawyer to write a promotional brochure, had a scale model of the buildings placed on public display, persuaded the Minister of the Interior to induce the Municipal Council to consider their proposal, and won the tightfisted Berger's support by convincing him that a company they proposed to organize to build the markets could get a large subsidy from the state. The Municipal Council found a number of flaws in the project, and it knew, too, that a shift to any new plan would bring additional delay and expense. In the end not a single councillor voted for the proposal. The decision was certainly justified, but twentieth century Paris may well regret the loss of one feature of Horeau's plan—a vast parking area (to accommodate 4,000 wagons and 800 horses) in the single

1 V. Baltard and F. Callet, *Monographie des Halles centrales de Paris* (Paris, 1863), pp. 7-9, 12-14.

huge cellar he proposed to build under the three pavilions.[2]

The Council also considered a plan to move the markets to the Left Bank near the Pont de la Tournelle and another to break them up into a number of small specialized markets to be located chiefly in outlying quarters. It rejected both and finally ended the dispute by readopting, with some modifications, the project drawn up in 1847 by the architects Baltard and Callet for the site Napoleon I had selected.[3]

With these matters settled and financing provided by the 50,000,000 franc loan approved by the National Assembly in August, 1851, Berger pushed work on the Central Markets rapidly forward. On September 15, 1851, Napoleon laid the initial stone of the first pavilion, and eighteen months later it was nearly completed. Then in June, 1853, all work was suddenly stopped. The new building with its heavy stone walls, small doorways, and narrow slit windows looked less like a market than a blockhouse intended to pacify a turbulent quarter. The people of the district, punning on the name of the porters of the markets, called it "le Fort de la Halle," and the building so dismayed the Emperor that he ordered suspension of the whole project until new plans could be drawn.[4]

Napoleon called on a number of architects to submit proposals, and he asked Haussmann, who had just taken over the prefecture, to receive and study the new projects preliminary to submitting them to him. The Emperor confided to Haussmann his fascination with the newly completed train shed of the Strasbourg Railway in Paris, a great roof of glass supported by a framework of iron, and he hoped that similar "umbrellas" of glass and iron might be used for the pavilions of the Central Markets. Haussmann, according to his own account, undertook to fulfill the Emperor's hopes and at the same time to help his old school-mate, the architect Baltard, reestablish himself after

[2] Baltard and Callet, *Halles centrales*, pp. 12-16; Charles Merruau, *Souvenirs de l'Hôtel de Ville de Paris, 1848-1852* (Paris, 1875), pp. 380-87; *Revue générale de l'architecture et des travaux publics* (Paris), VIII (1849-50), 154-55, 157, 159.

[3] Merruau, *Souvenirs*, pp. 381, 387; Baltard and Callet, *Halles centrales*, p. 14.

[4] *Moniteur universel*, Sept. 8, 1853; *Revue de l'architecture*, XI (1853), 224, XII (1854), 7-8; Baltard and Callet, *Halles centrales*, pp. 17-18; Merruau, *Souvenirs*, p. 443.

the disgrace of having his work publicly spurned by the Emperor. He called Baltard to his office, gave him a sketch of what Napoleon had in mind, and urged him to draw plans embodying the Emperor's ideas.[5]

"Iron! Iron!" Haussmann shouted. "Nothing but iron!"

But French architects and builders still looked on iron as an oddity, and an expensive oddity, too, and Baltard, a Grand Prix de Rome, found in his classic models no precedent for its use. His first plan was for a building with an iron roof supported by stone walls and stone columns. The Prefect rejected it. On the second the stone walls were gone, but the columns remained. Haussmann rejected it, too. On the third all was metal and glass except the stone foundations of the iron columns, the brick vaulting in the basement, and a light brick wall about six feet high at ground level to serve as a windbreak.

When the proposals of the competing architects were presented to the Emperor he examined them with mounting disappointment until at last he came to Baltard's drawings.

Then he burst out enthusiastically, "That's it! That's exactly it!"

He wanted to proceed immediately to construction, but Haussmann urged the preparation of more detailed plans before the final decision should be made. After these plans were drawn up Napoleon gave his final approval and decorated Baltard not knowing that he was also the architect of the unfortunate "Fort de la Halle."

In their own account Baltard and Callet minimized Haussmann's role and implied that the suggestion of a light, iron-work structure came originally from them. Haussmann was indignant at what he regarded as Baltard's gross ingratitude. Some years later, after his retirement, Haussmann retained Baltard to direct repair work on two houses he owned in the south of France, and Baltard compounded his earlier ingratitude by sending his former superior a bill that Haussmann regarded as outrageously high.[6]

The architect's new plans for the markets called for a group

---

[5] *Revue de l'architecture*, XXII (1854), 7-8; G. E. Haussmann, *Mémoires* (Paris, 1890-93), III, 478-83.

[6] Baltard and Callet, *Halles centrales*, p. 18; Haussmann, *Mémoires*, III, 487-88.

of six pavilions divided by three covered streets and, on the opposite side of a broad central avenue (later named the Rue Baltard), a group of four pavilions similarly separated by two covered streets. In 1857 Haussmann and Baltard agreed to add two pavilions to the second group. Together they provided a market space of twenty-one acres, ten times the area available in 1850, and nearly half of it was covered. Gas lights permitted night-time operations, and a special reservoir assured a normal flow of water to all outlets in the markets for several days should the supply from the public mains be interrupted. In the cellar plans Baltard made provision for access to the markets by an underground railway connecting with the trunk lines into the city, and underground passageways between the pavilions were actually built, but the remainder of the railway project never materialized. The first group of six pavilions was opened in 1858, and four of the second group were completed before the end of the Empire. Together with the remaining two, not added until the 1930's, the ten pavilions of the Second Empire continue to serve as the city's central market nearly a century later. Baltard's first stone pavilion was torn down in the late 1860's, and one of his iron and glass structures arose in its place.[7]

Baltard in two other buildings reaffirmed his grasp of the possibilities of structural iron. The three pavilions he designed for the livestock market at La Villette were umbrellas of glass and iron like the Central Markets. Later in the Church of Saint-Augustin he adapted an iron framework to a classical building. When Haussmann assigned to him the design of a church to occupy the conspicuous site at the junction of the Boulevard Malesherbes and the Avenue de Friedland, Baltard faced the problem of erecting a structure in the traditional cruciform plan and with adequate capacity on a site that was too narrow to permit the use of buttresses or heavy walls. He solved the problem by enclosing virtually all the site within curtain walls and by supporting the roof and dome on a framework of iron. Faithful to his Beaux Arts training he made the building look like a conventional church, even to the extent

[7] Baltard and Callet, *Halles centrales*, pp. 18-21; *Revue de l'architecture*, XV (1857), 103-04, XX (1862), 280-81, XXII (1864), 213; Adolphe Joanne, *Paris illustré en 1870 et 1877* (3d edit.; Paris, [n.d.]), p. 1003.

of having massive stone piers in the nave, but he left undis-
guised beside them the slender iron pillars that actually carried
the weight of the roof, and he left the iron arches of the roof
exposed, too. The exterior of the church was conventional in
appearance, although people complained that the finial looked
like a cast iron stove set atop the dome.[8]

The completion of the Louvre and its junction with the
Tuileries Palace, like the construction of the Central Markets,
was another of those accomplishments that Napoleon III would
regard as typical of his regime—the completion of a major
project long considered by preceding governments and always
postponed. Over the course of six centuries successive monarchs
had rebuilt and added to the original fortress of the Louvre
and built the adjacent Palace of the Tuileries. Napoleon I had
ordered the filling of the break in the great quadrangle of the
two palaces by the construction of a gallery along the new Rue
de Rivoli, but at the end of the Empire the new gallery extended only from the Tuileries to the Rue de Rohan, and a
gap of about 800 feet remained. It was filled with a confused
mass of old buildings that extended southward across the area
between the two palaces and formed the frightening slum that
Balzac described in *Cousine Bette*.

The republican government in 1848 took up the project
again, and the Law of October 4, 1849, on the extension of the
Rue de Rivoli and the clearing of the area between the Louvre
and the Tuileries, was introduced in the National Assembly
under the title, "Law on the completion of the Louvre,"
although it only prepared the way for that object. After the
Coup d'Etat in 1851 and with the clearing authorized by the
law of 1849 nearly completed, Napoleon decreed the joining of
the two palaces along the Rue de Rivoli and the erection of
additional wings proposed by the architect Visconti. To cover
the costs he allocated to the project more than 26,000,000
francs from state funds.[9]

While incomplete the two palaces had stood as a challenge to
architects as well as to ambitious rulers, for the effort to connect

8 Haussmann, *Mémoires*, III, 484; *Builder* (London), XXIV (1866), 27; Joanne,
Paris, pp. 322-24, 1018.
9 *Moniteur*, Oct. 5, 1849; Merruau, *Souvenirs*, p. 487.

them posed a difficult problem of harmonizing two ill-compatible masses. The Louvre and the Tuileries had been built as separate palaces with no thought of their being joined, and they did not lie on parallel axes. The problem of connecting them without producing an irregularity of line apparent to the eye had exercised the ingenuity of many French architects. Visconti solved it by building, in addition to the gallery along the Rue de Rivoli, two large wings (extending into the recently cleared area) that limited the view of the older buildings and drew one's attention away from the sections where the conflicting axes were most apparent. He was so successful that even today with the Tuileries Palace gone it is a rare visitor who is aware that the two wings of the Louvre are not parallel. At the same time Visconti's buildings met Louis Napoleon's practical requirements of accommodations for two ministries, additional galleries for the museum of the Louvre, and stables and coach houses for 140 horses and fifty carriages.[10]

The project quickly served Napoleon's purposes of providing employment in the capital and of advertising his good works. Although authorized only in March, 1852, excavations began in May, and the first stone was formally laid two months later. In 1853 as many as three thousand men were employed on the project, and it continued to furnish many hundreds of jobs until completed in 1857. It was a conspicuous project and attracted much popular attention. In the middle fifties a stop at the Louvre to see how the work was progressing became an established part of the usual Sunday promenade. Napoleon himself was a frequent visitor, and he often suggested changes or additions in the building, so often indeed that the Minister of State, who was responsible for the budget of the project, had to instruct the architect to report to him after each imperial visit the changes proposed by the Emperor together with estimates of their probable costs.[11]

[10] *Builder*, x (1852), 443, xii (1854), 131, 139; *Revue de l'architecture*, x (1852), 180-81; Louis Hautecoeur, *Histoire du Louvre* (Paris, [n.d.]), pp. 85, 96-98; Christiane Aulanier, *Le Nouveau Louvre de Napoleon III* (Paris, [1953]), pp. 12-13.

[11] *Moniteur*, Jan. 31, 1854, Feb. 28, 1855, Feb. 18, 1856; *Revue de l'architecture*, x (1852), 180, xiii (1855), 85; Aulanier, *Nouveau Louvre*, pp. 14-15.

Napoleon made the termination of the project the occasion for an elaborate inaugural ceremony. The Emperor and the Empress, the princes and princesses of the imperial family, the ministers, the "Great Officers of the Crown," and the marshals and admirals of France all took part. The mint struck a commemorative medal, and the Emperor presented duplicates of it to some fifty workmen who had participated in the building. That evening the Minister of State, Fould, presided over a banquet for the architects, contractors, and workers.[12]

Visconti did not live to see the palace completed. He died in 1853 when work was only well started. His successor, Hector Lefuel, put an additional story on his buildings and embellished their façades and an adjoining façade of one of older parts of the Louvre with elaborate sculptured ornamentation inspired by Lescot's and Lemercier's decoration in the sixteenth and seventeenth centuries of one façade on the palace's inner court.[13] But Lefuel lacked their genius, and he lacked the sculptor Goujon, who had worked with Lescot. Lefuel's ornamentation has been severely criticized for its extravagance, and to the taste of a century later it is unfortunate when compared with the more restrained ornamentation of the two palaces in earlier reigns. Yet Lefuel expressed the taste of the Second Empire— a taste that admired display and rich effects. Compared with Perrault's magnificent colonnaded façade on the east front of the old Louvre Lefuel's façades are excessive. Beside Garnier's new opera house (or the Albert Memorial in London, a contemporaneous creation) they are less offensive.

On the east side of the palace, opposite Perrault's façade, clearing of old buildings in the fifties left a large open space broken only by the Church of Saint-Germain l'Auxerrois. Fould proposed to Haussmann that it, too, be demolished, but the Prefect opposed the suggestion even though he admitted that the church "recalls a date that I execrate." On Saint Bartholomew's Day, August 24, 1572, during the religious wars Catholics had used the bell of the church to give the signal for the

12 *Moniteur*, Aug. 15, 1857.
13 Hautecoeur, *Histoire du Louvre*, pp. 98-100; Yvan Christ, *Le Louvre et les Tuileries* (Paris, 1949), pp. 105-06.

massacre of Protestants in Paris. Haussmann was a Protestant, and if he demolished the building, "no one," he declared, "would see it as anything but an act of revenge for the Saint Bartholomew's Massacre." The church was allowed to stand, and it remains today on the Place du Louvre. Because it stood at one side of the *place* Haussmann attempted to balance it by building the adjacent *mairie* of the first arrondissement in similar style and mass. A contemporary guidebook described the result as "the heaviest, the most ridiculous, the most absurd structure in all Paris."[14]

Another act of violence almost as well-known as the Saint Bartholomew's Massacre influenced the building of one of the great monuments of the Second Empire. The Opera House was inspired by an attempt to assassinate the Emperor. On the evening of January 14, 1858, an Italian named Orsini hurled three bombs at the imperial carriage as it drew up to the entrance of the old opera house on the Rue Le Peletier. The explosions left the Emperor and the Empress unharmed but killed or wounded several of their escort and injured scores of persons in the crowd gathered to watch the Emperor's arrival. In the following weeks the government took severe repressive measures against all opposition elements in France, and Haussmann conceived the idea of reducing the danger of repetition of the Orsini attack by moving the opera to a site on the Boulevard des Capucines with more spacious and more easily guarded approaches.[15]

Replacement of the old opera house was overdue. Built of used materials in 1821 as a temporary home for the national Academy of Music, it was, four decades later, in danger of collapse and a fire hazard, and it could not be adapted to the installation of modern stage machinery. Nonetheless, when the Legislative Body got wind of Haussmann's plan, several members were alarmed by what looked to them like another foolish extravagance. The Budget Committee asked the President of the Council of State for an explanation of the government's intentions, and he reassured them that the cabinet had made no

14 Haussmann, *Mémoires*, III, 500-02; Joanne, *Paris*, p. 138.
15 *Moniteur*, Sept. 18, 1858.

decision on the building of a new opera house nor on the selection of a site.[16]

Undeterred by this non-committal reply Haussmann with the approval of the Municipal Council went ahead with acquisition of land on the location he favored, sponsors of rival sites put forward their claims, and in April, 1860, the Prefect appointed a committee to study the various proposals. One project, with startling disregard for the past, would have put the new structure on the west side of the Place Vendôme in the axis of a new avenue running eastward out of the *place*, through the garden of the Palais Royal, to the Central Markets. Another plan proposed to place the opera house and another similar building (perhaps for the *Comédie Française*) on opposite sides of the entrance to the Avenue des Champs Elysées across the Place de la Concorde from the Tuileries Garden. The committee reasonably feared that the juxtaposition of two such attractions would produce formidable traffic congestion twice each evening. A third plan would put the new structure on the present site of the Hôtel Crillon and the adjoining buildings behind Gabriel's classic façade on the Place de la Concorde west of the Rue Royale, and still another would place it across the Rue Boissy d'Anglas where the American Embassy is now located.[17]

After considering all the proposals the committee recommended Haussmann's site on the Boulevard des Capucines, which suggests that its inquiries were only a bit of window-dressing, but the Prefect's location had advantages of accessibility (the committee noted the city's intention to build the Avenue de l'Opéra, from the Boulevard des Capucines to the Rue Saint-Honoré, and other streets around the site); the site could be cleared without sacrifice or disfigurement of architectural monuments; and it could be used without loss of precious park space. The government followed the committee's recommendation, and in September, 1860, authorized construc-

16 Archives nationales (Paris), C 1059, Corps législatif, Session 1859, Dossier No. 19; C 1077, Corps législatif, Session 1861, Dossier No. 187; Claude Rambuteau, *Memoirs* (N.Y., 1908), p. 304; *Moniteur*, Sept. 18, 1858.

17 *Revue de l'architecture*, XVIII (1860), 89; Arch. nat., C 1077, Dossier No. 187.

tion of the new opera house on the Boulevard des Capucines where it now stands.[18]

Before the site was fixed the Minister of State Fould had commissioned an architect named Rohault de Fleury to draw plans for the opera house, and in cooperation with the municipal administration the architect also prescribed the design of the façades that builders on the adjacent streets were required to follow. By the autumn of 1860 work had started on the neighboring buildings, but the opera house itself was still only on paper when, in November, 1860, Count Walewski (a man with the unusual distinction of being the illegitimate son of Napoleon I and the husband of Napoleon III's current favorite) succeeded Fould in the Ministry of State. The new minister scrapped Fleury's plans, and though it was too late to change the design of the facing buildings, he announced an open competition to choose an architect for the opera house. With the commission as architect of a great building to rise in the heart of the capital as the glittering first prize, there was no dearth of competitors. Although they had but a month to prepare plans, they submitted some 170 projects before the closing date on January 31, 1861. The jury, which included Walewski and Lefuel, architect of the new Louvre, found none of them acceptable and withheld the first prize until the completion of a second competition among the top five contestants. In that round the jury's choice fell upon Charles Garnier, a little-known young architect who had won fifth prize in the first competition.[19]

Garnier soon had working plans ready, and before the year was out construction had started. For six years it went on, concealed behind the high wooden screens that Parisian builders commonly erected around their structures. When workmen removed the screens and scaffolding from the south front in 1867, Parisians and visitors alike flocked to see it, and it rivalled the Universal Exposition of that year as an attraction. But this was only a tantalizing lifting of a corner of the curtain. Not

[18] *Ibid.; Recueil général des Senatus-consultes, décrets et arrêtés*, Series XI, Vol. VIII (1860), 531.

[19] Haussmann, *Mémoires*, III, 503-04; *Moniteur*, Dec. 31, 1860, June 9, 1861; *Revue de l'architecture*, XIX (1861), 19, 82-84, 103, 105-06.

until 1869 were all the façades uncovered and the statuary groups put in place. That autumn a trade journal reported that the building was to be completed before the end of the following summer, but in February, 1870, an English visitor with some difficulty obtained permission to visit the interior, and he found it completely empty with only a few iron columns to mark the positions of the boxes, lobbies, and staircases. Few Frenchmen knew it at the time, but the building was only a shell. The construction of the elaborate interior was left to the succeeding government and was completed only in 1874.[20]

The Orsini attack on the Emperor influenced the design of the new opera house as well as its location. One of the conditions set for architects in the competition opened in 1860 was that the imperial box should have a private entry through a vestibule into which the Emperor's party could drive and avoid stopping and alighting in the street. On both lateral façades Garnier placed pavilions penetrated by carriage ramps. The entry on the west side was reserved for the Emperor, and immediately above it Garnier put a reception room, dressing rooms for both the Emperor and the Empress, and a corridor leading to the imperial box. Napoleon never used his private entry, since the building was not completed until after his exile and death, and it now fills a less glamorous role as the quarters for the museum and library of the Opera.

The Opera, like the Louvre, was much criticized for its artistic shortcomings. It looked like a sideboard overloaded with knicknacks, someone remarked, and most observers agreed that whatever it looked like it was ill-adapted to its site. The architect Garnier himself admitted that he knew of no building, ancient or modern, that had a more deplorable situation. The structure seemed to be buried in a rock quarry, he declared, so closely was it enclosed by the buildings around it, and from some angles, owing to the slope of the ground, it suggested a crate about to slide off a tipping raft. When he walked by, Garnier said, he always found himself leaning in the opposite

20 *Revue de l'architecture*, xxv (1867), 141; *Builder*, xxv (1867), 751, xxvii (1869), 409, 681; xxviii (1870), 121.

direction, trying to get the raft back to a level position. In his own defense Garnier protested that he had had no voice in the selection of the site nor in the planning of the adjacent streets and buildings. Indeed, the structure rests in a setting conceived for another building. When Garnier became the architect the positions of the bounding streets were already determined and the design of the facing buildings fixed, drawn up by Rohault de Fleury as a setting for the opera house he planned. Garnier could not change them. He was, however, responsible for the lavish ornamentation of the façades of the Opera House with sculpture, gilding, and vari-colored stone. The unveiling of the nude figures of Carpeaux's "La Danse" on the south front produced loud protest, and rumor was that a few persons had sworn to destroy it if it were not removed, but the only damage done was a stain from a bottle of ink some zealot hurled at the figures. This particular protest against "La Danse" was an expression of moral indignation (suggesting, incidentally, that the Second Empire was perhaps more Victorian than its reputation), but most of the criticism of the exterior was on aesthetic grounds—the ornamentation offended good taste by its excesses. Garnier quipped that he was building a theater, not a morgue or a prison, and no one would want it plain and severe.[21]

"If I ever build a penitentiary," he declared, "I assure you I will produce a façade so mournful that it will be less sad to be behind it than in front of it."[22]

On the Ile de La Cité Haussmann did not quite achieve his ambition of demolishing every private building on the island and making it the exclusive preserve of law, religion, and medicine, but he came very close to it.[23] In all of old Paris no other area of comparable size was so completely altered by new or remodeled buildings. In 1850, aside from the Cathedral, the Palace of Justice, and two buildings of the Public Relief Administration, the island was covered with a mass of old houses into which crowded more than 14,000 residents, making it one

[21] Charles Garnier, Le Nouvel Opéra de Paris (Paris, 1878-81), I, 9, 28, 102-04, 106-07; Builder, XXVII (1869), 682, 720, 781.
[22] Garnier, Nouvel Opéra, I, 22.
[23] Haussmann, Mémoires, III, 554.

of the worst slums of Paris. In 1870 only two small triangles of houses remained, one between the cathedral and the north branch of the river and the other opposite the new west front of the Palace of Justice, and but a few hundred people made their homes on the island.

Work on remodeling and enlarging the sprawling Palace of Justice began under the July Monarchy, and it continued throughout the Empire. The most conspicuous changes were the addition of a wing at the western extremity of the older portions of the palace and the construction of a new building for the Prefecture of Police on the south side adjoining the Quai des Orfèvres. The western wing had a monumental though little known façade facing the Place Dauphine and partially hidden by houses adjoining it. The architect, Joseph Louis Duc, planned to demolish all the buildings between the palace and the Pont Neuf and to create a large open space before the façade, but the plan remained unrealized when the Empire fell. The screening buildings were, however, eventually cleared away, though two rows of seventeenth century houses were left to define the limits of the new Place Dauphine.[24]

Demolition of the cafés and wine shops on the opposite side of the Palace of Justice opened up the more familiar view of the palace from the east. This area was cleared to make way for three new public buildings: the domed Tribunal of Commerce on the corner of the Quai de la Cité, a headquarters for the Paris Guard and the municipal fire department near the Pont Saint-Michel, and behind it a large barracks, presently used by the Prefecture of Police.[25]

The east front of this barracks now faces the great west façade of the Cathedral across the spacious Place du Parvis Notre-Dame. The restoration of the Cathedral, the work of Viollet-le-Duc, was completed during the Second Empire, but the undertaking was initiated by the government of Louis

24 Préfecture de la Seine, *Documents relatifs aux travaux du Palais de Justice et la reconstruction de la Préfecture de Police* (Paris, 1858), pp. 215-18, 237, 245, 247-48, 273, 280, 289; Joanne, *Paris*, pp. 907-08.
25 Haussmann, *Mémoires*, II, 487-88.

Philippe in the 1840's, and the imperial regime could claim credit only for continuing it.[26] On the other hand, the Baroque Place du Parvis, scarcely an appropriate setting for a medieval cathedral, and the new Hôtel Dieu on the north side of the Place were imperial conceptions. In 1850 the area of the square was only partially cleared. On the north stood the central offices of the Public Relief Administration and on the south one building of the old Hôtel Dieu, a municipal hospital. The Relief Administration moved to new quarters on the Avenue Victoria opposite the City Hall in 1858, but the need for hospital space saved its old building from the wreckers. The nearby pavilion of the Hôtel Dieu was falling into ruin and marked for demolition, and its patients were transferred to the old office building until a new hospital could be completed. The removal of these buildings and the landscaping of the Place were not finally accomplished until 1882.[27]

The Hôtel Dieu, largest of the municipal hospitals in 1850, consisted of several poorly coordinated buildings erected over many decades as funds happened to be available. One large building overhung the Seine on the south side of the Place du Parvis Notre-Dame, and across the river stood another large building and several smaller structures adjoining the Church of Saint-Julien le Pauvre, which served as the chapel of the hospital. A foot bridge connected the buildings on opposite banks of the river. Demands to replace this haphazard complex of buildings with a rationally designed structure were heard at least as early as the latter eighteenth century, and the growing pressure on charity hospitals produced by rising population and especially by the cholera epidemic in 1831 gave the demands new urgency in the 1830's. The first result then, however, was the construction of a new hospital on the Boulevard de la Chapelle, and not until 1864 did officials of the Relief

[26] Viollet-le-Duc was one of the most famous architects of the time and a personal friend of the Emperor, but he played no significant role in the rebuilding of Paris, his medieval taste having little in common with the academic classic style favored by Haussmann and Napoleon for Paris. In his memoirs the Prefect did not even mention him or the restoration of Notre-Dame.

[27] Haussmann, *Mémoires*, II, 430-31; Département de la Seine, *Les Travaux de Paris, 1789-1889; atlas* (Paris, 1889), Pl. XIII.

Administration announce plans to replace the old Hôtel Dieu.[28]

This announcement at once set off disputes over both the size and the location of the new hospital. The Emperor wanted to keep it in its historic place near the cathedral, and in 1865 he approved the preparation of a site covering four and a half acres between the Place du Parvis Notre-Dame on the south and the present Quai aux Fleurs on the north and between the Rue d'Arcole and the Rue de la Cité. The surgeons protested that their patients needed fresh air for their convalescence and urged that the hospital be built outside the city. The government spokesman replied that the river, the Place du Parvis Notre-Dame, the widened streets on the east and west fronts, the spacious interior courtyards, and mechanical ventilation assured plenty of air in the hospital. The medical doctors in general supported the government, but many of them urged that the size of the new hospital be reduced from the proposed 800 beds to 600 or even 400. So insistent were their protests that the Emperor ordered the planned four-story hospital cut to three stories, reducing the number of beds to 600. The Emperor also rejected the architect's original plan for the exterior of the building, substituting for his thirteenth century Gothic a simpler design with more window space. Construction began in 1868 and terminated a decade later. The dispute over the hospital's size revived in the seventies, and the partisans of a smaller hospital succeeded in getting the Relief Administration to eliminate the third story on the wings of the building, reducing the capacity to 400 or 450 beds.[29]

Erection of new buildings was not the exclusive province of the public authorities. Private entrepreneurs built them by the score during the Second Empire and even undertook to erect all the buildings on long stretches of newly opened streets. In 1854, for example, the Pereire brothers, two Parisian bankers, formed the *Compagnie des Immeubles et de l'Hôtel de la Rue*

---

[28] Joanne, *Paris*, pp. 936, 938-39; Galignani, *New Paris Guide* (Paris, 1845), p. 315; Armand Husson, *Etude sur les hôpitaux* (Paris, 1862), pp. 26-44; Arch. nat., C 1102, Corps législatif, Session 1865, Dossier No. 55.

[29] *Moniteur*, Aug. 24, 1864, July 1, 2, 1856; Arch. nat., C 1102, Dossier No. 55; Caisse des Travaux de Paris, *Compte moral et financier des opérations*, Année 1866, pp. 60-61; *Revue de l'architecture*, xxx (1873), 180-81; Haussmann, *Mémoires*, II, 521-26.

de Rivoli to buy the land and build along a quarter mile of the north side of the new Rue de Rivoli, and the company put up the familiar arcaded buildings that now stand there, including the Hôtel du Louvre and the Louvre department store. From the Rue de Rivoli the company, its name changed to the *Compagnie immobilière de Paris,* moved on to other construction jobs, and in the fifties and sixties it erected buildings on the Avenue des Champs Elysées, around the new opera house, on the Rue Lafayette, the Boulevard Malesherbes, and the Boulevard du Prince Eugène. The annual report to stockholders in 1867 stated that the company currently owned 102 buildings on the Boulevard du Prince Eugène alone.[30]

The company built to sell, and it disposed of most of its buildings once they were completed, but it continued to hold the Hôtel du Louvre, a large hostelry of 600 rooms, which it operated as one of the leading hotels of imperial Paris. So successful was it that the Pereires built an even larger hotel, the famous Grand Hôtel on the Boulevard des Capucines and the new Place de l'Opéra. A lavish and luxurious establishment, it was a fitting neighbor for Garnier's opera house. It had 700 guest rooms, seventy public rooms. Six hundred persons could sit down simultaneously in its elaborately decorated main dining room (and buy dinner for six francs!), and the hotel's guests enjoyed the unusual conveniences of elevators and central heating.[31]

The typical structure erected by private builders along the new avenues was an apartment building of six or seven stories. The ground floor was commonly given over to shops and a prominent entrance way, usually wide enough to admit a carriage; the entrance opened onto a passage to an inner court, whence stairways led to the apartments on the floors above. Balconies with gilded iron railings set off the windows in the

---

[30] *Builder,* XII (1855), 76-77; *Revue de l'architecture,* XX (1862), 285; Arch. nat., F¹ᶜ III Seine 31, May 19, June 1, 1854. The activities of the *Compagnie immobilière* were recorded in the company's annual reports or in the annual reports of its parent company, the *Crédit mobilier,* published in the *Moniteur* about May 1 of each year.

[31] *Moniteur,* April 30, 1861; Karl Baedeker, *Paris et la France du Nord* (Coblenz, 1867), pp. 3-4; Joanne, *Paris,* p. lvi, and Appendix, pp. 40-51.

façade, and a continuous iron railing crowned the cornice. Ornamental stone work—caryatids and consoles supporting balconies, pilasters, sculptured relief in the window heads, and decorative medallions—were common to most buildings. On any one street they were all about the same height, for the law fixed a maximum height, varying with the width of streets, and owners, anxious for the largest possible return from their high cost lands, built to the maximum. Often they added an extra rentable story above the cornice line by having a Mansard roof with dormer windows opening into rooms immediately under the roof timbers. Hundreds of these structures still stand in Paris today.[32]

The public authorities encouraged private builders with tax exemptions and favorable credit facilities, but committed to a planned city, they imposed restrictions on them, too. Regulations inherited from earlier regimes and tightened after 1850 required builders to conform to established building lines and street elevations as well as to restrict the height of new structures. Nothing in these regulations, however, gave the government authority to enforce conformity to particular designs. If he chose, a builder could erect side by side a Renaissance palace, a Moorish castle, and a Greek temple. Both Napoleon and Haussmann were anxious to achieve uniformity in the houses lining their new streets in the tradition of classical city planning, and they succeeded in doing it largely by contractual means. The city and state owned large areas of land in Paris, much of it acquired by condemnation for public works, and when they sold it they would bind the buyer by contract to erect buildings with façades, and perhaps lawns and fences, conforming to plans prescribed by the city. When the *Compagnie des Immeubles de la Rue de Rivoli* purchased land along the new Rue de Rivoli in 1855 it contracted to build façades identical with those on the older portion of the street, and detailed drawings were attached to the contract. Similar requirements were imposed on buyers of land bordering the Place de l'Etoile, the Rond Point des Champs Elysées, the Place de l'Opéra, the Bois de Boulogne, the Park of Mon-

32 *Builder*, xvi (1858), 158-59, 798-99, xix (1861), 729, xxii (1864), 200, 219, 407.

ceau, the Avenue de l'Impératrice, and many other streets. The contracts bound all subsequent owners as well as the first, and they were not permitted to alter the street fronts of their property.[33]

Napoleon also undertook to enforce certain standards of maintenance for all buildings, new and old. A decree issued in 1852 required proprietors to clean or repaint the façades of their buildings at least once every ten years. The maximum fine of 100 francs for failure to comply could not have been a very strong impellent, but a foreign observer reported in 1861 that cleaning operations could be seen in progress throughout Paris every spring. Some professional cleaners were equipped with portable boilers and rubber hoses and used steam to loosen the accumulation of dirt.[34]

There is a puzzling paradox in these regulatory activities. Both Napoleon and Haussmann professed and actually demonstrated in many ways their desire to improve living conditions in Paris. Both were anxious to destroy the old slums, and they did destroy them in many parts of the city, but they did nothing to assure that new slums would not rise in the places of the old or in peripheral quarters of the city where slum dwellers from the old city moved. Their building regulations were concerned almost exclusively with appearances. Builders had to conform to certain standards of height and to erect prescribed façades, but behind those façades they were free to build crowded and airless tenements, and many of them did.

The failure to cope adequately with the slums made the relief offered by public parks and open spaces especially important to the well-being of the city. In 1850 there were no municipal parks except the neglected Champs Elysées and the Place des Vosges, not fifty acres in all. The gardens of the Tuileries, the Palais Royal, the Luxembourg, and the Jardin des Plantes were national property open to Parisians only on sufferance. All of them were formal gardens laid out on geo-

[33] Charles Lortsch, *Le Beauté de Paris et la loi* (Paris, 1912), pp. 33-35, 95-110, 118; Haussmann, *Mémoires*, III, 25, 76, 215, 229, 256.
[34] *Recueil général des lois, décrets et arrêtés*, Series x, Vol. v (1852), 342; *Builder*, XIX (1861), 402, XXVI (1868), 333.

metric lines. The English gardens now in the city are a legacy of the Second Empire.

The Emperor instructed Haussmann to use every opportunity that the transformation of Paris might present to create small parks throughout the city similar to the squares of London. He perhaps thought of them as a substitute for improved housing, for he maintained that they would benefit the public health and, by presenting a happy contrast with the crowded slums, gradually effect a revolution in working class morality. Haussmann did not share the latter hope, but he was convinced of the value of parks to public health. His administration created twenty-two enclosed landscaped squares (fifteen of them in the old city) that were actually small parks varying in size from a quarter of an acre to six and a half acres, and it planted with trees and flowers and furnished with fountains and benches many more limited areas, like the Place du Chatelet or the Place du Louvre, left by the crossings of new streets or the disengagement of buildings.[35]

The squares were not among the Second Empire's most famous creations in Paris. With a few exceptions they were little known outside their immediate quarters, but they filled a need for easily accessible neighborhood parks that the larger, better known parks did not. Unlike the London squares that inspired them they were maintained by the city and were freely open to all, and there was one of them within easy walking distance of every Parisian's door.

Napoleon's first and major venture in park building, the Bois de Boulogne, sprang less from his concern for the slumdwellers of Paris than from his interest in landscape architecture and from a personal ambition to give Paris a Hyde Park. He took a hand in drawing up plans for lakes and driveways and planting, and when the work was in progress he frequently drove over from Saint-Cloud to watch and give directions. The visits were no formal, royal inspections; he knew what he wanted done, and if necessary, he would get out of his carriage and drive stakes into the ground to make his points clear.[36] It

[35] Haussmann, *Mémoires*, III, 240-53; Adolphe Alphand, *Les Promenades de Paris* (Paris, 1867-73), pp. 211-18, 240-42.
[36] T. W. Evans, *Memoirs* (N.Y., 1905), p. 35; Haussmann, *Mémoires*, III, 172-73.

was not the behavior of a man solely moved by the humanitarian motives Haussmann ascribed to the Emperor. Had he been so motivated, moreover, he would certainly have started his park building near the crowded quarters of the old city, not three miles away.[37]

When Louis Napoleon saw the Bois de Boulogne in 1848 and referred to it as an "arid promenade," it was a state forest, famous, a guidebook said, "for duelling and suicides." The avenues that crossed it were long and straight, as in all state forests, to facilitate hunting and policing, and few of them were kept in good repair. No lakes or waterfalls, no lawns or gardens varied its expanse of trees, and on the west an unsightly wall cut the Bois off from the Plain of Longchamps and the river.

In July, 1852, Napoleon transferred the Bois from the national government to the city of Paris on condition that the city spend at least 2,000,000 francs on its improvement in the next four years and maintain it permanently as a park. Direction of the landscaping was confided in a man named Varé, formerly the gardener on an estate of Louis Napoleon's father. In the spring of 1853 workmen began to clear trees from the site of the elongated lake, resembling the Serpentine in Hyde Park, that the Emperor wanted near the eastern limits of the Bois. When Haussmann succeeded to the prefecture in June, 1853, he found excavations already in progress at several points of the site. At first struck by the inclination of the land between the two extremities of the lake, he grew alarmed when he learned that Varé was proceeding almost blindly, having no elevations whatever marked on his working plans. Haussmann ordered one of the municipal engineers to survey the site, and he reported back that Varé's lake would be dry at one end and would overflow at the other. Napoleon had his heart set on a Serpentine in his park, and he refused to believe the report. Only when it was confirmed by his own aide-de-camp, a colonel of engineers, did he accept Haussmann's substitute plan for two lakes on different levels. Varé lost his job, and Haussmann

[37] Galignani, Guide (1845), p. 440; Haussmann, Mémoires, III, 184-85; Alphand, Promenades, pp. 2-3.

brought to Paris Adolphe Alphand, the artistic and talented young engineer of the Corps des Ponts et Chaussées whom he had met in Bordeaux when he was Prefect of the Gironde, and placed him in charge of the entire operation of converting the Bois into a park.[38]

The two lakes, roadways around them, and adjoining lawns were completed in 1854, and satisfaction with them contributed to the decision to undertake much more extensive work in the park. An imperial decree in 1854 and the Law of April 13, 1855, authorized the city to purchase and add to the Bois all of the Plain of Longchamps on the west and the Park of Madrid adjoining it on the north and to subdivide and sell as building lots certain outlying portions of the Bois. After the acquisitions and sales were completed the park had an area of 2,100 acres, nearly 200 more than in the former state forest.[39]

At the end of 1854 Alphand had new plans ready, work was begun the following year, and by 1858 the Bois had become the park and promenade familiar to Parisians today. Alphand eliminated all of the straight roads of the state forest except two, the Allée de Longchamps and the Allée de la Reine Marguerite, and in their place put forty-three miles of curving carriage roads and bridle paths. For pedestrians he provided meandering footpaths, some of them staked out by the Emperor himself. More than half the park was left in woods, and Alphand and his chief gardener, Barillet-Deschamps, planted 400,000 new trees and shrubs. The "aridity" of the old forest was dissimulated by the two principal lakes that stem from Napoleon's original plans and by smaller lakes and artificially created streams and waterfalls. Water pumped from the Seine entered the two large lakes over cascades contrived of cut stone to have a rustic appearance. When it was first put into the larger lake water escaped through the permeable soil more rapidly than the available pumping capacity could replace it. Simple remedies failed, and municipal engineers had to drain the lake and install a cement and mortar lining. From the

38 Haussmann, *Mémoires*, III, 121-25; Alphand, *Promenades*, p. 3.
39 Arch. nat., C 1042, Corps législatif, Session 1855, Dossier No. 26; Alphand, *Promenades*, pp. 3-6; Haussmann, *Mémoires*, III, 184, 186-90, 207.

lake a brook carried the water thus conserved a mile and a half through the Bois, and on the west side of the park it fed the imposing Cascade of Longchamps. Here the fall was twenty-five feet, and the volume of water required so large, some 12,000 gallons a minute, that, like a theatrical performance, the cascade functioned only for an audience. The water was permitted to flow over only once daily at the popular promenade hour in the afternoon. During the remainder of the day the stream filled the reservoir above the fall to make possible this brief show.[40]

Under the Cascade of Longchamps Alphand built two grottos furnished with paths and stairways so promenaders might stroll through. Haussmann explained in his memoirs almost apologetically that public taste demanded a grotto in every park, and Alphand built others in the Bois de Vincennes and the Park of Monceau and put the most imposing one of all in the Park of the Buttes-Chaumont. The later ones were improved models with artificial stalactites and stalagmites.[41]

While the municipal gardeners and grotto builders were occupied with these projects, the municipal architects were busy furnishing the park with many new buildings, rebuilding or redecorating those already there, and providing for the public's comfort and convenience by the erection of restaurants and cafés, shelter houses, benches, sign posts, and docks for boaters on the lakes. The extension of the Bois brought into the city's possession several residences. One of them, the Villa de Longchamps, was lavishly remodeled and furnished on the express orders of the Emperor, according to Haussmann's account, and then turned over to the Prefect of the Seine as a summer residence. Haussmann, ever anxious to refute accusations of personal extravagance, claimed that he accepted it with reluctance and that it only added to the heavy financial burdens of his office.[42]

When plans for transformation of the Bois were in preparation, the Duke de Morny, Louis Napoleon's half-brother and

[40] Alphand, *Promenades*, pp. 4-5, 27-34, 42-44, 51-52; Haussman, *Mémoires*, III, 197-203.
[41] Alphand, *Promenades*, pp. 34-36, 166, 195, 202-03.
[42] *Ibid.*, pp. 65-68; Haussmann, *Mémoires*, III, 191-93, 203-04.

close political associate, urged the construction of a race track on the Plain of Longchamps. Morny, a leading member of the Jockey Club (the popular version of the imposing title, Society for the Encouragement of the Improvement of Horse Breeding in France) wanted a site for the club's races that might help to give them some of the popularity and vogue that the Derby had in England. He convinced the Emperor and Haussmann that a track on the edge of the fashionable promenade of the Bois de Boulogne would do it, and in 1854 the Emperor authorized the city to buy the southern portion of the Plain of Long- champs and to build a track with the national government bearing the expense equally with the city. Two years later the city granted the Jockey Club a fifty-year lease on the track, and the club undertook to build at its own expense the grandstands and other essential structures, to maintain the track and build- ings, and to pay to the city an annual rental of 12,000 francs. Morny's expectations were quickly realized after the track opened in 1857. Admission receipts more than tripled in the first decade of operation, and Longchamps became and still remains as famous as Ascot or Epsom as a center of racing and a rendezvous of fashionable society.[43]

To make the new park readily accessible the Emperor wanted a broad avenue leading to it from the city. The architect Hittorf, originally charged with the project, proposed an avenue between the Place de l'Etoile and the entry to the Bois at the Porte Dauphine and boldly suggested that it be 130 feet wide, about twenty feet wider than the main boulevards in the city. This impressed the expansive Haussmann as a petty conception, and he prescribed a magnificent avenue with a central carriage- way broad as a boulevard, bounded by planted areas almost as wide and by two roadways for use of residents. Property owners were forbidden to build within thirty-three feet of the road- ways, and from building line to building line the avenue was 460 feet wide. Completed in 1856 and named the Avenue de l'Impératrice (now the Avenue Foch) it became a fashionable

[43] Alphand, *Promenades*, pp. 3-4, 96-99; Haussmann, *Mémoires*, III, 186-89; Joanne, *Paris*, pp. 623-24, 626.

parade, and despite its generous width it was jammed every pleasant afternoon with carriages and horsemen.[44]

The transformation of the Bois de Boulogne into a city park stands among the most happy accomplishments of Napoleon III and Haussmann. It filled a need of the city hitherto without a large municipal park, and it was popular with Parisians of all classes, both the idle rich who used it daily and the popular crowds that came there on Sundays and holidays. "There are Parisian ladies," a contemporary columnist declared, "who would certainly die every evening if they could not take a drive around the lake [of the Bois de Boulogne] each day. For them it is no longer a mere habit, it is a necessity."[45] The Bois was, moreover, converted into its popular form at modest cost to the city. The municipal government's total expenditure on it was 14,352,000 francs, and it covered three quarters of that sum by the subsidy from the state for the Longchamps track and by income from the sale of land detached from the Bois. The net cost of the entire operation to the city was less than 3,500,000 francs.[46]

In a popular empire the chief fault of the Bois de Boulogne was its location. Situated beyond the western limits of the city it was too far removed from the crowded central and eastern quarters, and it benefited chiefly the well-to-do residents of the west end. Beyond the fortifications on the east of the city, however, lay a second state forest, the Bois de Vincennes. In the latter 1850's Napoleon, probably inspired by the success of the transformation of the Bois de Boulogne and anxious to avoid the appearance of neglecting eastern Paris, initiated work on Vincennes to transform it, too, into a popular park. The excavation of three small lakes, the creation of new paths and roadways, and the planting of trees and lawns were accomplished in two years, all at the expense of the Civil List. The city of Paris had no part in the project, but after the extension of the city's limits in 1860 the national government transferred the property

44 Haussmann, *Mémoires*, III, 496-97.
45 Quoted in *Dans les rues de Paris au temps des fiacres* (Paris, 1950), p. 32.
46 Haussmann, *Mémoires*, III, 207-08; Alphand, *Promenades*, p. 6.

to the city, and the municipal government assumed the obligation of transforming it into a park similar to the Bois de Boulogne. The Emperor, still retaining his interest in landscaping, did not give up his personal concern with the new park. The contract for the cession of the *bois* from state to city prescribed that all the city's projects for improving it must be approved by the Emperor.[47]

During the next five years the Bois de Vincennes submitted to the same kind of improvements that the Bois de Boulogne had experienced in the preceding decade, and in the end the eastern *bois*, too, emerged with miles of new roads and paths, lakes and streams, cascades and grottos, restaurants and cafés, shelters and benches, and even a race track and large grandstands.[48]

Although intended as an eastern counterpart of the Bois de Boulogne, the Bois de Vincennes was not quite the equal of the earlier park. It was slightly larger, but nearly a sixth of its surface was reserved for use as a training area and artillery range by the army. This reserved area together with the race track, which adjoined it on the south, cut the *bois* into two parts that had to be developed virtually as two different parks, and to visit the entire park one had to cross almost a mile of this bare intermediate expanse. The cost of Vincennes disappointed Haussmann, proud of the small charge the Bois de Boulogne had placed upon the city. The purchase of property to enlarge the park and the works carried out there cost nearly 24,000,000 francs, and the city recovered only half of it by the resale of land. The net cost of 12,000,000 francs made it more than three times as expensive as the Bois de Boulogne.[49]

Within the city Haussmann created three large municipal parks. The most interesting of them was on the Buttes-Chaumont, where Haussmann and Alphand took sixty-two acres of deserted lands, once the site of the gibbet of Montfaucon (for centuries the Parisian place of public execution) and until

47 Alphand, *Promenades*, pp. 156-60; Haussmann, *Mémoires*, III, 214-15; Arch. nat., C 1067, Corps législatif, Session 1860, Dossier No. 43.
48 Alphand, *Promenades*, pp. 160-70; Haussmann, *Mémoires*, III, 212-24.
49 Alphand, *Promenades*, pp. 171-72; Haussmann, *Mémoires*, III, 210-11, 214; Joanne, *Paris*, p. 278; Galignani, *New Paris Guide for 1863* (Paris, [1863]), p. 587.

1849 the depository of the city's sanitary sewage, and in three years converted them into a pleasant park serving the growing industrial districts of La Villette and Belleville on the northeast side of the city. The site, which included a number of abandoned quarries, was rocky and broken and almost free of vegetation. Adapting his plans to the terrain Alphand designed the park to resemble a mountainous landscape, and he hauled in top soil to support trees and shrubs and lawns. Water pumped from the Canal de l'Ourcq fed a waterfall more than 100 feet high, two streams running through the park, and a lake dug around the principal promontory. What Haussmann called "the inevitable grotto" was fashioned out of a former quarry, and there were the usual paths and roadways, buildings for restaurants and cafés, and shelter houses. The expense was proportionate to the difficulty of the project; the Park of the Buttes-Chaumont cost the city nearly twice as much as the Bois de Boulogne although it was only a twentieth the size.[50]

The Park of Monceau on the west side was not an entirely new creation of the Second Empire, but the park as it exists today dates from 1861. A park had long stood on that site, the property of the Orléans family, and during the July Monarchy the public might use it though only with passes obtained from the Intendant of the Civil List. In the 1850's, however, it was closed to the public.[51] When Haussmann in 1860 was preparing to put the new Boulevard Malesherbes across a corner of the park, the city purchased the entire property from the heirs and from the state, which had acquired some of it in 1852. Part the city resold for subdivision into building lots, and only twenty-one acres, about one-third the original area, became the municipal Park of Monceau. Alphand gave it the usual treatment, and in the late summer of 1861 it was opened to the public with new lawns, flower beds, trees and shrubs, a lake, a waterfall, and, of course, a grotto. Although it was the only municipal park within the old limits of the city, it was situated in a prosperous residential district of the west end, and it

[50] Alphand, *Promenades*, pp. 198-204; Haussmann, *Mémoires*, III, 232-38, 241-52; Galignani, *Guide for 1863*, p. 451.
[51] Galignani, *Guide* (1845), p. 201; Galignani, *New Paris Guide for 1855* (Paris, [1855]), p. 209.

remained as it had been under the July Monarchy largely a resort of the well-to-do.[52]

The Left Bank had no municipal park until the last years of the Empire. Its residents did have the use of the Luxembourg Garden and the Jardin des Plantes, but the city's tardiness in building the southern park long contemplated in plan did give credence to the old Left Bank complaint of neglect. In 1867 the municipal government purchased thirty-nine acres of land on the hill of Montsouris, a deserted area adjoining the fortifications about a mile and a half directly south of the Luxembourg Garden. Alphand created on the property three broad lawns, separated by intruding railroad tracks, which were bridged over at three points and concealed by planting. On one lawn he excavated a large lake, and all were planted with trees and shrubbery and furnished with paths and carriage roads. There was no waterfall and no grotto. The war interrupted work on this park in 1870, and it was not finally completed until 1878.[53]

Before the Park of Montsouris was begun Napoleon produced one of the noisiest tempests of the whole transformation of Paris by approving a project to reduce the size of the Luxembourg Garden. In preparation for the construction of new streets intended to improve communications between the quarters around the Luxembourg the Emperor in November, 1865, authorized the amputation of a strip of land some 250 feet wide along the western side of the garden and another strip from the nursery on the southern edge. Although residents of the adjoining quarters had wanted the new streets, they raised loud protest against the mutilation of the garden. One evening when the Emperor and the Empress came to the neighborhood to attend a performance at the Odéon they were greeted by a hostile crowd shouting protests and insults. Napoleon, ever sensitive to public opinion, inspected the site personally, and in February, 1866, he instructed the Minister of the Interior that the western side of the garden should be left intact, but

[52] Haussmann, *Mémoires*, III, 72-73, 232-34; Alphand, *Promenades*, pp. 191-97; Joanne, *Paris*, pp. 208, 211.

[53] Haussmann, *Mémoires*, III, 237-39; Alphand, *Promenades*, pp. 204-05.

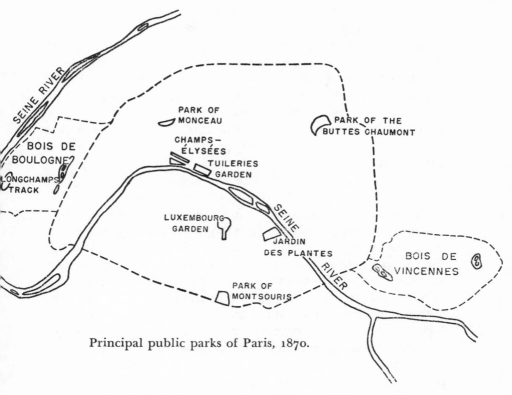

Principal public parks of Paris, 1870.

all of the nursery south of the present Rue Auguste Comte was to be cut off.[54]

The storm continued to rage. In 1866 the Senate received four petitions protesting the change, one of them with more than 10,000 signatures, and a deputy in the Legislative Body formally questioned the ministry on the matter. Charges were made that the government was planning to sell the land in order to balance the budget and that its next move would be to start selling off the Tuileries Garden! The Senate considered the petitions but declined to act on them, and the government went ahead with its plans. The remnant of the nursery became the English garden that still enchants visitors in the southwest corner of the Luxembourg Garden, and the city transformed

[54] *Moniteur*, Nov. 28, 1865, Feb. 21, Aug. 17, 1866; Michel Chevalier, "Journal," *Revue des deux mondes*, 102d Year (1932), XII, 178.

the roadway between the garden and the Square of the Observatory into two tree-lined avenues divided by lawns and walks. These offered some compensation to the disgruntled neighborhood but not to everyone's satisfaction. Protests were heard again in the Legislative Body in 1868 and 1869, and Adolphe Joanne, the publisher of the guidebooks that bear his name and the author of one of the petitions against the changes in the Luxembourg Garden, noted in his Paris guide for 1870 that the nursery was still mourned by "all the residents of the Luxembourg quarter."[55]

However regrettable to some devotees of the garden, the Luxembourg's loss of ten acres was small compared with the total park area Napoleon III and Haussmann gave to Paris. When Haussmann resigned in 1870 Paris had 4,500 acres of municipal parks; only twenty years earlier there had been but forty-seven. In 1850 those forty-seven acres together with other parks in the city ordinarily open to the public provided an acre of recreation area for every 5,000 inhabitants; in 1870 there was an acre for every 390 inhabitants. The Regional Survey of New York in 1928 recommended one acre of park for 300 to 500 inhabitants as a reasonable standard, and in 1925 Manhattan had only one for every 1,130 of its residents. The Emperor and Haussmann had not done badly for Paris.[56]

[55] *Moniteur*, June 2, July 1, 1866; *J.O.*, Mar. 13, 1869; Arch. nat., C 1133, Corps législatif, Session 1869, Dossier No. 139; Haussmann, *Mémoires*, III, 247; Alphand, *Promenades*, pp. 233-34; Joanne, *Paris*, pp. 201-02.

[56] *J.O.*, Supplément, May 1869, p. 7; L. Hanmer, *Public Recreation (Regional Survey of New York and Its Environs*, Vol. v) (N.Y., 1928), pp. 40, 133.

V · A BATTLE FOR WATER

THE IMPROVEMENT OF THE WATER SUPPLY stood high among Haussmann's aims from the first months of his career as Prefect of the Seine.

Many before him realized that the city needed more water and a better system for distributing it. Water pipes too few in number and too limited in dimensions and the elevation of parts of the city restricted daily consumption to little more than half the 27,000,000 gallons the city had at its disposal. Even with supplemental supplies from private wells the quantity available to consumers fell short of the modest standards of other large cities, and well water, contaminated by seepage from cemeteries and cesspools, was unsuitable for most domestic purposes. In the middle 1830's and again in 1849 the Municipal Council had heard proposals to install water turbines utilizing the fall in the Seine in its passage through Paris to pump more river water into the city's reservoirs, and in 1848 the city built a new steam pumping station on the Left Bank just above the Pont d'Austerlitz. Three years later it began the installation of new pumps and steam engines in the old pumping station on the Seine at Chaillot. Authorizations for new water mains became a frequent item of business at meetings of the Municipal Council in the early 1850's, and in the spring before Haussmann arrived in Paris, Berger, his predecessor, proposed the construction of three new reservoirs. Private business, too, was interested in the problem, for money could be made in selling water. In 1853 five different companies presented plans to the city for taking over all or part of the municipal water supply system, and they all proposed to make heavy expenditure on expanding it.[1]

[1] Eugène Belgrand, *Les Travaux souterrains de Paris* (Paris, 1873-77), IV, 60-62; *Moniteur universel*, Dec. 5, 7, 1854.

Louis Napoleon had little personal interest in water supply. It had no place in the plans he had drawn up for transforming the city, and not until nine months after he had given those plans to Haussmann did he discuss the water problem with the Prefect. Then he suggested that the city accept the proposal of a group of financiers headed by the banker Charles Laffitte to assume responsibility for the city's water supply. Haussmann objected. He pointed out the perils of placing so vital a public service entirely in private hands. (He had, perhaps, heard of The Manhattan Company, an organization of bankers that in 1799 had obtained the sole right to supply New York with water and had brought the city good banking service but little water.) He also urged upon the Emperor his conviction that the city ought to be supplied with spring water, not more river water as all the private projects proposed. River water, which amounted to 98 per cent of the Parisian supply, was acceptable for monumental fountains and for cleaning streets and sewers, but for drinking and cooking and washing Parisians deserved better than those hard and troubled waters. Spring water free of both chemical impurities and organic matter and uniformly cool was the ideal for domestic consumption. Knowing the Emperor's interest in Roman history Haussmann astutely recalled to him the great aqueducts that had carried fresh spring water over long distances to Rome. The Emperor listened intently to his Prefect's spirited discourse, and when Haussmann finished he asked a few questions, slipped the papers on Laffitte's proposal back into a drawer of his desk, and told the Prefect to prepare a project based on his own ideas.[2]

Preparation of plans was the simpler part of Haussmann's task. He had also to sell his ideas on spring water to the Parisians. The commonly accepted view, shared by a majority of the Municipal Council and by the Director of Public Works, looked to the Seine as the obvious source of increased water supply. It was immediately at hand, and no costly aqueducts were required to move its waters to Paris. Although inferior to spring water in quality, river water had satisfied Parisians for a long time, and it could be improved by filtering; and there

[2] G. E. Haussmann, *Mémoires* (Paris, 1890-93), III, 294-301.

was even a widely accepted belief that Parisians had a special liking for river water despite its shortcomings and would not readily exchange it for spring water.[3] A similar prejudice had once flourished in New York. "Spring water is like the wind"; ran a popular saying there, "nothing substantial to it; nothing to bite down on."

Haussmann knew these arguments, but he was more impressed by his observation that everyone who could afford it used river water only after it had been filtered, and filters on merchant fountains filled so quickly in some seasons of the year that they had to be cleaned daily. In the years ahead pollution would grow worse as expanding population and industry discharged more and more wastes into the Seine and its tributaries above Paris. Filters offered no solution, he believed, because a public filtering system to treat all water for domestic consumption would be prohibitively expensive. Moreover, river water had to be pumped mechanically, and Haussmann feared to leave the city's water supply dependent on the continuous operation of complicated machinery. Spring water, if found at sufficient elevation, could be distributed by gravity alone, completely independent of mechanical power. It would require no filtering, nor would it reach the extremes of hot and cold that characterized river water. But in the spring of 1854 it appeared that the river-water majority in the Municipal Council with near-sighted practicality would withhold its support from any plan for improved water supply that did not draw on the obvious source of the Seine.[4]

Haussmann refused to give in until he was convinced that supplying the city with spring water was a practical impossibility. He recalled his former associate in the Department of the Yonne, Eugène Belgrand, the young engineer of the *Corps des Ponts et Chaussées*, who had piped water from mountain springs to two towns of the department. Belgrand was now in charge of the Hydrometric Service of the Seine River Basin, and Haussmann in April, 1854, asked him for a report on

[3] Belgrand, *Travaux*, IV, 3-4; *Documents rélatifs aux eaux de Paris* (Paris, 1867), p. 390 (hereafter cited as *Documents*); Haussmann, *Mémoires*, III, 315.
[4] Belgrand, *Travaux*, I, 469, 480, 486-87; IV, 2-3; *Moniteur*, Dec. 6, 1854.

springs in the basin whose waters might be diverted to Paris. Only those springs should be considered, Haussmann explained, whose waters fulfilled three conditions. They had to be of good quality, and that meant reasonably free of chemical and organic impurities and uniformly cool the year around. Secondly, they had to have sufficient elevation at their source to flow to Paris without mechanical aids and arrive at least 230 feet above sea level. Finally, the sources had to be capable of a very large yield, somewhere around 26,000,000 gallons a day. Belgrand warned Haussmann that all springs within a radius of sixty miles of Paris were tainted by gypsum deposits. For satisfactory drinking water he would have to go beyond those limits. Good water, the Prefect assured him, was the first object; he had a free hand to seek it anywhere in the Seine Basin.[5]

Belgrand began his search by first eliminating all the springs whose waters were clearly inferior in quality or inadequate in volume. Then he ruled out those that could be used only at excessive cost because of the distance or the difficulty of the terrain separating them from Paris or because established holders of water rights would demand heavy indemnities. After these exclusions he had remaining the springs in two large areas: the valley of the Eure River some sixty miles west of Paris and the chalk soil districts of Champagne, about one hundred miles east of Paris. Louis XIV had once been interested in the Eure valley near Chartres as a source of water supply for Versailles, but the aqueduct he started was never completed, and Belgrand found that at the point where the springs could be practically captured and diverted to Paris the flow was insufficient, less than half the 26,000,000 gallons daily that he sought. Additional springs could be tied in but at excessive cost. Only Champagne remained, and there near Chalons in the Department of the Marne Belgrand found a group of springs that appeared to meet all the essential requirements.[6]

5 Belgrand, *Travaux*, I, 157, IV, 3; Haussmann, *Mémoires*, III, 301-303; *Moniteur*, Dec. 6, 1854.

6 Eugène Belgrand, *Recherches statistiques sur les sources du bassin de la Seine qu'il est possible de conduire à Paris* (Paris, 1854), pp. 28, 31, 74-75; Belgrand, *Travaux*, I, 102-06; Haussmann, *Mémoires*, III, 303-10.

Early in July, 1854, he handed his first report to Haussmann. In the springs that fed the Somme and the Soude rivers, two small tributaries of the Marne between Chalons and Epernay, Paris could take the fresh water it needed. Almost totally free of offending chemical or organic matter it excelled river water in quality, and the altitude of the area would permit it to flow by gravity to reservoirs in Paris at the prescribed elevation of 230 feet. The cost of acquiring the necessary property and of building an aqueduct 107 miles long Belgrand estimated at 22,000,000 francs. He hedged on the quantity of water available. The city could count, he thought, on a minimum of 23,000,000 gallons a day, but he had lacked time for exact measurements, and his estimate might be wrong. Nevertheless, if the actual yield should fall short by as much as a third, other nearby springs could be tapped to make up the deficit. In the succeeding weeks further studies quieted his doubts, and in October he advised Haussmann that the minimum flow of the Somme-Soude springs exceeded 35,000,000 gallons daily.[7]

Two weeks after Belgrand submitted his original report a municipal engineer, A. A. Mille, handed Haussmann a memorandum on his observations in Great Britain. At the same time he had given Belgrand his assignment Haussmann had sent Mille to Britain to study sewage disposal practices, but Mille also examined sources of water supply in several cities. He reported back that although London drew its water from the Thames, British authorities frowned on rivers as sources for city water supply, preferring either springs or controlled watersheds such as Liverpool and Manchester had developed.[8]

Once Haussmann had this technical data from Belgrand and Mille in hand he put his case before the Municipal Council. On August 4, 1854, he presented to the Council the first of his four famous memoranda on water supply. He reviewed for the councillors the history of the city's water supply system, its present capacities, and the proposals then pending before the Council for improvements. All of these plans looked to the

[7] Belgrand, *Travaux*, I, 106-07, IV, 3; Belgrand, *Recherches*, pp. 49-71, 75, 76, 83, 86; Haussmann, *Mémoires*, III, 311-13.

[8] A. A. Mille, *Rapport sur la mode d'assainissement des villes en Angleterre et en Ecosse* (Paris, 1854), pp. 32-33 *Moniteur*, Dec. 6, 1854.

Seine for increased supplies, and the waters of the Seine and, indeed, all the water the city had at its disposal in 1854, failed to meet recognized standards of water for domestic consumption. Men looked with disdain, he said, on the Romans, who built aqueducts to bring water from distant sources by natural flow. But, Haussmann asked his hearers, were not "error and barbarism" on the side of those who believed the acme of progress to be the use of steam engines to pump polluted river water into the public mains, leaving the city's supply at the mercy of a broken wheel or a dying fire?[9]

Haussmann then played his trump card—Belgrand's report, which showed that it was possible to bring spring water from the Somme and the Soude valleys to Paris in quantity and at reasonable cost. Knowing that 22,000,000 francs (Belgrand's estimate) might not look reasonable to the economy-minded Council, he quickly explained that the annual interest on that capital would be only a fraction more than the cost of the coal required to pump the same quantity of water from the river, and to the latter cost would have to be added capital charges for pumps and filtering equipment, wages, and maintenance costs. The final cost of a gallon of Somme-Soude water delivered in Paris would be only half the cost of a gallon of water pumped from the Seine. A reasonable expectation of increased revenue from the sale of the additional water supply, moreover, justified a much larger outlay than 22,000,000 francs.[10]

Haussmann then proceeded to recommend a larger outlay. If the elevation of the new waters on arrival in Paris were raised from 230 to 260 feet, all floors of even the highest situated houses in Paris could be supplied. Belgrand had advised the Prefect that if the slope of the aqueduct were slightly reduced it could be brought into Paris at the higher elevation; there would be some loss in capacity, but an increase in the diameter of the conduit would readily make it up. The additional cost, Belgrand said, would not be more than 3,000,000 francs, a sum that Haussmann characteristically passed on to

9 *Moniteur,* Aug. 4, 1854; *Documents,* pp. 9-42, 80-81. Haussmann's memorandum was reprinted in the *Moniteur,* Dec. 5, 6, and 7, 1854.

10 *Moniteur,* Dec. 6, 1854.

the Municipal Council as "a little more than 2 millions."[11]

Belgrand's report did not consider distribution of water, but Haussmann told the Council that he envisaged two distinct systems of water mains in Paris. One would distribute water from the rivers and nearby springs to the so-called "public service" outlets (public fountains, curb-side taps for street cleaning, fire hydrants, and watering troughs). Haussmann estimated that the requirements of this service would shortly reach 29,000,000 gallons a day, nearly double the existing consumption. Waters from the Ourcq Canal, the city's artesian well in Grenelle, and the springs in the environs could supply more than 28,000,000 gallons, and the remainder could be pumped from the Seine. The requirements of the "private service," which included industrial, domestic, and institutional consumers, would rise to 24,000,000 gallons once water were piped to every apartment in the city, and to fill this demand Haussmann would distribute the new waters from Champagne through a second and wholly independent system of mains. The use of two distribution systems would assure more dependable flow to both services in times of peak load, and it would keep the high quality of spring water undiluted.[12]

Haussmann presented this proposal only as a suggestion requiring no action by the Council, but he did ask the councillors to examine Belgrand's preliminary plans on the Somme-Soude derivation, and, if they judged them worthy of serious consideration, to authorize a complete study of the whole project. The Council immediately referred the matter to a committee, but showed no further disposition to act quickly on it. Perhaps if Haussmann had been content to imply that his opponents were merely mistaken and not mistaken barbarians he would have gotten more rapid action. Not until January 12, 1855, did the Council accept his recommendation. It then authorized the Prefect to prepare definite plans and detailed estimates of materials and costs for the project, but it cautioned the Prefect that it also wanted reassurance that these particular sources in the Somme-Soude valleys could be relied upon to fill the city's

[11] *Documents*, pp. 43-44; Belgrand, *Recherches*, pp. 87-88.
[12] *Documents*, pp. 44-53.

needs. At the same time the Council opened a credit for the creation of a new municipal office to make the studies it had authorized.[13]

Haussmann immediately laid before the Minister of Public Works a request that Belgrand be permanently assigned to the city's engineering staff, and seven weeks later, on March 1, Belgrand became the head of the newly created municipal Water Service. His task was to re-study the whole problem of bringing spring water to Paris, to reach a definite decision on the best springs to use, and to draw up working plans, specifications, and estimates for the derivation that the new studies showed to be the most desirable.[14]

Through the remainder of 1855 and half the following year Belgrand tested and measured the springs of the Seine Basin, while two assistants worked on the plans and specifications for the Somme-Soude project. He was prepared to stop his assistants should he discover better sources to supply Paris, but the complete studies reaffirmed his earlier judgment. The nearest springs fulfilling all the essential requirements were those in the valleys of the Somme and the Soude. The second best group he located in the valley of the Vanne River, a tributary of the Yonne (which flowed into the Seine a few miles above Fontainebleau). Situated in the same chalk soils as the Somme-Soude springs they had nearly the same high quality and the same potential flow, but they could be delivered in Paris at only 230 feet above sea level. Either group could be supplemented, Belgrand reported, by tapping secondary sources along the line of the aqueducts to Paris, and he recommended specific springs that could be readily tied in. He was confident, however, of the reliability of either group to deliver the desired 26,000,000 gallons a day. In 1855, a dry year, he found the flow of each to be more than that amount. In 1857, when the water in the Seine in Paris dropped to the lowest level since records of river stages were first kept in 1719, the springs of neither area were seriously affected. The following year the drought continued,

[13] *Moniteur*, Dec. 7, 1854, Jan. 18, 1855; *Documents*, pp. 85-88; Haussmann, *Mémoires*, III, 328-31.
[14] *Moniteur*, Jan. 28, 1859; Haussmann, *Mémoires*, III, 338-39.

and in the Somme and Soude valleys the higher springs went dry and others diminished in volume, but Belgrand regarded this as an aberration that might not recur even once in a century. Further investigations convinced him that underlying the existing springs was an accessible sheet of water that no drought could seriously diminish. Haussmann was satisfied with his engineer's explanations, and in 1858 he accepted Belgrand's detailed plans for the Somme-Soude aqueduct and his preliminary recommendations on reservoirs and mains for distribution of the new water in Paris.[15]

Perhaps Haussmann chose July, 1858, to present these plans to the Municipal Council simply because that was the earliest he could have them ready, but the date was in the middle of the driest summer the city had experienced. The river level fell lower than ever before, thirty-three inches below the zero point of the scale on the Pont de la Tournelle, fifteen inches lower than in the preceding year, and the volume of water flowing through Paris dropped off 40 per cent from the usual minimum in the dry season. That summer any offer of 26,000,000 gallons of water would be hard to resist.[16]

Haussmann made the offer in his second major memorandum on water supply, dated July 16, 1858, a veritable book covering the field from a review of the water system of ancient Rome to suggestions on water rates for future consumers of spring water from the Somme and Soude valleys. The heart of the memorandum was the Prefect's recommendation that the city acquire the springs of the Somme-Soude and build an aqueduct to carry their waters to Paris. The springs could furnish at least 26,000,000 gallons a day, but if necessary in dry years, up to half of that desired quantity could be drawn from the springs of three other rivers, the Berle, the Dhuis, and the Sourdon, all adjoining the proposed line of the aqueduct and easily turned into it. The plans for the aqueduct, even as briefly outlined in Haussmann's memorandum, revealed a formidable construction project. A masonry conduit with a minimum cross-

[15] *Moniteur*, Jan. 28, 29, 1859; *Documents*, pp. 276-77; Haussmann, *Mémoires*, III, 383-85.

[16] *Moniteur*, Jan. 27, 1859; *Documents*, pp. 153-55, 277.

section dimension of five feet over the first half of its length and nearly seven feet over the second half was to run from Conflans at the junction of the Somme and the Soude 114 miles down the valley of the Marne to a reservoir on the hill of Chaumont on the east of Paris. The maintenance of an even slope over more than 100 miles would require the construction of eighteen miles of tunnels, four miles of bridges, and four and a half miles of siphons. The total cost, Haussmann believed, would not exceed 26,000,000 francs, but on the insistence of the General Council of the *Corps des Ponts et Chaussées* he raised the top limit to 30,000,000.[17]

The Somme-Soude project was intended to supply Paris only within its boundaries of 1858. When the contemplated annexation of the suburbs inside the fortifications should take place, the city would require not only more water but also water at a higher elevation, for the suburbs included the heights of Montmartre and Belleville overlooking the old city. Belgrand's Water Service was prepared to meet the demands for additional quantity from the springs of the Vanne, and the spring waters of the Dhuis or the Sourdon valleys could be brought to Paris at elevations suitable to supply all the highest areas on which houses were likely to be built. But these problems were still in the future. To meet present needs Haussmann asked the Council to authorize the immediate execution of the Somme-Soude project.[18]

In the same memorandum Haussmann presented Belgrand's preliminary plans for a dual system of water distribution. Belgrand proposed a network of 330 miles of standardized mains and pipes to carry the "new waters" of the Somme-Soude springs to every street in the city and an independent system less than half as long to supply the public services with "old waters" of the Ourcq and the other sources already in use. The six small existing reservoirs and a dozen large mains would suffice for a time as the principal elements of the public network, but the private network would require a number of large

[17] *Moniteur*, Jan. 29, 1859. Haussmann's second memorandum was reprinted in the *Moniteur*, Jan. 27, 28, 29, Feb. 3, 5, and 7, 1859.
[18] *Moniteur*, Feb. 3, 1859.

new mains and three reservoirs. The reservoir newly completed at Passy to store river water raised by the pumps of Chaillot could be tied into the system, and two others would have to be built. One would be placed atop the hill of Chaumont adjoining the site where Alphand later created the Park of the Buttes-Chaumont and the other on the Left Bank adjoining another of Alphand's parks, the Park of Montsouris. Each would have a capacity of 26,000,000 gallons, more than twice the capacity of all the old reservoirs combined.[19]

When he presented the second memorandum on water and observed its favorable reception Haussmann thought that his case for spring water was finally won, and in March of the following year when the Municipal Council unanimously approved the Somme-Soude project he confidently expected that he would soon start work on the new aqueduct. He had convinced the Municipal Council, and he had quieted opposition in his own engineering staff by dismissing Dupuit, the municipal Director of Public Works, who opposed the use of spring water.[20] But he underestimated the variety and the strength of resistance outside the Municipal Council and administration. He had still to contend with widespread popular prejudice against spring water, to fight anew the battle with partisans of river water, and to win over the property owners of the Somme and the Soude valleys.

When the public learned of the projects to bring spring water to Paris, the city was beset with rumors of dire consequences for the public health. Spring water, Parisians heard, caused many ills, from tooth decay to cancer of the stomach. One rumor had it that these waters produced goiters in women, and the rumor was so persistent that an official committee investigating one of Belgrand's projects felt obliged to inquire into its validity. Medical opinion, it found, was divided on the cause of goiters, but the spring waters in which the city was interested possessed no qualities that were even suspect. The editor of *La Patrie*, a newspaper that had spread the report, appeared before the committee and readily admitted that he knew nothing about the particular springs the city proposed

[19] *Moniteur*, Feb. 3, 1859.
[20] *Documents*, pp. 293, 296; Haussmann, *Mémoires*, III, 110-11.

to use and that the information he did have was based on nothing but hearsay.[21]

The old claim that Parisians disliked spring water cropped up again and was sufficiently credited to demand new refutation. It was based, the same committee decided, on the preference of Parisians for Seine water over the hard and tainted waters of the Belleville and Pré Saint-Gervais springs, but it ignored the equally obvious fact that they used good quality spring water whenever they could get it. On holidays Parisians flocked to the springs of Meudon, Sceaux, and Montmorency and drank their waters with obvious relish.[22]

Popular preference for Seine water was largely a myth, but the Seine, like the Hudson in New York City, had a tenacious appeal as a source of water. In New York the advocates of pumping water from the Hudson had opposed the construction of the Croton Aqueduct in the 1830's, and men of the same conviction opposed extension of the Delaware system in 1955.

Haussmann in his first memorandum in 1854 had pointed out the many deficiencies of the Seine as a source of water supply, and four years later in his second memorandum he demonstrated that the specific projects for raising water from the river ranged from the impractical to the ridiculous. One would flood all the river ports of the city, and another had a derivation canal that would leave the river bed in Paris completely dry during four months of the year! The Municipal Council's Committee on Water, after independent studies of its own, concurred in Haussmann's judgment, and in 1859 rejected all proposals to draw on the Seine. Still undeterred the river-water men revised their projects and insisted on a new hearing. The General Council of the *Ponts et Chaussées* urged that they be heard, and Haussmann, fearing that to leave them unanswered might undermine public confidence in the Somme-Soude project, ordered the municipal engineers to prepare plans and estimates for pumping 26,000,000 gallons of Seine water daily into the Parisian reservoirs. Their report showed that that quantity of water could be pumped from the river and filtered, but no engineer could guarantee that filtering

---

21 Belgrand, *Travaux*, I, 131; *Documents*, pp. 396-400, 426-27.
22 *Ibid.*, pp. 390-93.

1. A typical narrow street of old Paris—the Rue des Marmousets, eliminated by demolitions for the new Hôtel Dieu in the 1860's. (Photograph in the Bibliothèque Historique de la Ville de Paris, Paris.)

2. The Boulevard Richard Lenoir, with the Canal Saint-Martin under the roadway. (Adolphe Joanne, *Paris illustrée en 1870 et 1877*, 3rd ed., Paris, [n.d.], p. 73.)

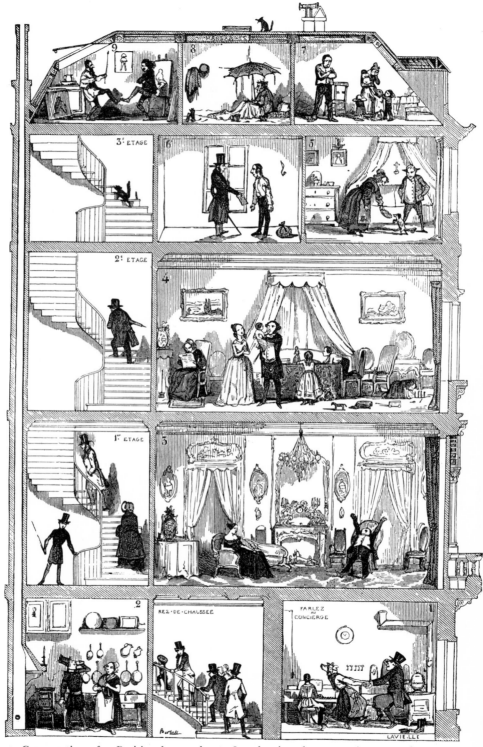

3. Cross section of a Parisian house about 1850 showing the economic status of tenants varying by floors. (Edmund Texier, *Tableau de Paris*, Paris, 1852, I, 65.)

C. MERYON, D.S.

4. Water pumping station on the Pont Notre-Dame seen from the **Right Bank**, 1852. The towers of the cathedral are in the background.
(Etching by Charles Meryon, Yale Art Gallery.)

The Post Office employing chimney sweeps to deliver letters addressed to the surveyors engaged in triangulating the city.

The giraffe used in surveying the district around the zoo.

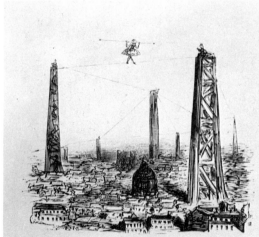

Madame Saqui, the celebrated aerialist, entrusted with maintaining communications among the surveyors during the triangulation project.

Using artillery to send the surveyors to their offices.

5. The cartoonist Cham comments on the towers erected for the triangulation of Paris. (Cham, pseudonym for Amédée de Noé, *Croquis contemporains*, Paris, [n.d.], Part 3.

6. "But here is where I live—and I don't even find my wife." Daumier looks at the construction boom in 1852. (*Charivari*, Paris, December 10, 1852.)

7. "Good! There's another house being pulled down. I'm going to raise all my tenants' rents 200 francs." Daumier satirizes landlords who profiteered on the housing shortage created by demolitions for public works, 1854. (*Charivari*, Paris, February 21, 1854.)

8. Demolitions for the Rue de Rennes. The church of Saint-Germain des Prés is on the right.
(*L'Illustration*, Paris, LI, 89, February 8, 1868.)

9. Demolitions for the Avenue de l'Opéra. The new Opera House is in the background. (Photograph in the Bibliothèque Historique de la Ville de Paris, Paris.)

10. The principal façade of the new Opera House. The photograph dates from about the end of the Second Empire. (*Vue de Paris en photographie*, a bound volume of photographs in the New York Public Library.)

11. The architects' sketch of the Central Markets.
The two pavilions on the far left next to the round Halle aux Blés were not built during the Second Empire.
(V. Baltard and F. Callet, *Monographie des Halles Centrales*, Paris, 1863, Pl. 1.)

12. Clearing of the area between the Louvre and the Tuileries, 1852. (Photograph in the Bibliothèque Historique de la Ville de Paris, Paris.)

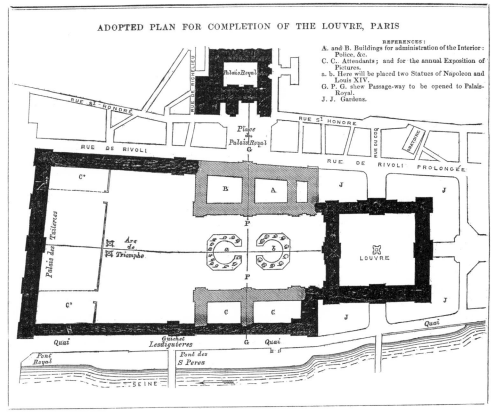

ADOPTED PLAN FOR COMPLETION OF THE LOUVRE, PARIS

REFERENCES:
A. and B. Buildings for administration of the Interior: Police, &c.
C. C.. Attendants; and for the annual Exposition of Pictures.
a. b. Here will be placed two Statues of Napoleon and Louis XIV.
G. P. G. shew Passage-way to be opened to Palais-Royal.
J. J. Gardens.

13. Ground plan of the Louvre and Tuileries palaces showing additions made by Napoleon III, 1852-57. (*The Builder*, London, x, 443, July 10, 1852.)

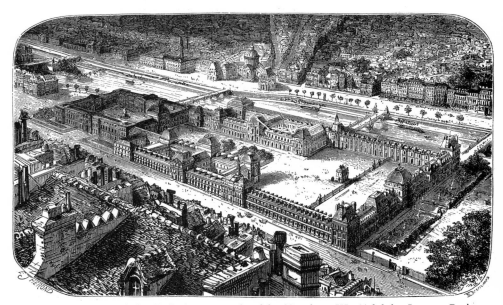

14. The Louvre and the Tuileries as completed by Napoleon III. (Adolphe Joanne, *Paris illustrée en 1870 et 1877*, 3rd ed., Paris, [n.d.].)

15. The Ile de la Cité seen from the **R**ight **B**ank when clearings for the new Hôtel Dieu were in progress, 1867. (Photograph in the Bibliothèque Historique de la Ville de Paris, Paris.)

16. Typical Parisian apartment house erected during the Second Empire.
(*The Builder*, London, XVI, 159, March 6, 1858.)

17. Plan of the **Bois de Boulogne** after its transformation in the 1850's. (Adolphe Alphand, *Les Promenades de Paris*, Paris, 1867-73, Atlas, Pl. 2.)

18. Bird's-eye view of the Park of the Buttes-Chaumont, built on the site of abandoned quarries in northeast Paris.
(Adolphe Alphand, *Les Promenades de Paris*, Paris, 1867-73, Text, p. 199. Fig. 306.)

19. Cholera protests to Haussmann that demolition of old houses in Paris has left him homeless—a jibe at critics of Haussmann who complained that public works had created a housing shortage. (*L'Illustration*, Paris, March 13, 1869, p. 172.)

How heartless! Haussmann is gone, and that mason still sings.

Sorry to see you go, ex-prefect.

20. Construction workers mourn the dismissal of Haussmann as Prefect
of the Seine, 1870. (Cham, pseudonym for Amédée de Noé, *Les Folies
Parisiennes*, Paris, 1883, p. 161.)

would clarify the water, and it could never remove dissolved impurities nor assure a constant temperature. The initial cost of the pumping station and filtering plant would be less than the cost of a long aqueduct, but comparison of annual charges for operations, maintenance, depreciation, and interest clearly showed the aqueduct to be the cheaper of the two. The best the Seine could offer, Haussmann told the Municipal Council in 1860, was inferior water at higher cost.[23]

The Loire River, too, had its champions. When Haussmann wrote his first memorandum on water supply he had before him a proposal to bring waters of the Loire to Paris, but he had summarily dismissed it as fantastic. Even the financial wizardry attributed to him by his enemies could not have devised means to finance a derivation canal ninety-five feet wide running across 150 miles of hilly country and a storage reservoir covering 500 acres. The reservoir alone would cost 80,000,000 francs. Haussmann was indignant that he had to waste even a footnote on such an ill-conceived scheme. But a river full of water, lying 250 feet above the highest point in Paris had an allure not easily destroyed. In 1859 a government engineer proposed a new project that interested the General Council of the *Ponts et Chaussées*. When the Council recommended that Haussmann consider it along with the new proposals on the Seine he ordered the municipal engineers to draw up a practical plan for tapping the Loire and to give him estimates of the cost. He was annoyed that the time of his engineers had to be taken to put the vague conceptions of impractical men into working plans when at best the outcome would be a supply of water far inferior in quality to that he knew could be had from the springs of Champagne. But the Water Service's study of the Loire derivation did clearly establish for all to see that the cost of the project would be higher than the cost of either the Seine or the Somme Soude projects and that the waters of the Loire were of poor quality (during nearly half of each year they were filled with a fine sand that could not be filtered out). It had even less to offer than the Seine.[24]

[23] *Moniteur*, Jan. 27, 1859; *Documents*, pp. 249-62, 296, 300, 316-19.
[24] *Documents*, pp. 119-20, 262-65, 302-06, 310-16.

Belgrand, too, grew annoyed at the persistence of the advocates of river water, and he grew especially tired of being told that London used filtered river water. He declared somewhat petulantly that what satisfied Londoners would not satisfy Parisians. The English insisted on *clear* water, he knew, but they drank so much beer and tea that they did not know or care how their water tasted. The French, he said, demanded water that was good to taste as well as to look at![25]

For a time the projects for tapping the rivers stood in Haussmann's path, but he did succeed in removing them. The opposition of the property owners of the Somme-Soude raised an obstacle that he could never remove. He knew as early as 1856 that residents of the Department of the Marne objected to the derivation of the Somme-Soude springs, but in his second memorandum he had dismissed their opposition as groundless and, by implication, not very serious. The following year he found, however, that individual proprietors refused to sell the spring sites, claiming that the water was essential to the fertility of their land. When he tried to get officials of the national government to schedule hearings in the Department of the Marne as the first routine step toward condemning the required property, he could get no action. The interested persons in the department had organized to resist the taking of any water, and they carried their protests to the Minister of Public Works, the Minister of the Interior, and the Council of State. Haussmann was accustomed to such opposition and equally accustomed to breaking through it, but he had always had the personal support of the Emperor, and this time he lacked it. The deputy of Epernay in the Department of the Marne took his constituents' grievances to the Tuileries, and when the Emperor went out to military maneuvers at Chalons in the Marne they showered him personally with their protests. Napoleon never had any personal interest in Haussmann's project, and he was always sensitive to public opinion. He gave Haussmann no backing in the dispute and finally asked him to use some other springs.

[25] Belgrand, *Travaux*, I, 471, 475.

This particular project, he had apparently concluded, was not worth the opposition of even a handful of voters.[26]

Haussmann ultimately abandoned the Somme-Soude derivation, one of the few defeats he ever suffered on a major project. In 1860, however, he admitted only a postponement and concealed his reversal behind a proposal that he presented to the Municipal Council in April, 1860, to tap springs in the valleys of the Dhuis and Surmelin rivers, small tributaries of the Marne near Chateau-Thierry in the Department of the Aisne.[27]

The annexation of the suburbs on January 1, 1860, brought into the city, he explained, large areas on the Right Bank that lay above the elevation at which the Somme-Soude waters could be brought to Paris. He had foreseen this in his second memorandum and pointed out higher springs, including those of the Dhuis, that could be used to supply these quarters, and in 1859 the city had begun to buy up springs in the Dhuis valley and in the adjoining valley of the Surmelin. The original proposals of 1858 had envisaged tying them into the Somme-Soude aqueduct when it was completed, but Haussmann now recommended that the city first build an aqueduct from the Dhuis and the Surmelin valleys. It would bring the city 10,000,000 gallons of water a day at an elevation permitting distribution to any part of the city. The derivation of the Somme-Soude springs could be completed later, to bring the total daily supply of spring water up to the desired 26,000,000 gallons. But while he told this to the Municipal Council Haussmann privately ordered Belgrand to prepare working plans for tapping the springs of the Vanne River valley, and he intended to substitute them for the Somme-Soude springs.[28]

When Haussmann eventually admitted the abandonment of the Somme-Soude project he attributed his decision to pressure from the Emperor, who had been influenced by residents of the Marne. His decision was at least made easier by his grow-

[26] *Moniteur*, Jan. 29, 1859; Archives nationales (Paris), BB30 384 Paris 7, 1859, BB30 384 Paris 8, 1861, 1862; *Documents*, pp. 284-86, 322-23; Haussmann, *Mémoires*, III, 380-82.

[27] *Documents*, pp. 299-305, 322; Haussmann, *Mémoires*, III, 383.

[28] *Documents*, pp. 320-21, 324, 332; Belgrand, *Travaux*, IV, 93; Haussmann, *Mémoires*, III, 392.

ing doubt of the reported capacities of the Somme-Soude springs. Belgrand had estimated a minimum yield of 26,000,000 gallons a day, and the project Haussmann presented to the Municipal Council in 1858 was based on the assumption that the city could always take at least half that quantity. In the dry season of that dry year, however, the yield dropped to 6,000,000 gallons. Belgrand did not inform the Prefect immediately, and both Haussmann and the Municipal Council continued to act on the assumption that the engineer's original estimates were correct. The Council learned of the failing supply in 1859 but accepted Belgrand's judgment that the low level of 1858 was unlikely to recur, and even if it should, the loss could be made up from deeper springs or from springs of nearby valleys. By the time Haussmann presented his third memorandum in April, 1860, he no longer shared this optimistic view. He kept his doubts to himself, because, he said, he wanted to make no slur upon Belgrand's professional reputation, nor did he care to aid his enemies by revealing a mistake that might, but for fortuitous delays, have cost the city millions of francs. In the years ahead the drought grew worse, and the city was fortunate, Haussmann believed, to be free of any dependence on the Somme-Soude springs.[29]

The Municipal Council, knowing nothing in 1860 of Haussmann's misgivings, received the proposal on the Dhuis and the Surmelin as an adjunct of the Somme-Soude derivation it had already approved. On May 18, 1860, just a month after they had heard the Prefect's recommendation, the councillors voted to accept it and at the same time expressed their wish to see the Somme-Soude project pushed forward along with the new one. Public hearings, the solicitation of authority from the central government, the expropriation of lands, and the letting of contracts required more than two years. Property-owners and communes along the Dhuis protested against the city's taking water, and owners of land crossed by the aqueduct complained of illegal expropriation, but here the protests and complaints were largely maneuvers to win bigger indemnities.

[29] *Documents*, pp. 156-57, 276-77; Haussmann, *Mémoires*, III, 383-85, 392; *Moniteur*, Feb. 10, 1866.

Among the 1,250 property owners affected fewer than 100 refused the city's offers to buy, and these few hold-outs accepted the indemnities fixed by expropriation juries without further objection. Along the Surmelin the proprietors were more tenacious, but if they, too, were playing for larger indemnities they overplayed their hands, for the city regarded their demands as unreasonable, suspended work on that part of the project and never resumed it.[30]

On September 1, 1862, workmen finally broke ground for the new reservoir on the heights of Ménilmontant that was to receive the new waters. Construction of the aqueduct began at the end of June, 1863, and it was pushed so vigorously, the prolonged drought giving an added spur, that just twenty-seven months later on October 1, 1865, the first spring water from the Dhuis flowed into the mains of Paris.[31]

The aqueduct over most of its length was an oval shaped masonry conduit with a maximum cross-section of about six feet. Extending eighty-one miles down the valley of the Marne to Paris it required thirty-two tunnels, the longest nearly half a mile in length, to carry it under hills and nearly as many bridges and eleven miles of siphons to move it across valleys. The cost added up to nearly 18,500,000 francs, 4,500,000 francs more than the original estimate.[32]

In 1862 when work on the project was only started an architect proposed the erection of a monumental fountain as elaborate as the cascade at Saint-Cloud "to welcome" the waters of the Dhuis on arrival in Paris. When they did finally reach Paris in 1865 many Parisians surely felt like erecting a monument to them. They came at the end of a dry summer that had put a heavier strain on the city's water supply than any experienced before. The level of the Seine fell below the intake of the Chaillot pumps. The Canal Saint-Martin and the Canal Saint-Denis, which were fed by the Ourcq Canal, had to be closed to navigation, and the city's use of Ourcq River waters was cut

[30] *Documents*, pp. 331, 334-35, 339-40; Haussmann, *Mémoires*, III, 399; Arch. nat., BB[30] 371 Amiens 4, 1863; BB[30] 384 Paris 9, 1863.
[31] *Moniteur*, Feb. 10, 1866; Belgrand, *Travaux*, IV, 142-43.
[32] Belgrand, *Travaux*, IV, 115-16, 138-40, 144; Haussmann, *Mémoires*, III, 400.

10 to 15 per cent. The administration stopped the monumental fountains, suspended the washing of gutters and sewers and the sprinkling of the dusty macadam pavements, and limited the operation of the public drinking-water fountains, which usually ran continuously. Some high points in the city were without running water for months. The arrival of the waters from the Dhuis valley brought temporary relief, permitting the resumption of all services except the monumental fountains, but it did not solve the city's water problem, and it filled only a fraction of the city's need for spring water. In 1865 Belgrand estimated this need at 37,000,000 gallons a day. The springs of the Dhuis yielded only 5,000,000, half the volume Haussmann had counted on, and 32,000,000 gallons short of the need.[33]

Late in 1865 Haussmann offered a new solution. In his fourth and final memorandum on water supply he presented to the Municipal Council plans for tapping the springs of the valley of the Vanne that he had instructed Belgrand to prepare five years earlier when he lost faith in the Somme-Soude springs. Without making any public announcement of the derivation project the city had been since 1859 quietly buying up the springs in the Vanne valley, and by the end of 1865 it owned thirteen springs that ordinarily yielded more than 32,000,000 gallons of water a day. Their flow had declined in the dry years, but they had proved more dependable through the long drought since 1857 than the springs of the Somme and the Soude, and even at its lowest point the flow was enough to meet the city's most pressing requirements. Together with the water Haussmann expected to obtain from the Surmelin springs and from two new artesian wells, it would fill most of the gap between demand and supply. If necessary, the city could also buy additional springs in the Vanne valley. The water was of high quality, and it could, the Prefect believed, be taken without serious local opposition, for the city had bought up the properties likely to suffer from loss of water as well as the springs themselves. Much of the affected area, moreover, was marshy

[33] *Revue générale de l'architecture et des travaux publics* (Paris), xx (1862), 163-64; *Documents*, pp. 307, 320; Belgrand, *Travaux*, iv, 87-88, 143; *Moniteur*, Feb. 10, 1866.

and would benefit from drainage. The aqueduct would run some 108 miles from the Department of the Aube to a reservoir on the hill of Montrouge just inside the southern limits of Paris. The estimated cost of the entire project was 31,600,000 francs, nearly double the estimate on the derivation of the Dhuis and the Surmelin.[34]

The serious water shortage and a renewed outbreak of cholera in Paris late in 1865 proclaimed the need for haste, but hearings and other preliminaries of the new project took up more than a year, and it was November, 1867, before the contracts were let and construction companies started to work.[35]

Haussmann had judged the potential local opposition correctly except in one case. The town of Sens in the Department of the Yonne fought a bitter battle with the city over water rights and indemnities, using in the course of four long years every weapon from conferences with Haussmann to a petition to the Emperor and a legal appeal to the highest court in France. In the end the small town (population around 10,000) boldly but vainly petitioned the courts to declare the expropriations for the Vanne derivation illegal and called upon the Legislative Body to force the capital city to stop the entire Vanne project.[36] Construction meanwhile went on unhindered, and when the Franco-Prussian War interrupted building operations in the summer of 1870 only a fifth of the aqueduct remained to be built. After the war the need to arrange additional financing delayed resumption of work, and not until August, 1874, did the first waters of the Vanne reach Paris. Regular distribution began nine months later.[37]

The Vanne aqueduct crossed broken terrain and was a more complex structure than the aqueduct from the Dhuis valley. Nearly half its length was in siphons, tunnels, or bridges. Twenty-one tunnels, six of them more than a mile long, led the conduit under hills. Sixteen major siphons included one

[34] *Moniteur*, Feb. 10, 1866; Haussmann, *Mémoires*, III, 400-01; Belgrand, *Travaux*, I, 163, 168-70; Arch. nat., C 1145, Corps législatif, Session 1870, Dossier No. 259-60.

[35] Belgrand, *Travaux*, IV, 199, 236.

[36] Arch. nat., BB30 384 Paris 10, 1866, 1867, 1868; C 1145, Dossier No. 259-60.

[37] Belgrand, *Travaux*, IV, 236; Département de la Seine, *Dérivation des sources de la vallée de la Vanne* (Paris, 1871), pp. 17, 41.

running for more than two miles across the valley of the Yonne River and two others more than a mile long. Among the many bridges one is a familiar sight to residents of suburbs south of Paris. The bridge over Bièvre River in the suburb of Arcueil-Cachan dominates the valley, and in an age grown accustomed to engineering prodigies its seventy-seven arches rising up to 125 feet above the valley floor are still impressive. The cost of the aqueduct and the reservoir of Montrouge exceeded the original estimates by 50 per cent. It fell just short of 46,000,000 francs.[38]

When Haussmann resigned early in 1870 his battle for water was won. At the moment the city had only 5,000,000 gallons of spring water at its disposal each day, but the Municipal Council and administration were committed, as Haussmann wished, to the use of springs alone to supply the city's private consumers. The rising aqueduct of the Vanne would shortly add 26,000,000 gallons to the available supply, and in the next half century under the Republic the city, still following the lead of the prefect the republicans professed to scorn, tapped the springs of three additional river valleys and raised the daily flow of spring water into the city to some 80,000,000 gallons. In the battle for water this was Haussmann's great victory.

But he also won other victories. To the supply of water for the public services he added twice as much as all his predecessors combined. All of it came from rivers, and to raise it he completed the new pumps at Chaillot, enlarged the pumping station on the Quai d'Austerlitz, established new pumps on the Marne, and from private owners purchased six additional pumping plants. Two venerable pumps, one of them a landmark in central Paris since the reign of Louis XIV, fell victim of the improvements. The ancient pump house that had disfigured the Pont Nôtre-Dame since 1670, and the pumps (built by James Watt) at Gros-Caillou on the Left Bank near the Pont de l'Alma were dismantled and removed in 1858. The water lost with the removal of these old installations was small and the combined capacity of the new pumps very large—55,000,000 gallons a day. Continued dry weather in the summer months

---

[38] Belgrand, *Travaux*, IV, 199, 231-33, 238.

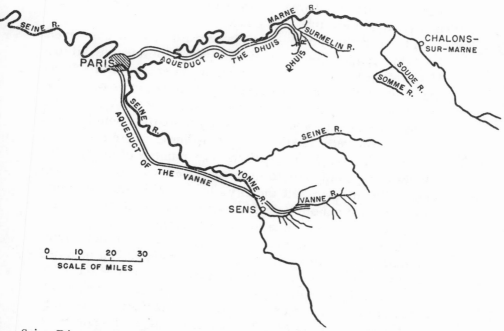

Seine River Basin and the aqueducts built by Haussmann and Belgrand.

during the sixties handicapped the water supply dependent on the Seine and the Marne, and in his final years as prefect Haussmann looked again to the Loire River, this time with favor. He negotiated with a private company that proposed to build a derivation canal from the Loire to Paris and to sell the city some 100,000,000 gallons daily, but nothing came of the project.[39]

In 1850 the total water supply of the city had amounted to only 27,000,000 gallons a day. If it could have been distributed, the average supply for each of the city's inhabitants would have been but twenty-six gallons daily. When Haussmann left the prefecture in 1870 he had raised the average to fifty gallons, and the completion of the derivation of the Vanne added

[39] Haussmann, *Mémoires*, II, 515-16, III, 402-03; Belgrand, *Travaux*, III, 256-57, 290-93, IV, 71-73, 79-85, 379, 382-83; *Moniteur*, May 8, 1858, Dec. 11, 1867: Arch. nat., C 1134, Corps législatif, Session 1869, Dossier No. 140.

another fourteen. Three quarters of a century later London had yet to achieve that abundance.[40]

In the distribution of water Haussmann's record was mixed, his achievements being balanced by one conspicuous failure. His professed aim was to put running water into every dwelling, and to that end he made important improvements. Between 1854 and 1870 the combined length of the city's water mains were doubled and their capacity more than doubled, and most of them were installed in sewer galleries where they could be readily inspected and repaired. The number of houses with city water piped directly to them rose from 6,000 to more than 34,000. But in 1870 half the city's houses still lacked running water, and many more lacked it above the ground floor. Haussmann's water program like his slum clearance was incomplete. He cleared slums but did nothing to assure that new slums would not replace them. He made water available, but he failed to apply any sanction that would assure its equitable and wide distribution. Subscription to city water was left at the option of each proprietor, and he was required to pay water rates only if he chose to take water. Many landlords decided against the expense. Had Haussmann made subscription obligatory and collected the rates in taxes, as he considered doing, the abundance of water he gave to the city would have been a much more general benefit.[41]

[40] *J.O.*, Supplément, May 1869, p. 7; Haussmann, *Mémoires*, II, 515-16.
[41] Haussmann, *Mémoires*, II, 516-17, III, 370-71; *Moniteur*, Dec. 7, 1854; Seine, *Dérivation de la Vanne*, p. 33.

VI · PARIS UNDERGROUND

NAPOLEON III ONCE ASKED EDWIN CHADWICK, Britain's great public health crusader, what he thought of his improvements in Paris.

"Sir," he replied, "it was said of Augustus that he found Rome brick and left it marble. May it be said of you that you found Paris stinking and left it sweet."[1]

Whether Chadwick meant to praise Napoleon for work accomplished or to exhort him to new efforts is uncertain, but the statement did bluntly summarize an aspect of Napoleon III's transformation of Paris that is often forgotten—the construction of an efficient system of sewers. At mid-century Paris was, as Chadwick affirmed, a smelly city, and much of the trouble lay in its drainage. Most streets lacked underground drains. Those in existence were too small and frequently overflowed and flooded low-lying areas. The Seine itself was an open sewer flowing through the center of the city. In 1870 the imperial administration left Paris, if not sweet smelling, at least sweeter than it was two decades earlier. Haussmann and the engineer Belgrand gave virtually every street in old Paris its own underground drain and substantially extended the network of street drains in the annexed zone, and they built a comprehensive system of collectors that carried waste water to the Seine well below Paris and ended pollution of the river within the city.

This revolution in Paris underground was the conception of Haussmann and Belgrand. Chadwick's statement, if he intended it as praise, might better have been directed to them. Louis Napoleon backed their efforts, but he never exhibited much personal interest in sewers and drains. He proposed none in

[1] Quoted in G. M. Young, *Victorian England: Portrait of an Age* (London, 1936), p. 11.

the plan for the transformation of Paris that he gave to Haussmann in 1853, and before that time he had put no pressure
on Haussmann's predecessor to build new sewers or even to
improve the old. Nine months passed after Haussmann had
assumed the office of Prefect of the Seine before the Emperor
even discussed the subject with him, and then Haussmann
raised it. The Emperor had called the Prefect to the Tuileries
to consider the banker Laffitte's proposal to take over the water
supply of Paris, and Haussmann used the occasion to impress
upon the Emperor his serious anxiety over the related problem of sewers, particularly the pollution of the Seine by the
city's sewage in its course through Paris. The interview concluded with Napoleon's giving Haussmann a free hand to
prepare definite proposals for improvement of both the city's
water supply and its sewerage.[2]

The science of sanitary engineering was in its infancy, and
there was no well-marked path for Haussmann to follow. In
the 1830's the querulous Mrs. Trollope, objecting to offensive
odors in Paris, declared petulantly, "It really appears to me
that almost the only thing in the world which other men do,
but which Frenchmen cannot is the making of sewers and
drains."[3] She was not quite right. Haussmann's and Belgrand's
predecessors in Paris had accomplished important improvements in sewerage that suggested the directions their program
might take. In the twenties a municipal engineer had developed
a low cost method of building sewers of cement and rough
stone, and the city had used it in constructing some sixty miles
of new lines during the two following decades. Another engineer had introduced a rational pattern into the location of new
street drains and had prepared the first map and statistics of
the existing lines. To carry all waste water to the river below
the city the Prefect Berger and his Director of Public Works,
Dupuit, had started construction of the first collectors, one
under the Rue de Rivoli and another under the quais of the
Left Bank. The design of these galleries was revolutionary, and

2 G. E. Haussmann, *Mémoires* (Paris, 1890-93), III, 294, 297-301; Eugène Belgrand, *Les Travaux souterrains de Paris* (Paris, 1873-77), v, iii-vi.
3 Frances Trollope, *Paris and the Parisians in 1835* (London, 1836), I, 117.

Belgrand copied it in all the collectors he built during the Empire.[4]

These were useful beginnings. In a modest moment Haussmann himself declared that the Rue de Rivoli collector was "the point of departure for a revolution in Paris sewers." But the actual accomplishment before his time was small and uncoordinated in any comprehensive plan. The 260 miles of streets still had fewer than 100 miles of sewers, and they lacked the capacity to handle heavy rains. Their dimensions had been determined by the size of a man, facility in cleaning being the designer's first consideration; Haussmann could find no indication that any effort had ever been made to compute in advance of construction how much water a gallery might be required to carry. The experiment of pumping liquids from cesspoools directly into gutters and sewers, instituted in 1850, had not proved wholly satisfactory, for the liquids were not as odorless as expected, and they compounded the offensive smell of household and industrial waste water already there. The collectors begun under the Rue de Rivoli and the quais of the Left Bank proved to be defective in elevation. The least high water flooded the first completed section on the Left Bank rendering it useless, and it had to be abandoned. If the Rue de Rivoli collector were continued to Chaillot, it, too, Haussmann and Belgrand later discovered, would be subject to frequent flooding. The slope required to assure an adequate velocity in the channel of the collector was greater than the slope of the river bed through Paris, and as the collector was continued downstream parallel to the river it came ever closer to the level of the water in the river. Haussmann's engineers computed that the collector, if built to Chaillot as planned, would emerge at the river bank only about forty inches above the low river stage. If continued on to the fortifications, it would join the stream at about the level of low water. At least once yearly high waters would flood the collector, stop the flow, and back up sewage into the streets.[5]

[4] Belgrand, *Travaux*, v, 30-38, 41; *Moniteur universel*, July 25, 1851, Sept. 15, 1852, Dec. 7, 1854; Haussmann, *Mémoires*, III, 316-17.

[5] *Moniteur*, Dec. 7, 1854, April 8, 1859; Haussmann, *Mémoires*, III, 297-98; Belgrand, *Travaux*, v, ix-x, 49-53, 94; Département de la Seine, *Rapport général*

Following his discussion with the Emperor on water and sewers in April, 1854, Haussmann had directed his attention primarily to water supply, and four months later when he presented his and Belgrand's proposals on water to the Municipal Council, he had ready only some suggestions of general policy on sewerage. His memorandum of August 4, 1854, recommended the tapping of distant springs that would double the city's supply of water, but Haussmann pointed out that this was only one face of the problem. Provision must also be made to remove the greater volume of water after it had been brought to the city and contaminated by use. He made only one recommendation for the construction of a particular sewer, but he did lay down certain objectives toward which the city should work. He urged first that every street should have its own covered drain and that every sewer should have dimensions carefully computed to carry the maximum rainfall ever known to fall in its drainage area. All galleries should also be built to accommodate water conduits and possibly gas pipes, too, in their vaults. Secondly, he recommended that all primary and secondary sewer lines be equipped with rails for cars used in cleaning as in the new Rue de Rivoli collector and that all the smaller street sewer and private connections be of a size permitting passage through them of wheelbarrows or portable containers for sanitary sewage. The sanitary sewage or nightsoil accumulated in cesspools, he thought, could then be removed underground through these passageways, and they might also be used for garbage collection, sparing the streets the daily piling of garbage on the curbs.[6]

He warned the Council that the contemplated increase in the city's water supply would further complicate the removal of sanitary sewage. When water was piped to every household, the volume of liquid discharged into cesspools would be greatly increased. If the system of manual disposal remained unchanged, there would have to be more frequent collections, which would multiply the noise and stench inevitable in the

sur les travaux du Conseil d'Hygiène et du Salubrité, 1849-1858 (Paris, 1861), p. 85.

[6] Moniteur, Dec. 7, 1854.

removal process. Landlords, moreover, would be faced with substantial increases in their operating costs, for nightsoil contractors charged by volume and made no distinction between liquid and solid. In the past many proprietors who had piped water to all floors of their apartment buildings found the consequent increase in removal costs prohibitive, and they eventually limited running water to the first floor.[7]

At the conclusion of his memorandum Haussmann asked the Municipal Council to authorize further study of the whole sewage problem in Paris along the lines he had suggested. Almost six months elapsed before it granted the authority, but the delay was owing more to differences over water supply than to any serious opposition to the sewer program.[8] The improvement of sewerage never became a political issue in Paris as did Haussmann's street building, nor did proposals to turn the whole matter over to private entrepreneurs raise any obstacles to his plans as they did in the case of water supply.

With the Council's endorsement in hand Haussmann placed Belgrand, who had assisted him in the preliminary water studies, at the head of the municipal Water Service, where he had charge of sewer construction and sewage disposal as well as the derivation and distribution of water. Three years later Haussmann presented to the Municipal Council his second memorandum on water and sewers, embodying recommendations that were the issue of Belgrand's studies.[9]

The Prefect's memorandum of 1858 made two specific recommendations on sewers: first, the construction of about 200 miles of underground street sewers to achieve the objective laid down in the first memorandum of giving every street its own covered drain; and second, the creation of a system of collectors to carry all waste water to the Seine below Paris. All were to be storm sewers, sanitary sewage still being left for manual removal, although liquids from cesspools might be run directly into the sewers if properly disinfected.[10]

Before the Empire fell Haussmann had completed more than

---

[7] *Moniteur*, Dec. 7, 1854; Belgrand, *Travaux*, v, 322.
[8] Haussmann, *Mémoires*, III, 327-32.
[9] *Ibid.*, III, 333, 339.   [10] *Moniteur*, Feb. 5, 1859.

200 miles of sewers, but he fell short of his aim of a drain for every street, for the annexation of the suburbs in 1860 had added to the mileage of city streets. In 1870 Paris had 348 miles of sewers, four times the total in 1851, but the length of its streets then exceeded 500 miles. The many streets that remained unserved were particularly in the poorer quarters of the annexed zone. Proprietors were supposed to share the expense of building sewers adjoining their property, and in poor districts they resisted new construction.[11]

The installation of connections between individual buildings and the city sewer lines also fell short of the administration's aims, and here, too, the deficiency was largely in the newly annexed quarters. The decree of March 26, 1852, gave proprietors of existing buildings ten years in which to build connections, and they took full advantage of the period of grace and a little more. In the early 1860's they bestirred themselves, and in the old city they generally built the sewers as required without resistance. So many were built in 1862 and 1863 that the Prefect had to issue new regulations to protect the public against obstacles to traffic and the danger of cave-ins during construction. In the poorer districts of the annexed area, however, few proprietors had complied with the law before the deadline in 1870. Haussmann's successor in February, 1870, authorized less costly connecting galleries, but little more was accomplished before the Empire's end six months later.[12]

But length and numbers alone were not the whole measure of the new sewers. They were superior to the old lines in other ways. Since the First Empire municipal engineers had recognized the advantages of sewer galleries large enough to carry water pipes under their vaults, but the added expense of enlarging the old heavy-walled, vertical-sided galleries was prohibitive. The galleries built after 1855 were egg-shaped, made of hydraulic cement, and their walls were but half as thick as those of the old style sewers. A given amount of building material used in a gallery of the new design produced a cross-

11 Haussmann, *Mémoires*, II, 517; *Documents rélatifs aux eaux de Paris* (Paris, 1861), p. 390.
12 Belgrand, *Travaux*, V, 42-43, 162-63; *Moniteur*, Dec. 4, 1862, Dec. 6, 1863.

section about 50 per cent larger than it would in an old style gallery. In these larger vaults was space for water mains, and later they provided protected and accessible positions for electric, telegraph, and telephone wires and for the pneumatic tubes that carried letters about the city at high speed. For the first time, moreover, the dimensions of sewers were related to the volume of water they would be required to carry. Belgrand computed the cross-section required for each 250 acres of area that a sewer must drain, and the new lines were built and most of the old rebuilt according to that formula.[13]

Haussmann's extension of the network of street sewers and individual house connections was an accelerated continuation of the work begun before his time. His second recommendation in the memorandum of July, 1858, on collectors was both more original and more typical of his flair for grand projects. Previously engineers had planned one collector on each bank parallel with the river. Haussmann and Belgrand proposed a system of eleven collectors covering the whole city, and they had already begun construction of its major component, the great general collector that would receive the flow of all the others and carry it to the Seine at Asnières, below Paris.

The Collector of Asnières was a solution to the problem raised by the discovery that no collector following the river could have sufficient incline and sufficient length to carry it beyond the city and still emerge above flood stage. It took advantage of the peculiar course of the Seine below Paris, where the river doubles back on itself in a great bend around Boulogne and flows northeastward for a few miles, coming at Asnières within two miles of the city's northwestern limits. In 1857 Haussmann recommended to the Municipal Council the construction of a primary collector from the Place de la Concorde to the Place de la Madeleine and thence northwestward under the hill of Monceau to the river at Asnières. The distance was six-tenths of a mile less than the distance along the river from the Place de la Concorde to the fortifications, and, what was more important, the outfall at Asnières, being nine miles further downstream, could be nearly seven feet

[13] Belgrand, *Travaux*, v, 39-45; *Moniteur*, Feb. 5, 1859.

lower than at Chaillot, the proposed outfall of the Rue de Rivoli sewer. The city's engineers could build the collector with the requisite incline and still bring it out on the river's edge at an elevation safely above flood stage. The construction of the collector and its tributaries would permit the closing of all regular connections between the sewers and the river within the city.[14]

The idea was a brilliant solution to the problem of ending contamination of the Seine in Paris. Haussmann claimed it occurred to him after many months of thought. Reconciliation of the river's slight slope with his desire to free the river of sewage long seemed impossible. Then one sleepless night as he sat staring at a plan of Paris this simple solution suddenly struck him. Belgrand disagreed, but lacking his chief's flair for the dramatic he had no tale of midnight inspiration. He simply affirmed that the idea was his.[15]

The execution of the plans for the collectors began in the spring of 1857 when Belgrand asked for bids on the construction of the Collector of Asnières, the *Cloaca Maxima* of the system.[16] (Haussmann frequently used the Roman name and often referred to the Roman sewers in his reports, in part because he had to go back that far to find a precedent for what he was attempting, but also, certainly, because he hoped the Roman comparison would heighten the appeal of his program to the Emperor.) Belgrand's specifications called for a larger gallery than any previously built for a sewer. It was elliptical in shape with a maximum interior width of about eighteen feet and a maximum height of nearly fourteen-and-a-half feet. As in the Rue de Rivoli Collector a channel for the flow of water ran between two footways; the channel was more than eleven feet wide and four feet deep, three times as wide and nearly twice as deep as the channel of the Rue de Rivoli Collector.

The gallery presented some formidable construction problems. The water table under much of the Right Bank of Paris, including the area through which the collector would pass,

14 *Moniteur*, Apr. 7, 1857; Belgrand, *Travaux*, v, 49-54.

15 Haussmann, *Mémoires*, iii, 298-99; Belgrand, *Travaux*, v, 50.

16 The following account of the construction of the Collector of Asnières is based on Belgrand's own account in his *Travaux*, v, 66-68, 76-91.

was unusually high and turned the strata of sand and gravel a few yards below the surface into quicksand. The walls of a trench or tunnel cut through it would not stand up, and excavations caused shifts in the soil that endangered foundations of nearby buildings. On the portion of the collector between the Rue de la Pépinière near the Church of Saint-Augustin and the fortifications, involving work in this perilous soil, there was but one bidder, and Belgrand considered his bid prohibitively high. Armed with authority from Haussmann to seek new bids he negotiated directly with the principal contractors of Paris, but he could get no better price, and many contractors even when directly importuned refused to bid on the job.

The villain of the piece was, of course, not the contractors, who were only reasonably cautious, but the high water layer, and Belgrand undertook to eliminate the villain. He dug a series of pits along the course of the collector, installed a steam engine and pump at each, and pumped out the water, lowering the water level by eight feet. The sand and gravel layer, once drained of water, had enough consistency to permit construction of the gallery with no more than ordinary hazard. The city itself then built the section that tunnelled under the hill of Monceau from the Rue de la Pépinière to the fortifications and completed it before the end of 1858 at approximately estimated cost and without serious accident. A private contractor built the adjoining portion between the fortifications and the river in the last eight months of 1857. Belgrand held up work on the section under the new Boulevard Malesherbes until 1860, when it could be combined with construction of the boulevard itself, but the trunk under the Rue Royale and a temporary junction gallery around the Boulevard Malesherbes were built in 1858-59, permitting the immediate diversion of the Rue de Rivoli Collector into the new general collector. Two years later Haussmann reported to the Municipal Council that the Collector of Asnières was completed and in use over its entire length.[17]

Two independent conduits were built into the structure of the collector under the footways. One connected with soil drainage pipes to carry off sub-surface water and keep it below

[17] *Moniteur*, Dec. 12, 1861.

the level of cellars. The other, anticipating a decision of the Municipal Council to run all toilet waste into sewers, was intended to carry this waste matter independently of the sewer channel. It reflected Haussmann's determination to keep his fine new collector uncontaminated, but the Municipal Council never made the expected decision, and the second conduit was actually built in only a part of the general collector and in none of the secondary collectors.[18]

In the memorandum of July, 1858, Haussmann had recommended the construction of five new secondary collectors on the Right Bank and their integration, together with the two already there, into a system of tributaries of the General Collector of Asnières. His administration subsequently built three of the new collectors approximately as planned and one additional that was independent of the general system.

The two principal tributaries followed the main depressions in the relief of the Right Bank. The Collector of the Quais, completed in 1863, started at the junction of the Canal Saint-Martin and the Seine and ran along the river edge to the Place de la Concorde, where it emptied into the Collector of Asnières. It drained the area between the Rue de Rivoli and the river and handled the overflow of the Rue de Rivoli sewer, which had proved too small for the demand put upon it. Through the lateral gallery under the Boulevard de Sébastopol and the Boulevard de Strasbourg the Collector of the Quais could also receive overflow from the collector at the foot of the northern hills. The Collector of the Quais itself was protected against overflow by emergency outlets directly into the river. The Collector of the Hills (des Coteaux) originally began at the Canal Saint-Martin and the new Boulevard du Prince Eugène (now the Boulevard Voltaire), described a broad arc through the depression between the inner ring of boulevards and the base of the northern hills and joined the general collector near the junction of the Boulevard Malesherbes and the Boulevard Haussmann. Between 1861 and 1866 Belgrand extended it from the Canal de l'Ourcq southeastward around the foot of the heights of Charonne almost to the fortifications opposite

18 *Moniteur*, April 8, 1857, Feb. 5, 1859.

the Bois de Vincennes. The Collector of the Rue de Rivoli continued in use from the Rue Saint-Antoine to the Place de la Concorde, and the short Collector des Petits-Champs drained the neighborhood between the Bibliothèque Nationale and the Place de la Madeleine.[19]

The Collector of the North, conceived after Haussmann presented the original plan in 1858, was independent of the general system. Built on the side of the heights of Belleville some sixty feet above the Collector of the Hills it intercepted rain water running down the hillside before it could enter the low ground below that suffered from frequent flooding. Belgrand ran it under the Boulevard de Belleville and the Boulevard de la Villette, through the depression between Belleville and La Villette, and thence northward to join a departmental sewer emptying into the Seine at Saint-Denis.[20]

For the Left Bank Haussmann proposed three collectors radiating like spokes of a wheel from the southern end of the Pont de la Concorde opposite the General Collector of Asnières. One was to drain the eastern quarters, the second the central quarters below the Hôtel des Invalides, and the third the western end of the Left Bank. A siphon across the river would connect them with the Collector of Asnières. The annexation of the suburbs in 1860 forced modification of this plan, for it brought into the city territory that was too far downstream to be drained by collectors terminating *upstream* at the Pont de la Concorde. The same problem arose on the opposite bank, where Belgrand had originally proposed a collector from Chaillot to the Place de la Concorde. The newly annexed areas might, of course, be drained directly into the river, but that would defeat Haussmann's primary purpose in building the system. The problem was taken up in a conference in Haussmann's office in 1864. Belgrand recommended a new collector from the southwest extremity of the city across Boulogne to the Seine opposite Saint-Cloud, but Haussmann would not hear of contaminating the river before it passed his cherished Bois de Boulogne. He suggested a collector starting at the Pont de

[19] Belgrand, *Travaux*, v, 55-57, 123-36, 133-34, 136.
[20] *Ibid.*, p. 56.

l'Alma and running north under the Place de l'Etoile to the river near the outfall of the Collector of Asnières. It would be practical only if the waste waters of the southwest quarters that lay downstream from the new collector could be brought upstream to it, and the ever resourceful Belgrand had a solution: an unsloped gallery in which the impact of entering water forced the flow in the channel. Haussmann was apparently satisfied that it was practical, for work started on the new collector in 1865 and was completed in 1868. The gallery followed the course the Prefect had proposed except that between the fortifications and the river it was turned to empty into the Collector of Asnières instead of going on to a separate outfall in the river. Belgrand's proposed collectors to drain the southwest quarters on both sides of the river remained unbuilt at the end of the Empire, and provisionally the waters of these districts continued to run directly into the Seine.[21]

The new collector under the Place de l'Etoile was called the Collector of the Bièvre, being regarded as a continuation of the principal collector of the Left Bank, which began at the Bièvre River on the east side of the city. Belgrand built most of the Left Bank section in the early 1860's while he was still pondering the problem of draining the southwest quarters, but he did not complete the final connecting links near the Rue Saint-Jacques and the Jardin des Plantes until 1867. A branch, the Collector Bosquet, was built between the Invalides and the Champs de Mars southward to the Boulevard du Montparnasse. It joined the main collector at its Left Bank terminus near the Pont de l'Alma.[22]

In 1868 Belgrand began work on the siphon under the Seine that was to connect the two sections of the Collector of the Bièvre. Its principal elements were two sheet iron tubes thirty-nine inches in diameter and 492 feet long, each composed of sections that were assembled on the river bank above the Pont de l'Alma and there joined together. Belgrand planned to lower the hermetically sealed tubes into the river, float them into position across the stream just above the bridge, and then sink

21 Belgrand, *Travaux*, v, 57, 94-97, 108-09, 140-42. *Moniteur*, Dec. 11, 1867.
22 Belgrand, *Travaux*, v, 106, *Atlas*, v, Pl. 2.

them onto a prepared bed. Maneuvering more than 110 tons of iron stretched over nearly 500 feet was no simple operation. Preparations for lowering the first tube thirteen feet down an incline from the river bank to the water took up the better part of two weeks at the end of July and early August, 1868, and even with those careful preparations workmen let it drop more than three feet. Happily the tube emerged undamaged. A week later on August 18 they lowered the second tube safely, and the two were anchored side by side in midstream and permanently fixed together with iron beams. They were then moved into position above the prepared bed, an operation complicated by the exceptionally low water in the river at the end of a dry summer. On August 26 before hundreds of spectators who came to watch the operations, the engineers in charge made the first attempt to submerge the huge structure, using iron weights to force it under water. Just below the surface it tipped, dumped some of the weights to the bottom of the river, and re-emerged. Operations had to be suspended until divers re-covered the lost weights. Not until September 1, after they had blocked all river traffic for more than a week, were the tubes successfully sunk. Divers fixed them in place with iron braces, and later two feet of concrete were poured over them. On November 2, 1868, municipal engineers turned the waters of the Left Bank section of the Collector of the Bièvre into the siphon.[23]

With the completion of this siphon and the Right Bank section of the Collector of the Bièvre in the same year Haussmann and Belgrand had finished the principal elements of their network of collectors, and they had come close to achieving their aim of freeing the Seine in Paris of all sewer water. Only the extreme southeast and southwest quarters and the two islands emptied their storm sewers directly into the river, and Belgrand had plans to bring those areas into the system. The new collectors with their large capacities and emergency flood gates also cut sharply into the number of days when flood waters of the Seine interrupted sewer service. Before they were

[23] Belgrand, *Travaux*, v, 112-14; *Moniteur*, Aug. 4, 12, 20, 23, 25, 29, Sept. 3, 1868.

built the city could expect fourteen to forty days of interrupted service each year. The collectors reduced the expectation to a maximum of ten days.[24]

During the Franco-Prussian War the collectors had some days of unforeseen disfavor with the public. When Parisians learned that the French armies were being routed in the east, rumor spread that Germans infiltrating the collectors might suddenly spring out of the earth in the center of Paris. Later the encirclement of the city by the besieging enemy changed the fantasy to a real threat, and the authorities built walls across the General Collector of Asnières to close it to potential invaders.[25]

An unmixed blessing for Paris at peace the collector system was a menace for the riverside communities downstream from the outfall. It concentrated at a single point all the evils of congestion and contamination that were formerly spread along several miles of the river in the city. An analysis of the water flowing from the general collector showed that in a year it carried 154,000 tons of solids and 77,000 tons of dissolved matter into the river. The solids included mud, sand, and gravel, coming especially from macadam streets, and organic matter, chiefly the leavings of curb side garbage collections and the less than perfect system of removing horse droppings. At the mouth of the collector the solids formed a delta that had to be dredged away periodically at the city's expense, and other foreign matter made a dark streak in the river visible miles downstream.[26]

Valuable fertilizers were being lost, and in the last years of the Empire the engineer Mille, the city's expert on solid sewage disposal, experimented with the use of the sewer water for irrigation and fertilization of gardens. In 1868 he obtained good results on a small plot at Clichy near the outlet of the general collector, and the following year the city pumped 1,300,000 gallons daily to the plain of Gennevilliers a short

[24] Belgrand, *Travaux*, v, 53, 119; *Moniteur*, Dec. 4, 1862.
[25] Maxime du Camp, *Paris: ses organes, ses fonctions et sa vie* (Paris, 1869-75), v, 343-44.
[26] Belgrand, *Travaux*, i, 484-86; *Annales des Ponts et Chaussées* (Paris), 1st, Part, 1869, 2d Semester, p. 559.

distance downstream and made it available without charge to any proprietor who would use it. By October, 1869, ninety acres in this area were being watered, and the formerly inhospitable soil began to produce a high yield of vegetables. Before the end of that year, Mille reported, rents of land had multiplied as much as five-fold. The experiment pointed the way toward a possible solution of the problem of river contamination, but several decades passed before more than a small fraction of the sewer water was used as Mille proposed.[27]

Haussmann in his memorandum of 1858 had laid down as one of the essential requirements of an acceptable system of sewers that the principal galleries be designed to permit the use of mechanical cleaning devices. Heretofore the sewers had been cleaned by hand. Men working with scrapers and using movable sluice-gates to produce a strong rush of water pushed mud, gravel, and other debris into piles under manholes; there it was hauled to the surface in buckets and loaded into carts for removal. When the Rue de Rivoli sewer was built, Dupuit, the engineer in charge, installed a rail on each of the footways so that cars straddling the channel could be run in the gallery itself to carry debris, and he also worked on the idea of a car with a kind of sluice gate projecting below it to obstruct the flow in the channel and produce a water action that would clean the channel. He built an experimental car, but the Prefect of Police, who then had sewer cleaning in his charge (although sewer construction came under the Prefect of the Department of the Seine) did nothing with it.[28]

Later Belgrand took up the idea, and in 1858 a newly built sluice car proved capable of an efficient job of cleaning. The device was a platform measuring about four by six feet, mounted on four wheels with a movable sluice gate suspended below it. The gate was slightly smaller than the cross section of the sewer channel, and near the lower end it had two small openings. Lowered into the channel it blocked the flow of water. When the difference in levels on opposite sides of the

[27] *Annales des Ponts et Chaussées*, 1st Part, 1869, 2d Semester, pp. 313-39, 344; Haussmann, *Mémoires*, III, 318-19; Archives nationales (Paris), C 1145, Corps législatif, Session 1870, Dossier No. 259-60.

[28] Belgrand, *Travaux*, v, 179, 184-86.

gate reached six or eight inches the water pouring through the two openings and around the edges of the gate produced an agitation that stirred up the sand and silt on the channel floor. The weight of the impounded water on the gate moved the car forward, and the gate and water together pushed the mass of stirred-up solids ahead as a spring wind blows dry sand along a beach. A bank of moving sand and sludge might extend 300 or more feet ahead of the car. In the Collector of Asnières the greater width of the channel precluded the use of straddling cars, but engineers applied the same technique of hydraulic cleaning there, using a boat instead of a car to carry the sluice gate. A single boat operating around the clock could traverse the three mile length of the general collector in from eight to twenty days. For more frequent cleaning several boats were operated simultaneously.[29]

On October 10, 1859, an imperial decree transferred to the Prefect of the Seine the responsibility for cleaning the sewers of Paris, and he applied the new method of cleaning to all the collectors. Sluice boats were used in the Collector of Asnières and the Collector of the Bièvre and in a section of the Collector of the Quais, sluice cars in all others. In the smaller sewers cleaning crews continued to use the old manual methods.[30]

The principle used in the sluice cars and boats Belgrand also applied to the cleaning of the siphon of the Pont de l'Alma. Every three days workmen placed in the upstream end of each tube a wooden ball a few inches smaller than the diameter of the tube. It backed up water behind it, and when it was released the water escaping around the sides stirred up any deposits in the siphon, and the weight of the impounded water forced the ball and all solid matter ahead of it through the tube and into the Right Bank section of the collector. The ordinary flow of the collector was sufficient to move the ball across the river in two and a half minutes, and it had enough power behind it to push out of the siphon on one occasion several hides

29 Belgrand, *Travaux*, v, 187-89; Adolphe Joanne, *Paris illustré en 1870 et 1877* (3d edit.; Paris, [n.d.]), p. 1039. Pictures of the cleaning cars and boats are printed in Belgrand, *Travaux: Atlas*, v, Pl. 6, 9, 10.

30 Belgrand, *Travaux*, v, 187.

lost by tanners in the upper waters of the Bièvre and lodged in the tubes.[31]

The Parisian system of collectors was unequalled in any other city in the world, and they attracted widespread interest. During the year of the Exposition of 1867 many visiting princes as well as lesser persons inspected them. Guidebooks recommended them to tourists, and Belgrand provided facilities for 400 visitors on stated visiting days and still did not satisfy the demand.[32] To this day the city continues to conduct public inspection trips through the collectors, and across the decades the visits have probably disappointed many thousands of visitors. To most literate men the sewers of Paris evoke one association—Hugo's unforgettable description of them in *Les Misérables*, but the visitors, riding comfortably in cars or boats, have seen not the dark and dangerous caverns through which Jean Valjean made his perilous escape in 1832 but the spacious, clean, and well-lighted galleries of the Second Empire.

To the second major problem of Parisian sewerage, the disposal of sanitary sewage, Haussmann's administration brought no new solution. Shortly after his first report on the matter in the memorandum of 1854 he sent Mille, who later made the irrigation experiments at Clichy and Gennevilliers, to Great Britain to study sewage disposal. Mille already favored both a system of general sewers that would handle all sewage, including nightsoil, and the use of sewage for fertilization, and he saw the method in operation in Britain and returned a convinced partisan. At La Villette he planted an experimental garden and irrigated it with water mixed with solids from the nightsoil reservoirs to simulate the contents of general sewers, and Haussmann admitted that the taste of the vegetables and fruit and the odor of the flowers he grew were impeccable. But the Prefect was not convinced. He believed that nightsoil solids would contaminate the slow-flowing, gravitational sewers of Paris and make them intolerable for cleaning crews, and

[31] *Ibid.*, v, 116-17, *Atlas*, v, Pl. 2.

[32] Joanne, *Paris*, p. 1038; Karl Baedeker, *Paris and its Environs* (Leipsig, 1876), pp. 251-52; Belgrand, *Travaux*, v, 209-10.

he also feared that the dilution of solids in water would cut their commercial value as fertilizers.[33]

By the time he wrote his second memorandum in 1858 the Prefect had eliminated Mille's method from the possible solutions. He then saw only two practical approaches. The first was an independent system of sanitary sewers. The discovery of a low cost method of installing concrete conduits in the solid structure of the new sewer galleries lowered the financial barrier that had been the primary obstacle to adoption of this method. Also, his belief that dilution of nightsoil in water would cut its commercial value as fertilizer, which had been another obstacle, had been proved erroneous. The second practical approach was through the use of separating devices that would permit continuous running of liquids into sewers and the manual removal through sewer galleries of the relatively small quantities of solids. Both methods still had important shortcomings, and the Prefect was unwilling to recommend either one of them to the Council. The new sewer galleries under construction left the way open for the adoption of either method. The galleries were all large enough to allow underground removal of solids from separators, and conduits for sanitary sewage were to be built into the sewer structures. In fact, the conduits were installed only in a part of the Collector of Asnières, and in his subsequent reports to the Municipal Council Haussmann said no more about them.[34]

The only changes his administration actually made in the system of sanitary sewage disposal inherited from the preceding regime were experimental adaptations of the separator system. The Prefect authorized municipal engineers to tolerate permanent connections that would permit continuous running of toilet liquids into the sewers if the proprietor in each case replaced his cesspool with a separator. Proprietors were reluctant, however, to adopt the procedure on so provisional a basis, suspecting that the city was only experimenting at their expense. Even after Haussmann gave formal authorization there was no rush to adopt the new method. In 1871, Belgrand reported, not

[33] Haussmann, *Mémoires*, III, 300, 317-19, 325-26.
[34] *Moniteur*, Feb. 5, 1859.

one house in ten had separators and direct sewer connections in operation.[35]

Throughout the Second Empire most sanitary sewage continued to be removed by the old odorous and noisy manual method. The task grew with the city, and in 1864 it required fifty teams of five men each at work nightly. The service remained in the hands of private companies and was still expensive enough to discourage many proprietors from distributing running water in their apartments, and the cost apparently moved some thousands to resort to illegal methods of disposal. They used permeable cesspools, had nightsoil removed by unauthorized nightmen, or even buried it in courtyards and gardens. Belgrand declared in 1871 that nearly 7,700 of the city's 68,000 houses had never had any legal disposal service.[36]

For a related problem of Paris underground Haussmann proposed a characteristically revolutionary solution and uncharacteristically got almost nowhere with it. The problem was the growing need for burial space in locations where seepage would not pollute wells or river. Haussmann's solution was a single, immense municipal cemetery in the open country thirteen miles beyond the fortifications, connected with the city by its own private railway. A decree of the first Napoleon had forbidden burials within the city, and in the first quarter of the century the municipal administration had established three cemeteries in the unsettled adjoining communes, the cemeteries of Montmartre, Père Lachaise, and Montparnasse. When Haussmann became Prefect in 1853 they were no longer isolated from settled areas as the Napoleonic decree had intended, and in 1860 the annexation of the suburbs brought them within the city itself. An article of the law of annexation exempted them from Napoleon I's decree, but two considerations more imperative than law moved Haussmann to try to supplant them. They were rapidly filling to capacity, and organic matter from thousands of decomposing bodies polluted sub-surface water that fed wells and ran into the river.[37]

[35] Belgrand, *Travaux*, v, 277, 287, 312-17, 324.
[36] Belgrand, *Travaux*, v, 269, 273, 322, 324-25.
[37] Haussmann, *Mémoires*, III, 404-05; *Moniteur*, Apr. 3, 1867.

The need for space became acute following an order of Napoleon III in 1853 putting an end to the mass charity graves in which coffins were stacked seven deep. The Emperor wanted an individual grave for each body, but in the existing cemeteries lack of space required that coffins be laid side by side in long common graves, and even this method, requiring seven times as much area as the old, was rapidly consuming the remaining space in the cemeteries, for nearly three-fourths of the burials in Paris were in charity graves. The establishment of a new cemetery beyond the fortifications at Ivry in 1853 eased the pressure temporarily, but in the 1860's the city in order to find space was obliged to reclaim charitable burial plots at the end of five years in order to re-use them. This was no permanent solution, and even as an expedient it was unfortunate. The soil did not have an unlimited capacity to absorb decomposing animal matter, and its continued re-use created a threat to public health. The well-to-do, moreover, could purchase long-term or perpetual leases in the municipal cemeteries. The indigent dead had only five years of undisturbed peace. In an Empire that professed to be dedicated to equality it was incongruous to forbid the poor equality even in death. Haussmann wanted to be able to guarantee every Parisian, rich or poor, an individual grave for at least thirty years and preferably fifty, and he estimated that for a population of 3,000,000, the city's maximum possible population (which, he believed, would be reached in from ten to twenty years) he must have at least 1,200 acres of new burial lands.[38]

In 1864 the Prefect appointed a commission of three engineers, including Belgrand, to investigate possible locations. Late that year they reported on three sites and recommended particularly one at Méry-sur-Oise near Pontoise, thirteen miles northwest of Paris. The land was sandy and unsuitable to agriculture but favorable to rapid decay. It could be purchased for a moderate price. The commissioners favored the location of a single large cemetery on this site to serve all Paris and the construction of a railroad to connect it with funerary stations to be

[38] Haussmann, *Mémoires*, III, 315-19, 441-42; *Moniteur*, Apr. 6, 1867.

built in each of the three major cemeteries within the city. In 1865 agents for the municipal government began quietly to take options on the purchase of the land, and early the following year Haussmann first publicly revealed the plan when he asked the Municipal Council to approve the purchase of 1,270 acres of land at Méry.[39]

The Council approved, but the public announcement of the project was followed by a chorus of protests, most of them groundless. Parisians whose families were all buried in the provinces solemnly denounced the closing of the old cemeteries as a violation of their ancestral burial places. One of several petitioners who asked the Senate to stop the project declared that the distant cemetery outraged the Parisian respect for the dead. Bodies would be shipped off like so many trunks; family and friends could not witness the final interment; and they could not visit graves of their dead. This was a popular line of complaint, and Haussmann and his aides were obliged to offer public explanations. Funeral services would be conducted as usual, and the processions would still go to the three interior cemeteries. There the coffins would be placed aboard special funeral cars, and as many mourners as chose could accompany the body to Méry and join in graveside services. The city would provide frequent trains for persons wishing to visit graves and extra sections would be run on All Saints' Day and All Souls' Day, the traditional occasions for remembering the dead. The railroad would, moreover, be reserved exclusively for cemetery traffic. Fares would be nominal, and the city would furnish free tickets for the indigent. Other objections came from persons who favored several cemeteries near the city, and from rural proprietors who wanted the funeral railroad kept away from their property. The Senate rejected the protests, and public hearings in the two interested departments, the Seine and the Seine-et-Oise, where the site was located, ended in endorsement of the project.[40]

In 1867 Haussmann submitted the plans to the Emperor, and

[39] Haussmann, *Mémoires*, III, 427-36; *Moniteur*, Apr. 3, 1867.
[40] Haussmann, *Mémoires*, III, 438-39; *Moniteur*, Apr. 3, 6, 1867; Du Camp, *Paris*, v, 166-67.

they progressed no further during the Empire. Napoleon himself, never convinced that they offered the best solution to the burial problem and beset with more pressing difficulties that threatened the existence of the regime, offered no strong support. Haussmann's star was already in the descendant. The attack that led to his dismissal in 1870 had already grown warm, and his enemies found in the Mèry cemetery a controversial issue that, like the changes he proposed in the Montmartre Cemetery, might be used to pilory him as a man not only scornful of the law but disrespectful of the dead. In 1869 when the attack on the Prefect reached a climax in a long and bitter debate in the Legislative Body over his financial methods, an opposition speaker brought up the Méry cemetery project and accused Haussmann of breaking the law in buying the land without authority from the legislature. The government was on the defensive in this debate, for the nominal attack on Haussmann was an assault on the whole imperial regime, and Rouher, the government's principal spokesman, was no friend of Haussmann. He sought to appease the opposition on this issue with the promise that nothing further would be done toward establishing the Méry cemetery or building the connecting railroad without consulting the Legislative Body. No more was heard of it from the government before the Empire fell.[41]

Haussmann's defeat on the Méry cemetery was a minor reverse when weighed in the balance against the successes in his program for Paris underground, and he might well have been pleased with the whole record. At the end of the Empire sewage no longer ran in the streets of the old city, no longer coated the pavement with ice in the winter; low areas and cellars were rarely flooded; and the Seine passed through Paris largely uncontaminated.

But these were negative benefits that could readily be taken for granted, and the different situation two decades earlier was easily forgotten. Haussmann lamented that the public thought

41 Haussmann, *Mémoires*, III, 465-69; Arch. nat., 45 AP 1 (Rouher Papers), Rouher's notes on cabinet meeting, Aug. 8, 1868; *Journal officiel de l'Empire français*, Mar. 11, 1869.

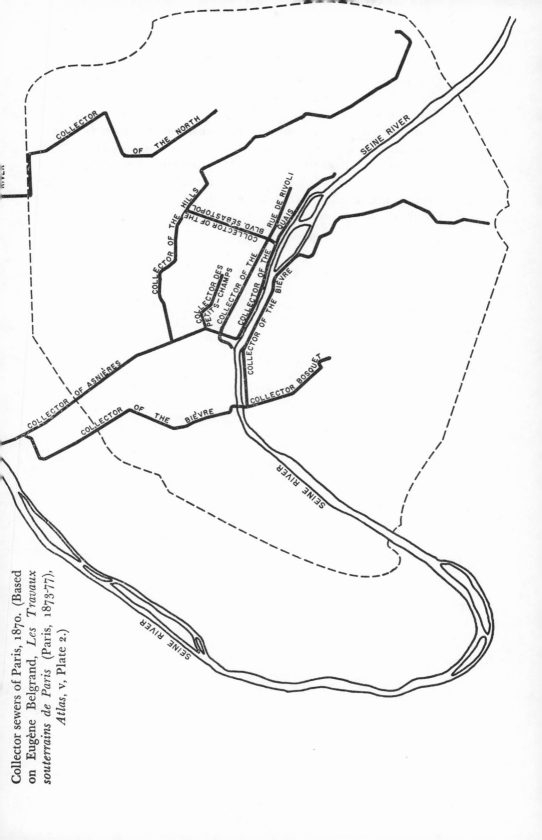

Collector sewers of Paris, 1870. (Based on Eugène Belgrand, *Les Travaux souterrains de Paris* (Paris, 1873-77), *Atlas*, v, Plate 2.)

of his sewer improvements only in terms of torn-up streets and obstructions to traffic. Once they were completed and excavations filled, people forgot them, giving no thought to the sewers' contribution to their convenience and health.[42] One may regret that Chadwick did not compliment Haussmann instead of Napoleon on making Paris sweet. Napoleon would have been more pleased had Chadwick praised him as a builder in marble. Haussmann would have been grateful for the compliment as Chadwick offered it.

[42] *Moniteur*, Dec. 4, 1862.

NAPOLEON III'S ASPIRATION to give Paris streets and parks and public services suitable for a city of its size was an heroic task when he first drew up his plans after 1848. In the years that followed it became ever greater as growing population multiplied the city's needs. When Napoleon conceived his ambitious projects the city had about a million inhabitants, and in the entire preceding century the number had risen by scarcely half a million. In the next decade alone the population rose more than half a million, and in the two decades of the fifties and sixties, a little short of a million.

POPULATION OF PARIS
WITHIN THE CITY'S LEGAL LIMITS, 1762-1872

1762	600,000	1851	1,053,300	
	(estimate)	1856	1,174,300	
1801	547,800	1861	1,696,100	(after annexation of suburbs)
1817	714,000			
1831	785,900			
1836	899,300	1866	1,825,300	
1841	935,300	1872	1,851,800	
1846	1,053,900			

Source: Département de la Seine, Service de la Statistique municipale, *Résultats statistiques du dénombrement de 1896 pour la ville de Paris et le département de la Seine* (Paris, 1899), p. 426.

The increase was actually greater than the official figures show, for the census of 1872 missed the peak of the city's population during the Empire. That census came after the siege of the city in the Franco-Prussian War and after the insurrection of the Commune, when the population certainly declined. Haussmann estimated that Paris had 1,970,000 inhabitants in 1870, 120,000 more than recorded by the count of 1872.

The annexation of the suburbs in 1860 produced a misleadingly large increase in official population between 1856 and
1861, a distortion that may be corrected by substituting for the
official population statistics before 1860 the numbers actually
included within the new limits of 1860 in the earlier census
years. These figures and Haussmann's estimate for 1870 properly show the greatest upsurge of population coming in the

POPULATION WITHIN THE LIMITS OF PARIS
FIXED IN 1860, 1831-1870

Year	Population	Increase	Year	Population	Increase
1831	861,400		1851	1,277,100	50,100
1836	1,002,600	141,200	1856	1,538,600	261,500
1841	1,059,800	57,200	1861	1,696,100	157,500
1846	1,227,000	168,200	1866	1,825,300	129,200
			1870	1,970,000	*144,700

* Haussmann's estimate.

Sources: Louis Chevalier, *La Formation de la population parisienne au XIXᵉ
siècle* (Institut national d'Etudes démographiques, *Travaux et documents*, Cahier
No. 10) (Paris, 1950), p. 284; G. E. Haussmann, *Mémoires* (Paris, 1890-93), II, 448.

boom years immediately following Louis Napoleon's *Coup
d'Etat* and a sustained high rate of growth during the succeeding decade and a half of the Empire.

The principal source of the growing population was immigration from provincial departments to Paris. The excess
of births over deaths in the official limits of the city was only
119,000 between 1851 and 1870, and had the city depended
on this natural increase alone for its growth the population
would scarcely have exceeded 1,170,000 by the end of the
Empire. The annexation of the suburbs added between 350,000
and 400,000. Immigrants made up the remaining 400,000 to
450,000. Natural increase would have been even smaller but
for the effect of immigration on birth and death rates. Most of
the immigrants were young, and they gave Paris a population
structure heavily weighted in the years of greatest fecundity
and disproportionately small in the years of infancy when
mortality was high. The age groups above sixty, in which

mortality was also high, were unusually small, too, owing to Parisians' practice of retiring to the provinces.[1]

The rapid growth of the capital aroused grave concern in France, and the subtleties of birth and death rates were ordinarily ignored in the popular conclusion that the city grew by draining population out of the provinces. In May, 1848, the National Constituent Assembly, ordering an investigation of labor problems throughout France, specifically asked for an inquiry into the means that might be taken to stop emigration from the fields to the cities. Three years later some deputies opposed the bond issue to finance the building of the Central Markets and the Rue de Rivoli because the operations would attract more workers to Paris, and within a period of nine months in 1851 and 1852 the Academy of Moral and Political Sciences heard two learned discussions of the shift of population from country to city. But it was the publication of the results of the census of 1856 that produced the greatest concern. Although the total population of France had increased in the preceding five years, fifty-four of the nation's eighty-six departments had lost population. Among the minority of growing departments those that gained the most were urban, and at the top of the list stood the Department of the Seine.[2]

Anxiety over the lure of Paris ranged from dismay to outright alarm. The Goncourt brothers saw the city growing about them and were dismayed at the passing of the smaller, more tranquil Paris of their youth. Proudhon was irritated by the submersion of native Parisians in a sea of outlanders. Others with vivid memories of February and June, 1848, saw in the concentration of proletarian population in Paris a certain promise of revolution.[3] The city had been overrun by poor

[1] Département de la Seine, *Résultats statistiques du dénombrement de 1896 pour la ville de Paris et le département de la Seine* (Paris, 1899), p. 426; Département de la Seine, *Annuaire statistique de la ville de Paris*, I (1880), 313; Louis Chevalier, *La Formation de la population parisienne au XIXe siècle* (Institut national d'Etudes démographiques, *Travaux et documents*, Cahier No. 10) (Paris, 1950), pp. 48-51.

[2] Paris, Chambre de Commerce, *Statistique de l'industrie à Paris . . . pour les années 1847-1848* (Paris, 1851), Part I, p. 16; *Moniteur universel*, Apr. 2, Aug. 3, 1851, Jan. 13, 1852; France, *Annuaire statistique de la France*, IV (1881), 4-7.

[3] David H. Pinkney, "Migrations to Paris during the Second Empire," *Journal of Modern History*, XXV (1953), 1.

workers from the provinces who changed it from the capital of luxury and art, one alarmist warned, to "a formidable workers' city, . . . the permanent home of insurrection and civil war."[4]

Many looked anxiously to the opposite end of the shift of population. Scores of books and articles and speeches discussed and usually deplored the depopulation of the countryside. Countless official reports from the government's agents in the provinces expressed local concern over labor shortages in agriculture and the inability of rural proprietors to pay wages sufficient to hold workers against the attraction of the cities. Drastic remedies cropped up in the discussions: suppression of freedom of movement and the restriction of passports to property owners; revival of the gild system to reduce both social and physical mobility; and destruction of the railroads and telegraph lines and even of the big cities themselves.[5]

Political opponents of the Empire and Haussmann's enemies, ever alert for difficulties that might be blamed on the government or the Prefect, attributed the rapid increase in the city's population to the attraction of Haussmann's public works. The pull of Paris became irresistible, one Parisian editor, Louis Lazare, wrote, only when rural workers were convinced that in the capital they could live better and work less. In every hamlet of France when villagers gathered to hear the schoolmaster read the newspapers they were excited by the news of the millions of francs pouring into public works in the capital. The young men saw in Paris the opportunity of higher wages and easier work than their native villages could ever offer, and they went to the capital by the thousands.[6]

Haussmann retorted that the influx of population was none of his doing, and both he and spokesmen of the national government agreed that it was a direct consequence of the building of the railroads, which converged on Paris and poured into the city a steady stream of new inhabitants. There were other causes, both Haussmann and the government admitted: the attraction of an abundance of jobs, of charitable resources for

4 Louis Lazare, *La France et Paris* (Paris, 1872), p. 14.
5 Pinkney, "Migrations," p. 1; *Siècle* (Paris), Sept. 29, 1858.
6 *Moniteur*, July 23, 1867; *Journal officiel de l'Empire français*, Feb. 23, 27, 1869; Lazare, *France et Paris*, pp. 97, 100.

care of the poor, of free schools and nurseries, but in the Prefect's words "the principal and . . . effective cause" was the building of the railroads.[7]

In making their charges Lazare and other opponents of Haussmann and the Emperor were playing not alone on the anxiety over the "dangerous" growth of the city but also on popular resentment against rising rents. Haussmann attributed this rise to the demand for housing by new residents brought to Paris by the railroads. His enemies attributed it to the public works, which forced the demolition of hundreds of houses and at the same time increased the demand for housing by attracting more people to the city. In 1861 Lazare set forth this view and attacked the Prefect so vigorously that the police suppressed his paper, the *Revue municipale*. But he continued to make the charge in his books, and there were other voices ready to take it up. One deputy or another could be counted on to repeat the accusation in every parliamentary debate on the Parisian administration in the latter 1860's.[8]

The explanations offered by both Haussmann and his enemies were over simplifications. The railroads were not without influence, but there had been large movements into the capital before they were built—in the period 1831-36, for example, when more than 100,000 new residents established themselves in the city. The openings of rail lines connecting provincial departments with Paris were not uniformly followed by notable increases (insofar as they can be measured) in the numbers of natives of those departments in the capital. In some cases the numbers from a particular department actually declined after the opening of the railroad connection.[9]

Simple generalizations on the attractive power of higher wages are equally unsatisfactory to explain the city's growth. The average nominal wage in Paris was higher than in pro-

[7] *Moniteur*, Dec. 7, 1854, Nov. 30, 1857, Apr. 8, May 10, 1858; *J.O.*, Feb. 23, 1869; *J.O.*, Supplément, May 1869, p. 8.

[8] *Revue municipale* (Paris), Oct. 20, 1861, Feb. 26, 1862; Louis Lazare, *Les Quartiers pauvres de Paris* (Paris, 1869), pp. 56, 66, *Les Quartiers pauvres de Paris: le XXe arrondissement* (Paris, 1870), pp. 6-7, 94.

[9] *Moniteur*, June 13, Aug. 30, 1850, Aug. 21, 1851, July 19, 1852, May 30, 1854, Aug. 17, 1855; France, Ministère de la Justice, *Compte générale de l'administration de la justice criminelle en France*, Années 1841-1857, passim.

vincial France, but the difference was scarcely large enough to explain the city's attraction. Differences in real wages were even less, for food prices and rents were usually higher in Paris than in the provinces, though emigrants were probably impressed by higher money wages and did not inquire into differences in purchasing power. But it was not the departments with the lowest wages that sent the most emigrants to Paris.[10]

The city's attraction was strongest in the northern departments within 100 to 150 miles of the capital, generally the most richly endowed and prosperous section of the country. Estimates based on statistics of the department of origin of persons who died in Paris in 1833 show that two-thirds of the city's population born outside the Department of the Seine came from the area north of the Loire River and east of the Cherbourg peninsula. Elsewhere the pull of the capital was equally strong only in two departments of central France, the Creuse and the Cantal. In 1851 this geographic incidence (measured by the statistics of place of origin of persons arrested in the Department of the Seine) remained essentially unchanged. The city still drew chiefly on the northern third of the country, excluding Brittany, which was little affected although it was among the poorest of French provinces. In central France the island of contributing departments, composed of only the Creuse and the Cantal in 1833, now included several neighboring departments. In 1869, the last full year of the Empire, the capital's attraction was still strongest in the north, but the island in central France had become part of a peninsula of contiguous departments extending southward from Paris to the Aveyron. By 1869, too, the isolation of Brittany was breaking down, though the great influx of Bretons, which by the end of the century had made them one of the largest and most conspicuous provincial groups in Paris, did not begin until around 1880.[11]

Illustrations of how the city's attraction actually operated

10 Chevalier, *Formation*, pp. 48, 92-99.

11 France, *Administration de la justice criminelle*, Année 1851, pp. 278-79, Année 1869, p. 270; Chevalier, *Formation*, pp. 164-66, 207-11, 285; R. Musset, "La Population et l'émigration bretonne," *Annales de géographie*, xxxiie Année (1923), pp. 185-88.

both on individuals and on departments may be found in the histories of expanding industries that furnished an increasing number of jobs in Paris during the Empire. Among them no industry flourished more than the building trades. They were important in 1847, when they employed 12 per cent of Parisian workers, but in 1866, when Haussmann's building program neared its height, they provided jobs for 20 per cent of a much larger labor force.[12]

Construction workers in the capital were traditionally a regional group coming chiefly from departments of the Central Plateau, and because activity in the industry was seasonal the typical worker came up each spring for the building season and returned home in the autumn or early winter. Men from the same district made the trip in a group and every year followed the traditional route and stopped at the same places along the way. In Paris they lived together, and they tended to settle on streets near the City Hall, for the Place de Grève, on which it faced, served as an outdoor hiring hall where contractors came to recruit workers.[13]

Among the departments contributing heavily to the building trades was the Department of the Creuse, part of that island in central France where the capital's attraction was strong. It was a poor, thinly populated department, some 250 miles from Paris and without railroad connections to the capital until the middle of the 1850's. Yet even before the Second Empire it had been a department of heavy seasonal emigration. Each year some thousands of its men went out for six to nine months to find in the construction trades of cities a better living than the meager resources of their native department offered them. They worked chiefly as stone masons, and it became almost axiomatic that to be an able-bodied Creusois was to be a mason. Martin Nadaud, who left in his memoirs the classic description of the life of the migratory construction workers of the Creuse in the 1830's and 1840's, declared that in his time it was the ambition of every boy in the department to join the trek to

[12] Chevalier, *Formation*, p. 111.
[13] *Ibid.*, p. 238; Henry Clement, "Les Emigrants du Centre de France," *Reforme Sociale*, 1st Series, x (1885), 486-87; *Moniteur*, July 19, 1852.

Paris. Nadaud himself went up to the capital for the first time in 1830, when he was only fourteen years old, and his father and grandfather had been masons in Paris before him. It was an arduous trip in those days. Nadaud and his companions walked the 170 miles from their starting point in the Creuse to Orléans and continued on to the capital in wagons.[14]

In the 1840's the number of migrants rose sharply from some 15,000 annually at the beginning of the decade to more than 30,000 before depression and the Revolution of 1848 disrupted construction business. The stream of emigrants diminished for a time, but with Louis Napoleon's resolution of the political uncertainties of 1851 and his energetic revival of public works the stream grew wider than ever before. Forty thousand left the department for the building season of 1852, and none returned for lack of work. In the immediately succeeding years the annual exodus remained around that figure, but rose nearer 50,000 in the 1860's. In 1859 the Prefect of the Creuse estimated that one-half of the physically fit men of the department migrated, and in the final year of the Empire, the Procurer-general (the representative of the Ministry of Justice in the area) reported that in some districts of the Creuse fully two-thirds of the men left for the building season.[15]

No accurate measure has survived of the number of emigrating Creusois who came to Paris, but it was certainly a substantial majority of them. The Prefect and the Procurer-general invariably placed Paris and the Department of the Seine at the top of their lists of places attracting workers away from the department, and in 1868 a local newspaper in the Creuse mentioned, with some exaggeration, 40,000 Creusois going up to Paris each year. The number of natives of the Creuse arrested in the Department of the Seine rose from 259 in 1851 to 593 in the last full year of the Empire; no other department of similar size and distance from Paris contributed so many.[16]

14 Martin Nadaud, *Les Mémoires de Léonard, ançien garçon maçon* (Paris, 1912), pp. 31, 47-57, 80-81, 159.

15 A. Legoyt, *Du progrès des agglomérations urbaines et de l'émigration rurale* (Marseille, 1867), p. 67; *Conciliateur: journal des intérêts de la Creuse* (Guéret), Dec. 17, 1851; Archives nationales (Paris), BB30 378 Limoges, 1852-68, BB30 390 Limoges, 1870, Flc III Creuse 8, 1853-59.

16 Arch. nat., Flc III Creuse 8, 1853-59, BB30 378 Limoges, 1852-66, BB30 390

For growing numbers the seasonal migration became a change of residence. In 1856 some 8,000, about one in each five migrants, did not return to the Creuse at the close of the building season, and some remained for three or four years in succession. In the winter of 1862-63, when mild weather permitted uninterrupted work, most of the Creusois stayed on through the winter months both in Paris and in the other large cities. The practice of remaining in Paris for two or even more building seasons was not unknown earlier, but it apparently became much more common during the Second Empire, and the prolonged stays were frequently extended into permanent residence. In 1857 an anxious sub-prefect, deploring the seasonal migration out of his district, reported that it was no longer a purely masculine movement but that women and children were accompanying the men on the treks to the cities. A few years later the Procurer-general observed that the migrants had cut their sojourn at home shorter, and that the number who left in 1864 with no intention of returning at the end of the season was larger than ever before. Some construction workers had already moved their families to Paris or Lyon to live the year around. They clung to the hope of eventually returning and settling on land purchased with their savings, but they had in fact become residents of the cities.[17]

The declining population of the Creuse during the Second Empire affirmed this change in the migrations from the department. Throughout the first half of the nineteenth century the population had increased without interruption to 287,000 in 1851, but between 1851 and 1861 the department lost 6 per cent of its population. It recovered some in the sixties, but at the time of the census of 1872, although births had exceeded deaths in the two preceding decades, the department had 13,000 fewer residents than in 1851.[18]

The Creuse had few means to retain its sons at home. It

Limoges, 1870; France, *Administration de la justice criminelle*, Année 1851, p. 278, Année 1869, p. 270.

[17] Arch. nat., Fle III Creuse 8, 1857. 1858, BB30 378 Limoges, 1864, 1865; Nadaud, *Mémoires*, pp. 77, 82-83, 88, 119, 127, 156; Chambre de Commerce, *Statistique . . . 1847-1848*, Part I, p. 94.

[18] Pinkney, "Migrations," p. 5.

lacked significant natural resources, had few industries, and agriculture, the principal occupation, was handicapped by unfavorable climate and a rocky soil suitable for little but cattle raising. The wages paid in the department reflected its economic weakness. In 1859, a prosperous year, the prefect reported that the average daily wage for men in agriculture was 1.53 francs and in industry, where there were few jobs, 2.40 francs. In Paris the usual wages of construction workers ran between 3 and 5 francs a day in 1860, and the daily wage of a mason might go as high as 12 francs. Food prices were not significantly lower in the Creuse, and no subsidy helped stabilize the price of bread as in the capital. A peasant proprietor working the year around in the Creuse could scarcely support a family on the fruits of his work on the soil. A construction worker in seven or eight months in the city could earn enough to maintain himself and his family the year around.[19]

To the Creusois the thought of going to the city was neither strange nor frightening as it might have been to residents of other departments where emigration was not part of the local tradition. With the completion in the middle fifties of the railroad connection between Paris and La Souterrain in the northwest corner of the department the journey became relatively easy. Nadaud's first trip in 1830 took five days. By rail it could be done in twelve or thirteen hours, and the fare was only 21 francs. Nadaud referred to the opening of the railroad as the beginning of the "golden age" for the masons of the Creuse.[20]

The migratory workers themselves spread the word of opportunities in Paris. No Parisian paper was widely read, and the local press carried no appeals for workers and few items of news on public works and private building. Isolated cases of recruiting by contractors may have occurred in the department, but

---

19 Paris, Chambre de Commerce, *Statistique de l'industrie à Paris . . . pour l'année 1860* (Paris, 1864), pp. xxxvi, 107, 136; France, *Statistique de la France* (Paris and Strasbourg, 1835-73) 2d Series, xi, 88, 108-09, 120-21, 178; Arch. nat., Flc iii Creuse 8, 1853-59, BB30 378 Limoges, 1852-67; *Conciliateur*, Dec. 17, 1851; *Echo de la Creuse* (Guéret), July 20, 1870.

20 Nadaud, *Mémoires*, pp. 13, 55-57; N. Chaix, *L'Indicateur des chemins de fer*, No. 613 (May 5-12, 1861), p. 9; N. Chaix, *Recueil général des tarifs des chemins de fer*, No. 16 (Feb. 1860), p. 102.

had it been a common practice the officials concerned over de-population would surely have been exercised by it, and they did not, in fact, even mention it in their reports on the problem. Workers enjoying good pay and steady employment in Paris wrote to friends and relatives urging them to come to the city and even promising them work, but illiteracy must have limited these appeals narrowly. Most influential surely was the personal testimony of the migrant workers who came home from Paris with their pockets full of francs and their memories full of recollections of a flourishing and brilliant city.[21]

The migrant worker on his return to the Creuse was the center of interest in his community. Whenever he appeared in the village streets during the first two weeks after his arrival he found himself surrounded by his neighbors anxious to learn how much he had earned and to hear about what he had seen in Paris. In the evenings when friends gathered at home or in a village café, it was the workers from Paris among them who did the talking. But even more eloquent than their embellished descriptions of the city were the francs that the workers brought back with them. If a mason had a successful season, the village soon knew of it, and his earnings were common knowledge for all to marvel at and for the boys and young men to aspire to equal by taking the road to Paris. Even if they were not personally inspired to go, social pressure probably gave them an added push. An observer in the department a few decades later, when the seasonal migrations were still important, noted that the girls and young women shunned the stay-at-homes and lavished their attentions on the men back from Paris and the other cities.[22]

Departments that had no long tradition of migrations to Paris were also affected by the lure of the capital's public works. The Department of the Haute-Saône in eastern France near the Swiss frontier lost a tenth of its inhabitants between 1851 and 1856, and the anxious Prefect reported to the Minister of the Interior in the latter year, "What depopulates our fields,

21 Pinkney, "Migrations," p. 6; Chevalier, *Formation*, p. 217.
22 Nadaud, *Mémoires*, pp. 44, 80, 84-85, 168-70; Clement, "Emigrants du Centre," 2d Series, 1 (1886), 285.

much more than epidemics, much more than war and emigration abroad, is internal migrations to the big cities, the factories, and the railroad construction camps."[23] This unhappy department was the victim of technological change—the railroads and overseas competitors had disrupted its established agricultural markets in Switzerland and in the south of France, and its iron industry, based on small, high cost charcoal furnaces, could not compete with new coke-burning furnaces. The consequences for the department were low wages and declining employment. A carpenter or a mason might double his hourly wage by going to Paris, and the pay of unskilled construction workers and the promise of more steady employment on the seemingly endless works in Paris must have looked attractive to the agricultural laborer facing the low wages and dismal prospects of the Haute-Saône.[24]

Even in a prosperous department with full employment and high wages the pull of Paris was strong. In 1853, when the public works were just getting well underway, a sub-prefect in the Department of the Seine-et-Marne wrote a long report on the shortage of farm laborers in which he declared:

> The extraordinary stimulus given to buildings by the creation of immense projects in the center of Paris has depopulated the countryside. A few years ago the laborers employed by the state, the masons, the carpenters stopped their work in order to help with the harvest; this year not only have they not suspended their work but they have drawn after them the unskilled workers who find more lucrative employment as laborers on the construction projects.[25]

In 1857 the sub-prefect reported the same complaint from the farmers of this district, and the following year when the Legislative Body debated a subsidy for the Second Network of streets in Paris a deputy from the Seine-et-Marne protested that farmers in his department had to hire Belgians as agricultural

23 Arch. nat., F1c III Haute-Saône 9, July 16, 1856.
24 Arch. nat., BB30 373 Besançon, 1852-68, BB30 389 Besançon, 1868-69, BB30 390 Besançon, 1870, F1c III Haute-Saône 9, 1857, 1859; France, *Statistique de la France*, 2d Series, XI, 121, 192; Chambre de Commerce, *Statistique . . . 1860*, p. 458.
25 Arch. nat., F1c III Seine-et-Marne 7, Oct. 17, 1853.

laborers because Paris drew off all of the native workers. Yet the Seine-et-Marne enjoyed uninterrupted prosperity throughout the decades of the Second Empire. It had a rich soil and was almost exclusively agricultural, and Paris, about twenty-five miles away, provided a large and accessible market. On only three occasions did the Prefect or the Procurer-general mention any unemployment in the department, and then the troubles were localized and quickly passed. Farm laborers could earn wages that were high for agriculture (and they rose substantially during the Empire), but they fell short of the pay offered even to day laborers in Paris, and when construction was booming employment there was steady. One sub-prefect, mindful of the attraction of stable employment, called for public works in the Seine-et-Marne to prevent the departure of farm laborers during the off-season in agriculture.[26]

The metal trades, another of the expanding industries in Paris during the Second Empire, drew from all parts of the country but particularly from nearby departments and especially from urban communities. Many of the metal industries required workers with particular skills or at least with some special experience that farm workers did not ordinarily possess. Nor were the skills required the old craft skills like stone-cutting or carpentry that had become traditional in particular departments. Many of the men who eventually became metal workers in Paris got their first training and experience in the railroad repair shops that sprang up in French towns and cities as the railroad network was built in the 1840's and 1850's. Others had been blacksmiths and some, woodworkers. Typically they were men engaged in skilled occupations connected with urban centers, and the attraction of the Parisian industry was strongest in the more populous and urbanized departments close to the capital.[27]

The diverse commercial activities of Paris defy generalization, but certain of them offer illuminating examples of the manner in which a particular trade recruited new residents

[26] Arch. nat., BB[30] 383 Paris, 1852-60, BB[30] 384 Paris, 1860-68, BB[30] 389 Paris, 1868-69, BB[30] 390 Paris, 1869, F[1c] III Seine-et-Marne 6 and 7, 1852-59; *Moniteur*, May 10, 1858.
[27] Chevalier, *Formation*, pp. 232-33.

for the city. Wine retailers were a fixture of the Parisian scene then as now, the large and steadily employed population providing an abundance of customers. In the nineteenth century *bistro* proprietors came from all parts of France but chiefly from the wine producing departments of Burgundy and from the Creuse and the Cantal in the Central Plateau. The typical proprietor was of peasant origin and had worked on the family farm until about his twentieth year, when he came up to Paris and took a job with relatives or family friends from the same department who kept a hotel or *bistro*. After five to ten years as a waiter or domestic servant the newcomer would set up business for himself, borrowing most of the necessary capital from family or friends back home or perhaps from a wine producer in his native village who might supply him with wine for several years.[28]

The proprietors of the many small dry goods shops in the capital came chiefly from Paris itself and from the departments to the north and east of the city. Ordinarily those from outside Paris had worked in stores in the provinces before coming to the capital and some had been proprietors of shops in smaller cities. Others were former peddlers who had come regularly to Paris to replenish their stocks and on those visits learned of the opportunities in the city. In five or ten years a successful peddler could save enough to establish his own shop in Paris, and during the Second Empire Parisian wholesale houses often selected the best of the salesmen among their peddler customers and advanced them the capital to finance a store in the city.[29]

These views of particular occupations in Paris and of certain provincial departments suggest something of the complexity of the forces that brought provincial Frenchmen to the capital. The cases of the Creuse and the Seine-et-Marne and the metal industries show that the public works certainly played a part, despite the official denials. The railroads made movement out of the Creuse easier, they contributed to the economic dislocation that forced men out of the Haute-Saône, and they gave men training and experience that prepared them for jobs in the city. But local custom, family connections, possession of

28 *Ibid.*, pp. 227-29.   29 *Ibid.*, pp. 230-32.

certain skills, business contacts were important, too, and this
list leaves untouched many less measurable factors that certainly were influential—the centralization of the nation's administrative system in Paris, the location there of the great
higher schools of the national educational system, and the
concentration in Paris of virtually all the country's intellectual
and artistic life, creating the contrast, that continues today between "the unceasing fireworks" of the capital and "the mortal
boredom" of the provinces.

Increase in numbers was not the only significant change in
the population of Paris during the Second Empire. Its distribution within the city also changed. In 1850 the population was
heavily concentrated in the central core of the city—especially
within the inner ring of boulevards on the Right Bank and in
a similarly confined area on the opposite bank. In the next
two decades demolitions drove residents out of the central
quarters, and many of them were kept out by the high rents in
the buildings that arose along the newly opened streets. Between 1851 and 1856 the demolitions for the Central Markets
and for the Rue de Rivoli forced thousands from the crowded
quarters just north of the river. The population of the Arcis
quarter at the eastern end of the Rue de Rivoli fell from nearly
12,000 in 1851 to fewer than 4,000 in 1856, the Saint-Honoré
quarter at the opposite end from 11,600 to 8,000, and the population of the Markets quarter was cut almost exactly in half in
the same period. In the succeeding five years the changes cannot
be accurately measured because of the alteration of the administrative areas in which population was recorded, but in the
sixties the numbers in the old central quarters and in the immediately surrounding ring of arrondissements continued to
decline. Between 1861 and 1872 the ten central arrondissements
lost 33,000 inhabitants while the ten eccentric arrondissements
added more than 200,000.[30]

In the fifties much of the displaced population of the center
and many newcomers settled in the zone between the city's

---

[30] Seine, *Résultats du dénombrement, 1896*, pp. xvii, 438-41; *Siècle*, Apr. 21,
May 18, 1853; *Moniteur*, May 20, 1861; *J.O.*, Mar. 5, 6, 1869; *Revue générale de
l'architecture et des travaux publics* (Paris), XIII (1855), 134.

official limits at the *octroi* wall and the fortifications, particularly in the communes of Les Batignolles, Montmartre, La Chapelle, La Villette, and Belleville on the Right Bank, and in Ivry, Montrouge, and Vaugirard on the Left Bank. Between 1851 and 1856 the population in this zone rose by nearly two-thirds, more than five times the rate of increase in the city itself.[31]

This section had long been familiar to Parisian workers, who frequented it on holidays to take advantage of the lower prices in the cafés and restaurants, which had to pay no city entry tax on their wines and provisions, but workers had regarded taking a job there or moving there as a step down the social scale. Work was generally harder, wages lower, employment more uncertain. Martin Nadaud, for example, went beyond the barrier to find a job in 1840 only as a last resort when he could find no work in the city. By the fifties this attitude was changing. The railroad companies had established their repair shops, yards, freight stations, and fuel depots in the zone, providing employment for hundreds. New factories and commercial houses offered additional jobs, and the overflow of population from Paris brought in many residents who commuted to work in the city. Following the city's annexation of these suburbs Haussmann poured some hundreds of millions of francs into improving their streets, sewers, and water supply, and in providing them with schools and churches, but improvements did not catch up with the growing population. Critics complained of crowded shanty towns, masses of hovels fashioned of planks and tar paper, growing up on the extremities of the city in the sixties.[32]

In the same decade many of the communes beyond the fortifications grew more rapidly than the city itself. The metropolitan area of Paris, defined as the city and its suburbs in which the population had reached an urban density, included seven communes beyond the fortifications in 1851; by 1872 it

---

[31] Chevalier, *Formation*, p. 284.

[32] Chevalier, *Formation*, pp. 242-43, 247; Département de la Seine, *Aperçu historique* (Paris, 1913), pp. 101-02, 125-26, 164; *Moniteur*, Aug. 22, 1854, Mar. 20, 1861; *Siècle*, Apr. 11, July 9, 1856; *J.O.*, Mar. 5, 6, 1869.

had spread over twenty-six communes in the Department of the Seine and three in the Department of the Seine-et-Oise.[33]

One who seeks neat schemes of cause and effect in urban growth will be disappointed that there are few clear-cut connections between the spread of Parisian population during the Empire and improvements in public transportation. No revolutionary developments in urban or suburban transport services occurred during the period. The *Compagnie générale des Omnibus*, formed in 1854 by the merger of the ten existing bus companies in the capital, introduced larger buses equipped with seats on the roof at half the usual fare of 30 centimes. (Women were not permitted on the top level, and men were warned to exercise great caution in descending the steep stairway. One must always start with the left foot, and the consequence of a mistake, Baedeker warned, might be a fatal fall.) Within a decade of its founding the company doubled the number of buses in service, and its franchise required it to operate lines to all parts of the city even though some might be unprofitable. But the improved services effected no revolution in Parisians' riding habits. The average number of rides per inhabitant (thirty-nine in 1856) was still fewer than sixty-five in 1869. Service did not begin in the morning until 8 o'clock, a genteel hour that indicates how little the buses were intended for the mass of working Parisians.[34]

In 1854 an engineer named Loubat obtained permission from the city to build a tramway across Paris from Sèvres on the west to Vincennes on the east. He completed the line from Boulogne, on the Seine opposite Sèvres, to the Place de la Concorde, and because he had picked up the idea of the tramway in the United States it immediately acquired the popular name of the "Chemin de fer Américain" or simply "L'Américain." Even guidebooks of the time identified it by that name. Unfortunately for Loubat the city authorities withdrew per-

[33] Chevalier, *Formation*, pp. 249-62, 284; Louis Bonnier, "La Population de Paris en mouvement, 1800-1961," *Vie urbaine* (Paris), 1e Année (1919), pp. 7-76.

[34] Seine, *Annuaire statistique*, I, 521-24, 528; Alfred Martin, *Etudes historiques et statistiques sur les moyens de transport dans Paris* (Paris, 1894), p. 95; Galignani, *New Paris Guide for 1856* (Paris, [1856]), pp. 6-7; Karl Baedeker, *Paris et la France du Nord* (Coblenz, 1867), pp. 26-28.

mission to extend his rails further into the city, fearing that they might cause accidents on the busy streets of the central quarters. The terminus remained at the Place de la Concorde until 1866, when the *Compagnie générale des Omnibus*, which had taken over the line, decided to continue it to the Place du Palais Royal. It introduced cars equipped with two smooth wheels and two flanged wheels. The flanged wheels could be easily removed, and on each eastbound run the car stopped on the Cours la Reine, where it was jacked up and the flanged wheels replaced with smooth wheels. The car then proceeded on its way to the Place du Palais Royal as a bus. On the return trip the process was reversed, and the bus again became a tram car for the trip on to Boulogne! Except for a special line built for the Exposition of 1867 Loubat's tramway had no imitators during the Empire.[35]

"Omnibus boats" were another innovation of the Empire. Introduced by a private company in 1867 the boats provided regular passenger service on the Seine within the city's limits. This was not the first passenger boat service on the river, but it was the first to operate on regular schedule throughout the week. They ran for only three years during the Empire, however, and in that time effected no notable change in Parisians' habits.[36]

The first railroad out of Paris, to Saint-Germain-en-Laye, had been opened in 1837, and a number of other suburban lines were completed during the forties. They offered transportation that was cheap and dependable, and the trains were much faster than the carriages that formerly served the environs. Along the rail lines grew the first dormitory suburbs of Paris. On the west side Neuilly, Boulogne, Saint-Cloud, and other communes bordering the Seine became fashionable places of middle class residence in the 1850's. The more distant Versailles, apparently doomed to slow decay after the removal of the government to Paris in 1789, began to revive as a suburb of the capital. The opening of the railroads serving the com-

[35] Martin, *Etudes sur les transports*, pp. 90-91, 148-49; Seine, *Annuaire statistique*, I, 523-24; *Builder* (London), xviii (1860), 230, xxiv (1866), 139; Emile Fleury, *Souvenirs* (Paris, 1897), I, 342-43.
[36] Martin, *Etudes sur les transports*, p. 117.

munes around the Bois de Vincennes in 1859 started a similar though more limited development on the east side.[37] A Parisian architect writing in the 1860's observed that the traditional division of domestic architecture into two categories—"city" and "country"—was no longer admissible, for between the two was the new branch of "suburban" architecture, a bi-product of the railroads and the prosperity of the middle class.[38] Statistics of the purely suburban traffic on the railroads are lacking for the years of the Empire, but the increase in the population of some of the suburban communes served by the railroads suggests the quantitative importance of the move to the suburbs. Boulogne-sur-Seine had 7,600 inhabitants in 1851, 19,000 in 1872; Saint-Cloud, 3,800 in 1851, 9,000 in 1872; and in Versailles the population rose from 35,000 to 61,000 in the same period.[39]

In 1860 the Emperor and parliament incorporated a ring of suburbs into the city. By the Law of June 16, 1859, the official bounds were moved outward from the *octroi* wall on the present second ring of boulevards to the line of the encircling fortifications. The *octroi* wall dated from the last years of the *ancien régime* when Louis XVI permitted tax farmers to throw a barrier around the city to facilitate the collection of the entry tax on food, wine and spirits, and certain other commodities. The city had no fortified wall then and had been without one since Louis XIV, who intended to fight his wars on enemy territory, had ordered the demolition of the capital's fortifications. His successors in the nineteenth century, chastened by the experience of foreign invasion and the fall of the capital itself in 1814, were less confident and less audacious, and as confidence and audacity declined, interest in fortifications rose. It was that most cautious of French regimes, the July Monarchy, that re-built the fortifications of Paris. Government and

[37] *Moniteur*, Sept. 29, 1859; *Siècle*, July 9, 1864; *Builder*, XIX (1861), 695, 729, XXII (1864), 199-200; Myriem Foncin, "Versailles: étude de géographie historique," *Annales de géographie*, XXVIIIe Année (1919), 338.

[38] César Daly, *L'Architecture privée au XIXe siècle* (Paris, 1870), I, 10.

[39] Seine, *Résultats du dénombrement, 1896*, pp. 446-47; *Bulletin des lois de la République française*, 10th Series, Vol. 9, No. 533, Decree of May 10, 1852, p. 1387; 12th Series, Vol. 5, No. 114, Decree of Dec. 31, 1872, p. 642.

parliament debated the matter in the 1830's, and in 1840 the war scare over the Near Eastern Question, when France again stood alone against the old anti-Napoleonic coalition, provoked them into action. In September, 1840, two royal ordinances made the first appropriations and authorized the acquisition of the necessary land, and the following spring a third ordinance prescribed the construction of fifteen outlying forts and a continuous fortified wall around the city.[40]

A logical accompaniment of this decision would have been the shift of the capital's administrative limits to the new wall. But private interests in the suburbs opposed it, and rather than complicate a matter of national defense with debate over local issues parliament postponed action on annexation. Opponents of extension of the existing limits were reassured by Article 9 of the ordinance providing that the limits would be altered only by law, but parliament rejected without debate an amendment to forbid any change during the next twenty years, presumably in the expectation that the inevitable annexation must come long before 1861. But in the forties and early fifties no urgency seemed attached to the matter, and apprehension of strong opposition to any extension of the *octroi* deterred action. In 1852 shortly before the plebescite on the reestablishment of the Empire enemies of Louis Napoleon spread the rumor that Napoleon and the Prefect of the Seine would shortly move the *octroi* limits to the fortifications. A political maneuver to deprive Napoleon of votes in the suburbs where the change would increase taxes, it obviously worried the government, for on November 19, two days preceding the plebiscite, the *Moniteur* carried a categorical denial of the rumor.[41]

Political expedience might suggest continued postponement, but the growth of population in the suburban zone made the existing partition of the city increasingly unsatisfactory. Between 1851 and 1856 the suburban area acquired 140,000 new inhabitants. Les Batignolles with 44,000, Montmartre with 36,000—had become larger than most provincial capitals. Paris

[40] *Moniteur*, Sept. 17, 1840, Apr. 6, 1841; Galignani, *New Paris Guide* (Paris, 1845), p. 47.
[41] *Moniteur*, Nov. 19, 1852, Feb. 12, Apr. 4, 1859.

was being surrounded by a belt of eighteen independent cities, each with its own administration devoted to local interests. Each built its streets to facilitate connections with the nearest gate to Paris and gave little thought to communications with adjoining communes. At the boundaries of communes one found wide, paved streets broken off opposite unpaved lanes and blind alleys, well laid out quarters side by side with slums. Inadequate sanitary services (the suburbs had eight miles of sewers for 160 miles of streets) made the area a potential menace to public health in Paris, and insufficient police vitiated the effectiveness of the expensive police forces in the capital. (Paris had one policeman for every 300 inhabitants, the suburban zone one for every 5,100.)[42]

A committee of the Municipal Council of Paris and of the Departmental Commission of the Seine began study of the annexation in 1853, but not until 1859 did the government act. In February of that year the *Moniteur* printed the text of the proposed law of annexation, and the Emperor ordered that registers to receive protests and observations of individual citizens be opened for two weeks in all the arrondissements of Paris and in all the suburban communes affected by the law. At the close of that period the municipal councils in the interested communes, the councils of the two suburban arrondissements of the department, and the Departmental Commission were to meet and give their advice on the proposed law. Specially appointed committees would be heard on opinion in the fragments of communes that were to be annexed.[43]

These elaborate efforts to sound public opinion reflected the government's continuing anxiety that the annexation would be unpopular, but the inquiries revealed little hostility. From among the 1,600,000 persons affected some 2,100 asked for modifications in details but accepted the essentials of the law. Only 1,850 actually opposed the annexation, and nearly 1,500 of them were from La Villette, where businessmen and the municipal council, charging that the law would ruin industry

[42] Chevalier, *Formation*, p. 284; Seine, *Résultats du dénombrement, 1896*, pp. 446-47; *Moniteur*, Dec. 11, 1858, Feb. 12, Mar. 12, May 12, 1859.
[43] *Moniteur*, Feb. 12, 1858.

and commerce in the commune, joined in a vigorous protest. In all the remainder of the department, including Paris itself, fewer than 400 individuals were sufficiently concerned to object. Most of the protests came from industrial and commercial interests that feared the effect of added taxes on their operating costs, and to ease the transition to the new tax situation the government proposed a gradual imposition of the city's levies. Among the twenty-five municipal councils involved only two objected to annexation. Two others asked for delays, and the council of Bercy, the seat of the great wholesale wine markets, asked for special tax treatment for its commerce.[44]

When the Legislative Body debated the project in two sessions at the end of May, 1859, the opposition came largely from the chronic opponents of Haussmann and the imperial regime. Two deputies used the occasion to air their objections to the public works program and to municipal budgetary practices. Another asked that the new limits be extended to include all of Neuilly and the Bois de Boulogne, but the government declined, not wishing to deviate from the superior *octroi* wall provided by the fortifications. (The wall was too high to scale, too deep to tunnel under. Smugglers had been known to dig passages under the old *octroi* wall.) No amendments reached the house floor, and on the final ballot on the project only thirteen deputies cast opposing votes. The Senate approved the law a week later, and on June 16, 1859, the Emperor signed it. By its terms the city's boundaries and the *octroi* would be moved to the ring of fortifications on January 1, 1860, the old arrondissement and communal boundaries would be suppressed, and the enlarged city divided into twenty new arrondissements.[45]

At midnight on December 31, crowds gathered at the city gates to watch the departure of the *octroi* guards. Just before the hour some spectators went outside the old barriers and bought taxable goods for the pleasure of bringing them in tax free a few minutes later. The shift to the new order went off smoothly. The guards established themselves at the new

44 *Moniteur*, Mar. 12, Apr. 2, 3, 4, May 4, 1859; Arch. nat., C 1063, Corps législatif, Session 1859, Dossier No. 117.
45 *Moniteur*, May 27, 28, June 7, Nov. 3, 1859.

limits of the city, and within a few weeks workmen began demolition of the old wall. The two roadways adjoining the wall, one on the interior and the other on the exterior, were merged, straightened, and planted with trees to form the second ring of boulevards.[46]

Despite their earnest efforts to inform everyone affected by the measure and to hear all objections, the government and Haussmann had neglected one interested group. No one had told the city's horses of the change. They continued to stop unbidden for the *octroi* inspection at the old gates, and their drivers had to make them move on.[47]

[46] *Moniteur*, Jan. 3, Feb. 5, 1860; Oct. 31, 1864; Arch. nat., C 1070, Corps législatif, Session 1860, Dossier No. 200.
[47] *Echo agricole* (Paris), Jan. 4. 1860.

DURING THE WINTER OF 1867-68 readers of the Parisian newspaper *Le Temps* were entertained by a series of articles on the municipal finances of Paris by one of the paper's sharp-tongued contributors, the republican deputy, Jules Ferry. The substance of the articles was not original nor were they the most revealing of the many publications on the subject that appeared during the sixties, but they were cutting and witty, and in 1868 Ferry republished them as a booklet with an arresting title, *The Fantastic Accounts of Haussmann (Comptes fantastiques d'Haussmann)*, a pun on *Contes fantastiques d'Hoffmann*, a play presented at the Odéon in 1851 and later set to Offenbach's music.[1] When more analytical studies were forgotten, Ferry's work was remembered. The title found its way into popular histories, and Haussmann's financing of the rebuilding of Paris is still commonly seen darkly through the glass of Ferry's political pamphlet.

In fact, there was nothing fantastic about Haussmann's financing unless it were the size of his expenditures. In 1869 he added up the costs of rebuilding the city since 1851 and reported a sum of 2,500,000,000 francs. The equivalent in dollars, $500,000,000, appears modest enough in this age of astronomical budgets, but relative to the Parisian municipal budget in the middle of the nineteenth century, when the city's total expenditures were about 55,000,000 francs annually it was an immense sum.[2]

Haussmann's total of 2,500,000,000 francs was not an amount that he or the Emperor foresaw in advance and set out to find. Expenditures added up as the transformation of the city pro-

---

[1] *Temps* (Paris), Dec. 20, 24, 31, 1867, Jan. 10, Mar. 17, Apr. 11, May 5, 11, 1868; Jules Ferry, *Les Comptes fantastiques d'Haussmann* (Paris, 1868).
[2] *Journal officiel de l'Empire français*, Nov. 28, 1869.

gressed, and they surpassed preliminary estimates as plans were changed and as building costs and property values mounted. The methods of raising the necessary funds varied, too, with the situation of the money market, the climate of national politics, and the moods of the Legislative Body and the council of ministers.

In the first years the problem of raising the money was part of the larger national problem of financing public works to stimulate industrial recovery. A depression starting in 1847 had halted railroad building in France, and since 1842, the year of the first national railway law, railroad construction had been the mainstay of heavy industry. Iron production fell off by a third, coal production by a fifth; other industries suffered; and in 1848 revolution added to the dislocation. The following year, filled with political uncertainties, brought no significant recovery, and in 1850 heavy industry was still in the doldrums, and unemployment remained dangerously high. In Paris the building industry had been near a standstill since 1847, and construction workers looked vainly for jobs. To many Parisians this was particularly ominous, for popular report was that the fighters on the barricades of 1848 were chiefly unemployed construction workers.[3]

Around Louis Napoleon was a group of bankers, journalists, and engineers who had been influenced in the twenties and thirties by the ideas on public works of the Count de Saint-Simon and his followers and following these ideas they now proposed to end the depression by priming the pump with heavy expenditures on railroads and other public improvements. But the state lacked budgetary resources to spend on a sufficient scale, and the National Assembly was not disposed to borrow for that purpose. No banks in France had adequate funds except a handful of private banking houses, the so-called *Haute-Banque*, of which the Rothschild bank was the largest and most influential, and because of the obvious instability of

[3] Louis Girard, *La Politique des travaux publics du Second Empire* (Paris, 1951), pp. 6-79; *Moniteur universel*, Oct. 5, 7, 28, 1849, Aug. 5, 1851.

the Second Republic and the threat of political upheaval ahead they now shunned long-term investment.[4]

In 1851, although the coal and iron and construction industries were still in depression, signs of recovery appeared on the financial market. Capital was available again for safe investments, and trading in government bonds and in "blue chips" on the stock exchange showed the first signs of vitality in years. Louis Napoleon took advantage of the improved climate to force the Prefect of the Seine, Berger, to begin the public works that stood first among his plans for Paris—the construction of the Central Markets and the continuation of the Rue de Rivoli from the Louvre to the City Hall. Prodded into action by the President of the Republic, Berger first asked the National Assembly for a subsidy to assist in the financing, but the Assembly refused, and he then sought authority to float a 50,000,000 franc bond issue. The Assembly granted the authority and subsidized private builders by approving a twenty-year tax exemption on buildings erected along the new section of the Rue de Rivoli. The authorizing law gave reassurance to timid investors by earmarking the revenue from a municipal surtax on beverages for the retirement of the loan by the end of 1870, and to tempt capital out of hiding it permitted a generous interest rate of 6 per cent. Berger still thought he could not place so large a loan in the uncertain times, and he postponed the offering until the following year. The Bank of France, however, had confidence in the municipal finances and gave the city an advance of 20,000,000 francs against the proceeds of the loan.[5]

Berger was perhaps correct in his judgment of the prospects for the entire loan on the open market. In the summer and fall of 1851 many private investors still held back from long-term commitments, and their reluctance was inspired by the continuing political uncertainties and particularly by the fear of the crisis year of 1852. Louis Napoleon had been elected presi-

[4] Girard, *Politique*, pp. 37-46; Pierre Dupont-Ferrier, *Le Marché financier de Paris sous le Second Empire* (Paris, 1925), pp. 18-19, 69-70.

[5] Girard, *Politique*, pp. 80-81; Archives nationales (Paris), C 993, Assemblée nationale, Session 1851, Dossier No. 702; Charles Merruau, *Souvenirs de l'Hôtel de Ville de Paris, 1848-1852* (Paris, 1875), p. 485.

dent of the Republic in 1848 for a four-year term. The National
Assembly had been elected in 1849 for a three-year term.
Elections for both president and assembly would recur in 1852,
and the radical republicans and the socialists made it clear that
they intended to stage a comeback in that dual election year.
Moderate men had nightmares of a return to the radical social
experimentation of February and March 1848, when the republicans guaranteed every man a job, fixed maximum hours
of work, organized a labor parliament, and talked of abolishing
private ownership of capital. Louis Napoleon, who might be
able to divert the masses from these dangerous ways, was not
eligible for re-election. To men of property the prospect of
1852 was alarming.

But as 1851 wore on the country heard more and more reports that the ugly prospect would not be permitted to become
a reality, and early in December Louis Napoleon dissipated the
threat. He seized personal control of the government, dissolved
the assembly, and promulgated a new constitution that made
himself president for a ten-year term. The army rallied to his
support. The desultory opposition was broken in a few days,
and on December 21 a plebiscite brought him an overwhelming
popular endorsement.

In the business community Napoleon's action was like the
lifting of a flood gate. Investors suddenly regained confidence
in the future. Capital poured into the money market. The
dreaded year of crisis, 1852, became one of the greatest boom
years in French history. The Prince-President authorized new
railroad concessions by personal decree, and the most conservative bankers of Paris hurried forward to furnish the necessary
capital. Heavy industry again had orders, and employment
mounted. On the stock exchange investors and speculators produced a vigorous bull market. The combined value of the
shares of sixteen principal railroad companies rose more than
50 per cent in the six months after the *Coup d'Etat*. In April,
1852, Berger offered the municipal bonds that he had feared to
put on the market the preceding summer, and a single banking
house took the entire offering above par. The city realized

61,000,000 francs at a real interest rate of less than 5 per cent.[6]

Paris shared in the boom as Napoleon stepped up public building by decree. On December 10, 1851, he approved the construction of the Belt Railway around the city. Three days later he opened a credit of 2,100,000 francs to assist the city in clearing the area between the Louvre and the Tuileries, and on March 12, 1852, he ordered the completion and enlargement of the Louvre and allocated 26,000,000 francs to the project. In the same month came a decree authorizing the city to build the Boulevard de Strasbourg (with financial assistance from the state), and in quick succession followed authorizations for a part of the Rue des Ecoles, the Rue de Rennes, and additional sections of the Rue de Rivoli. In July the state transferred the Bois de Boulogne to the city on condition that the municipal government spend 2,000,000 francs in transforming it into a public park. Private building revived, too; the quantity of taxable building stone entering Paris in 1852 was nearly three times larger than in the preceding year. A pleased contemporary noted the contrast between 1848 and 1852:

No longer did bands of insurgents roam the streets but teams of masons, carpenters, and other artisans going to work; if paving stones were pulled up it was not to build barricades but to open the way for water and gas pipes; houses were no longer threatened by cannon or fire but by the rich indemnity of expropriation....[7]

The country was prosperous in 1852, and Louis Napoleon might take credit for ending the depression that two preceding regimes could not touch. But how long would the boom last? The private banking houses expected it to give way shortly to a period of deflation—a natural and healthy reaction in their opinion. But for Napoleon a depression would be politically dangerous. He had no legal right to the power he held. His position had a firm base only in popular support, and he had won that support by a promise of accomplishment and less than a year of fulfillment. If he could offer no more than a brief respite from depression, the prospects for his popularity and his tenure of power were dark indeed.

6 Girard, *Politique*, pp. 86-88; *Moniteur*, Apr. 4, 1852.
7 Merruau, *Souvenirs*, p. 496.

Napoleon had never shared the view, accepted by the July Monarchy, that the state must stand aside and let the economy take its "natural" course regardless of political and social consequences, and he now tried to forestall the threatening depression. Reassurance on the future might help, he believed, as it had in 1851, and, in October, 1852, when he was about to reestablish the Empire, he assured the country that the Empire would mean peace, not war, and he promised that his government would complete the railroads, reclaim wastelands, and build highways, ports, and canals. His Saint-Simonian advisers told him that private industry would continue to flourish so long as capital was readily available for continued expansion. The Rothschilds and the other conservative banking houses could not be counted on to furnish it, for they had no sympathy with inflationary finance. To meet the need for credit a group of political figures and more audacious bankers led by the Pereire brothers founded in November, 1852, the *Société générale du Crédit mobilier,* a novel banking institution intended to tap the capital resources of small and large investors alike and put them at the disposal of expanding industry. The founders envisioned it as a great central source of credit that would finance a constantly expanding economy and perpetuate the boom of 1852.[8]

In Paris Napoleon faced the same problem as in the country at large but in even more acute form. He never enjoyed in the capital the popularity he had in the provinces, and the threat of revolution was ever close at hand. Thousands of construction workers, a turbulent element in the population, were a constant reminder to him that he could not afford to let the building industry languish. He was, moreover, personally anxious to see his plans for reconstruction of the city accomplished, and he would probably have pushed on with them even had political considerations not given them a special urgency.

The vexing question was how to pay for the huge projects he wanted. Persigny, the Minister of the Interior after January, 1852, had an answer. An adventurer who attached himself to Louis Napoleon in the precarious days of exile, he had little

8 Girard, *Politique,* pp. 108-11; Dupont-Ferrier, *Marché financier,* p. 117.

use for the orthodox views of conservative finance. He was active in the founding of the *Crédit mobilier*, and in 1853 he
urged upon Berger, the Prefect of the Seine, his view that expenditures on public works were not expenditures at all but
investments readily recoverable in the rising tax revenues from
the growing population and from the increased property values
that the expenditures themselves created. The obvious course
for the city was to borrow money, "invest" it in public works,
and pay off the debt with the resulting higher tax yields. It
sounded like perpetual motion, and Berger, Persigny reported,
was almost speechless when he heard the proposal. He left the
room mumbling that he would not be a party to the ruin of
Paris.[9]

The Minister's ideas were common enough among the Saint-
Simonians around the Emperor, but the suggestion probably
did shock poor Berger. He was a man of conservative financial
views, and he thought the city had already borrowed to the
limit of prudence. At the moment the municipal budget had a
surplus, but he believed that the business boom would soon
end and the favorable balance vanish. Pressed by Persigny he
finally agreed to spend the surplus, about 4,000,000 francs
annually, directly on public works, but that sum would scarcely
make a beginning on the great program the Emperor and
Persigny had in mind, and Berger would not hear of using the
surpluses for annual payments of interest and amortization on
a long-term loan as Persigny wanted.[10]

Berger was clearly an intolerable barrier in the way of the
Emperor's program. Persigny undertook to find a successor,
and when he interviewed the candidates he told them of his
plans for financing public works in Paris and carefully noted
their reactions. His ideas appealed to Haussmann, so much so
that Haussmann later claimed them as his own, and he was
brought to Paris to succeed Berger not alone because he had
the energy and determination to accomplish the physical task
of transforming the city but also because he shared the official

9 Fialin Persigny, *Mémoires* (Paris, 1896), pp. 243-50.
10 G. E. Haussmann, *Mémoires* (Paris, 1890-93), II, 30, 32; Merruau, *Souvenirs*,
p. 165.

views on finance. He was to do for Paris what the Pereire brothers and the *Crédit mobilier* hoped to do for industry—by long-term borrowing against future income he would provide the means to perpetuate the construction boom in Paris.[11]

Installed in office Haussmann found the majority of the Municipal Council more sympathetic with Berger's financial ideas than with Persigny's. For more than a year he avoided any direct reference to new borrowing, and he was able temporarily to finance the public works program with proceeds from the loan of 1852 and with subsidies from the state. But at the same time he laid the groundwork for a long-term loan. Berger in his budgets had exaggerated the city's obligations and minimized its resources, hoping to convince the National Assembly that Paris was poor and in need of subsidies if it were to undertake substantial public works. Haussmann, wanting to borrow from private investors, undertook in his budgets to demonstrate that the city was rich and its securities a sound investment. Three weeks after his installation he reported to the Municipal Council that a realistic analysis of Berger's figures on the city's revenues and obligations in 1854 revealed a surplus of at least 10,000,000 francs available for public works. When the city's debt charges, then at a peak, declined after 1856, the annual surplus would be even larger. In his message on the budget of 1855 he estimated that over the next fifteen years the city would have at its disposal a total of 250,000,000 francs in surplus funds. His estimate assumed only continuation of current revenues, and there was good reason to believe that revenues would in fact increase more rapidly than ordinary budgetary expenses, making the surplus still larger.[12]

But this accumulation was far in the future, and by the beginning of 1855 Haussmann needed additional cash at once. The cost of the Central Markets and the Rue de Rivoli had exceeded appropriations by 15,000,000 francs, and new projects he had initiated would cost the city another 41,000,000. If the work were to be financed directly out of the annual budget-

[11] Persigny, *Mémoires*, pp. 250-52; Haussmann, *Mémoires*, II, 35-36.
[12] *Moniteur*, July 18, 30, 1853, July 20, 1854; Haussmann, *Mémoires*, II, 41-42, 245-53, 261-64; Girard, *Politique*, p. 117.

ary surpluses, it would have to be spread over several years, an impractical and costly procedure in his judgment. To avoid that Haussmann in February, 1855, proposed to the Municipal Council that the city meet the immediate need with a long-term loan of 60,000,000 francs to be repaid over forty years. The annual interest and amortization charge, 3,340,000 francs, was relatively modest, and the surplus in the budget could easily cover it. The council, sensitive to the appeal of such painless finance (without unpopular taxes to be voted as there were for Berger's loan of 1852), readily gave its consent. The Legislative Body approved, and on June 14, 1855, the city placed the bonds on sale.[13]

The loan of 1855 must have delighted Persigny, for it was an open defiance of the conservative banking community, "the artful, sceptical men . . . from the corridors of the Bourse" whom he had hoped Haussmann would confound. Larger in amount and redeemable over a longer period than any loan previously floated by the city, it proclaimed Haussmann's disdain of the bankers' warnings against excessive discounting of future revenues. He also spurned their services in floating the loan. Earlier municipal loans had been taken in their entirety by private banks, which resold them to their wealthy clients, but Haussmann announced that the city would sell these bonds directly to the public. To accommodate small investors they were issued in 500 franc denominations instead of 1,000 francs as in the past. They were offered below par, and the subscription price might be paid in modest installments over nearly two years. For lottery loving Frenchmen there was the added inducement of bonuses on the first bonds drawn for redemption each six months. The first bond in each semi-yearly drawing would carry a bonus of 100,000 francs, the next four 10,000 francs each, and the following ten 1,000 francs each.

The city set up a subscription office in the City Hall and one in the mayor's office of each of the twelve city wards. They opened at 9 o'clock on the morning of Thursday, June 14, 1855,

13 Arch. nat., C 1042, Corps législatif, Session 1855, Dossier No. 37; *Moniteur*, Apr. 16, June 5, 20, 1855.

and when they closed that afternoon the offering had been oversubscribed by some 20,000,000 francs.[14]

The proceeds from the loans of 1852 and 1855, subsidies from the state (which amounted to 53,000,000 francs by 1857), and the income from the resale of condemned property provided the financial means to sustain the construction boom in Paris. The country suffered from a depression after 1856, but the transformation of the capital continued unretarded. Municipal revenues, which came largely from consumption taxes, mounted with the growing population, and Haussmann saw the budgetary surplus increasing each year. In 1858 he decided to make a new levy on the surplus to finance the largest program of street construction he had yet proposed.

The street projects up to this time had been confined largely to the "Great Crossing" of Paris (the Rue de Rivoli and the Boulevard du Centre) and their accessory streets. The other parts of the Emperor's plan had scarcely been touched. Haussmann now moved on to them, presenting to the Municipal Council in March, 1858, a project for the construction of the so-called Second Network of twenty-one streets. The cost would be 180,000,000 francs, a sizeable sum, he admitted, but the streets, all vitally important, would have to be built eventually, and with land values rising the city would save money by building them at once. He asked the state for a subsidy of 60,000,000 francs, one third the estimated cost, justifying his request on the ground that the proposed streets had national significance— in joining together the capital's railway stations they were continuations of those new national highways, the railroads, and they contributed to the national security by facilitating the maintenance of public order in the capital.[15]

The ministry agreed to the subsidy (although a number of streets that Haussmann had wanted to include were eliminated), but the Legislative Body was not easily won over. Provincial deputies objected to spending so many millions in Paris when construction of railroads and highways was held up by lack of funds, and they raised the old spectre of revolution led by

[14] *Moniteur*, June 2, 20, 1855.
[15] Arch. nat., C 1058, Corps législatif, Session 1858, Dossier No. 169.

workers the construction would attract to Paris. One member of the parliamentary committee that examined the bill wanted to limit the subsidy to 36,000,000 francs, and a majority agreed that seven of the proposed streets were without national importance and accordingly cut the subsidy to 45,000,000 francs. The government persuaded them to restore 5,000,000, but they stopped at a total of 50,000,000, payable in ten annual installments. The Municipal Council had earlier protested that the 60,000,000 franc subsidy was inadequate, but it accepted the smaller amount and decided to proceed with the construction of all twenty-one streets. The city's share of the costs, 130,000,-000 francs, Haussmann intended to raise by annual levies on the budgetary surplus and by resale of condemned property.[16]

To this point in his career as Prefect of the Seine Haussmann's financial methods were above serious reproach. Loans and subsidies freely debated and approved by parliament, surpluses in the regular municipal budget, and income from the sale of property provided the means for the public works program. His critics thought he spent too much and borrowed too freely, that he was imprudently optimistic in estimating future revenues, but these were questions of judgment. In those days no one could charge him with keeping fantastic accounts.

The years that followed were more difficult. The transformation of Paris was only beginning in 1858. The Second Network weighed heavily on the budget for the next decade or more, and it did not include all the new streets that Napoleon wanted. Haussmann was determined to carry out the Emperor's wishes and to add a number of other streets that he himself believed essential. He never presented to the Municipal Council or to the Legislative Body any comprehensive plan for these additional streets, but he built them, nonetheless, simultaneously with the Second Network in the 1860's, and by 1869 they had cost the city 300,000,000 francs. At the same time Haussmann had to meet the expense of the sewer construction he had begun in 1857, and the costs of the aqueducts, reservoirs, and mains required for distribution of spring water in the city. The annexation of the suburbs in 1860 put an additional burden on

16 *Moniteur*, May 9, 10, Sept. 17, 18, 1858; Arch. nat., C 1058, Dossier No. 169.

the city budget; in the next decade the city spent 353,000,000 francs there and recovered only a fraction of it in additional tax revenues from the area.[17]

Haussmann had also to contend with rising costs that wrecked his estimates of expenses, The final cost of the Third Network was double his expectation, and the Second Network, which the municipal engineers said could be built for 180,000,000 francs, actually cost 410,000,000. One might easily conclude that Haussmann and his staff had deliberately misled the Legislative Body and the public, but the higher costs were owing largely to developments that no one could accurately foresee. Real estate values inflated rapidly in the 1860's. The Council of State in December, 1858, persuaded the Emperor to limit the city's authority to condemn property and thereby cut the profits from resale of land that Haussmann had counted on when he planned the Second Network. In the early sixties the courts handed down rulings that increased the city's obligation to pay indemnities to tenants in condemned buildings. The juries that fixed the indemnities in event of disagreement between the city and proprietors or tenants were largely independent of the administration, and they proved unpredictably generous in making awards. Some lawyers made a business of representing owners and tenants of condemned property, and one among them at least, to impress juries of the justice of his clients' claims for larger indemnities produced forged leases, false account books, "stocks" composed of empty boxes, and customers hired for the day of the jury's visit![18]

Another financial difficulty arose from the need to make very large temporary outlays of money that at times exceeded available appropriations. The purchase of property for the right-of-way of a new street, some of which was later resold, required a heavy immediate expenditure, perhaps more than the ultimate cost of the project. Adequate funds might eventually be forth-

[17] *Moniteur*, Dec. 11, 1867; *J.O.*, Apr. 14, Nov. 28, 1869; Haussmann, *Mémoires*, II, 304-05, 313-16.

[18] *Moniteur*, Dec. 11, 1867; *J.O.*, Apr. 14, 1869; Haussmann, *Mémoires*, II, 304-05, 308; Léon Say, *Examen critique de la situation financière de la ville de Paris* (Paris, 1861), pp. 29-33; Maxime du Camp, *Paris: ses organes, ses fonctions et sa vie* (Paris, 1869-75) VI, 255-56.

coming, but appropriations ordinarily were paid in periodic installments that rarely corresponded with the demands for cash at the beginning of a project. The city needed additional money for this temporary financing.

As the costs of the transformation of the city mounted the chances of meeting them by the simple and straightforward methods of the 1850's grew less and less likely. The budgetary surpluses could not equal the huge sums required. The Legislative Body had made clear in the discussion of the Second Network that it was not disposed to grant any more subsidies, and that disposition did not change in the 1860's, when the Emperor granted the parliament more authority and it became increasingly independent and critical. The only course open to Haussmann was borrowing, but several obstacles stood in the way of additional bond issues like those of the fifties. The sums Haussmann needed were enormously larger than the 110,000,-000 francs borrowed in 1852 and 1855, and the market for government and municipal bonds was not limitless. The national government with financing of its own to arrange could not permit the city to saturate the market, and while the Legislative Body remained unconvinced of the necessity of Haussmann's building program in Paris, he could not count on its approval of additional loans. Nor could he be sure, even if he passed these obstacles, that investors would snap up the city's bonds as they had in the prosperous years of 1852 and 1855.[19]

Haussmann did succeed in obtaining authorization for a large loan in 1860 and for another five years later, but for both he had to find extraordinary justification. He convinced the council of ministers that the first loan was necessary to meet the expense, unforeseen in 1858, of providing the essential streets and municipal services in the newly annexed suburbs. (Haussmann's claim that the annexation had upset his careful financial planning was less than flattering to himself, for the annexation had long been regarded as inevitable, and a committee of the Departmental Commission had been studying the problem since 1853.) The Legislative Body approved the loan

[19] Girard, *Politique*, pp. 167, 170-71; Arch. nat., 45 AP 19 (Rouher Papers), memorandum, Fould to Emperor, Jan. 1865.

of 1860 for 130,000,000 francs, though not without protest. Investors were sparing in their approval. The real interest rate on the bonds was somewhat lower than in 1855, but the Prefect again offered the inducements of small denominations, payment by installments, and redemption bonuses. The subscription offices confidently set up throughout the city opened on August 13, 1860, prepared for a rush of investors. When they closed more than a week later nearly half the bonds remained unsold. Not until October, 1862, did the city succeed in selling the remainder, and then only at a reduction from the original price and with the help of the *Crédit mobilier*, which took about a fifth of the entire offering.[20]

After that experience Haussmann had little taste for another large public bond issue. In 1864 he told the Municipal Council that no additional loan would be necessary for the completion of the public works to which the city was then committed: the resources on hand and in prospect would permit their completion within ten years. He recommended no acceleration of the program except to satisfy the Emperor's wish that the streets of the Second Network be finished before the opening of the exposition scheduled for 1867. That would require some additional working capital, but Haussmann was confident he could raise it without a new loan. In 1865, however, the national government urged the city to complete its entire program within five years. This clearly required additional financing, and Haussmann asked the government for authority to borrow 300,000,000 francs repayable over sixty years. The Minister of Finance Fould was dubious of the Prefect's estimate of the city's financial capabilities and induced the government to cut the total back to 250,000,000. The Legislative Body, with many protests, approved this amount. The Emperor personally authorized another 20,000,000 francs for "expenses," an arbitrary move that did not please a parliament already complaining of its lack of control over Haussmann's spending.[21]

[20] *Moniteur*, July 20, 22, Aug. 4, 5, Dec. 6, 1860, Dec. 12, 1861, Dec. 4, 1862; Arch. nat., C 1070, Corps législatif, Session 1860, Dossier No. 200, Gaston Cadoux, *Les Finances de la ville de Paris de 1789 à 1900* (Paris, 1900), pp. 256-59.

[21] Arch. nat., C 1102, Corps législatif, Session 1865, Dossier No. 55, 45 AP 19, memorandum, Fould to Emperor, Jan. 1865, note on finances of Paris by Fould, 1865; *Moniteur*, July 1, 2, 1865; *J.O.*, Nov. 28, 1869.

Recalling the difficulties with the preceding loan the Prefect took the precaution in 1865 of arranging with the *Crédit mobilier* to buy any bonds remaining unsold at the close of six days of public sale. After a single day he announced that the issue had been oversubscribed, but subscriptions from the *Crédit mobilier* accounted for more than a third of the total. Haussmann had, in fact, been obliged to revert in part to the practice of borrowing from banks with the difference that the *Crédit mobilier* replaced the old private banking houses.[22]

The two loans gave Haussmann more than 400,000,000 francs and put only a modest annual burden on the municipal budget, but most of the proceeds were earmarked for expenditure in the annexed zone, and Haussmann was not confining his activities there nor to the twenty-one streets of the Second Network. Construction was moving at a feverish pace. The number of condemnations for public works rose from 129 in 1858 to 398 in 1860, to 691 in 1865, and on to a peak of 848 the following year.[23] Parisians saw in progress about them costly projects like the Rue du Pont Neuf, the Rue Lafayette, the Boulevard Haussmann, and the Avenue d'Iéna that had never figured in any plan for which the city had sought public financing. Haussmann was obviously raising money by some means that escaped public scrutiny.

Suspicious deputies found they could do little about it. The very magnitude of the operations and the complexity of the records hampered parliamentary control. In the Legislative Body the republican deputy Ernest Picard delivered frequent denunciations of Haussmann's activities; the imperialist Devinck as frequently defended them; and the other deputies were left floating in a sea of conflicting figures. The Court of Accounts charged the Prefect with violation of accounting regulations. The Minister of Finance Fould protested to the Emperor and to Rouher, "the Vice-Emperor," that the city's published budgets were meaningless. As early as 1865 Picard warned that Haussmann was contracting "hidden loans." But the Prefect was carry-

---

[22] *Moniteur*, July 26, Aug. 12, 1865; Cadoux, *Finances*, p. 262.
[23] Maurice Halbwachs, *Les Expropriations et le prix des terrains à Paris (1860-1900)* (Paris, 1909), pp. 186, 188.

ing out an assignment that came to him directly from the Emperor, and he could defy lesser men.[24] "There is no power in France today," cried a deputy in 1864, "that can control the omnipotence of the Prefect of the Seine."[25]

In the early sixties Napoleon had begun to relax the authoritarian regime of the first years of the Empire. Starting with the session of 1861 he permitted the Legislative Body to make a reply to the opening address from the throne, and discussion of the reply gave deputies an opportunity to review and criticize imperial policies. Debates, which had formerly been revealed to the public only in official summaries, were published verbatim in the *Moniteur* for all to read. Opposition deputies, muffled by restrictions on freedom of assembly and press, could speak out in the Legislative Body and know that they would be heard throughout France.

The growing political battles of the sixties centered on the demand for the transfer of the essential political powers from the Emperor and his ministers to elected representatives of the people, and in this struggle Haussmann came to personify for the parliamentary opposition the kind of government they sought to abolish. Unhampered by an elected municipal council he spent the taxpayers' money without their consent, withheld information on the use of public funds, and defied efforts to control his activities. When the opposition dared not attack the Emperor personally they could attack his close associates and through them strike at the arbitrary regime itself. The Prefect made an ideal whipping boy. He had no significant political following. The liberal deputies from Paris (and presumably the public, too, since they regularly elected opposition deputies in the sixties) disliked him as an authoritarian, and the provincial deputies, who generally supported the Empire, objected to his extravagant spending in Paris. Even among the imperial ministers he could not count on certain support. His position depended solely on the favor of the Emperor, and

[24] *Moniteur*, May 27, 28, 1859, July 21, 1860, Mar. 20, 1861, May 16, 18, June 25, 1862, Apr. 29, 1863, May 27, 1864, Apr. 7, June 25, July 1, 1865, Apr. 12, 1867; Arch. nat., C 1088, Corps législatif, Session 1863, Dossier No. 39, 45 AP 19, Fould's memo., Jan. 1865, and note, 1865.

[25] *Moniteur*, May 27, 1864.

when an attack was made on Haussmann there was no mistaking the real target.

The hostile deputies seized every opportunity to denounce the Prefect, his work, and the irresponsible municipal government of Paris. Two opportunities came each year with the reply to the address from the throne and the authorization of the annual bond issue of the municipal Public Works Fund, and the deputies rarely failed to use them. Every bill relating to Paris directly or indirectly—the loan authorizations of 1860 and 1865 and the municipal government law of 1867, for example—set off a barrage of attacks. Each year Picard and his fellows found one law or another to which they could attach an amendment calling for the restoration of an elected municipal council in the capital. Much of the petty obstructionism to particular public works projects recounted in earlier chapters is comprehensible only as part of the political battle centering on Haussmann. The government's decision to reduce the size of the Luxembourg Garden, the vexed questions of the location and cost of the new opera house, the site and size of the new Hôtel Dieu, Haussmann's proposed bridge across the corner of the Cemetery of Montmartre, and his project for the cemetery at Méry-sur-Oise were not debated simply on their merits but were used to discredit the Prefect and the authoritarian regime he represented.[26]

On these occasions the Prefect's enemies aired many complaints against him, but until the latter 1860's they looked vainly for a vulnerable point in his record. But vulnerable points did exist. Since 1858 he had been evading public control of a part of his expenditure by questionable use of a floating debt, and in the sixties, using a method of raising funds that long escaped even public detection, he contracted a short-term debt of half a billion francs without any preliminary authorization from the Legislative Body!

In 1858, a few weeks after the legislature had granted a subsidy for the Second Network, the Emperor authorized the city to establish the municipal Public Works Fund, (*Caisse des Tra-*

26 Summaries and stenographic reports of parliamentary debates in the *Moniteur*, 1858-1867.

vaux de Paris). Its nominal purpose was to relieve the city's budget of temporary financial obligations and detailed accounting connected with public works. It provided funds for the purchase of property needed for new projects and temporarily held title to portions that would be resold. It received and held contractors' deposits to guarantee performance, which were ordinarily refunded when projects were completed, acted as the city's disbursing agent for payments on public works contracts, and it might temporarily provide the necessary funds until appropriations became available. Nominally all its operations were self-liquidating, but the fund required working capital, and the Emperor gave it power to issue bonds in its own name. Its maximum bonded indebtedness was fixed annually by law, but no time limit was set for its liquidation. In practice the fund enabled the city to maintain a floating debt independent of the municipal budget.[27]

From the beginning some deputies suspected that it was a device for evading public control of Haussmann's expenditures. In the legislative session of 1859 the Budget Committee, which was asked to approve the bond issue in 1859 and 1860, first tried to restrict the fund to the purchase of property needed for authorized public works, forbidding it to make any expenditures for new construction. Failing that, the committee asked that the fund be limited to financing works expressly approved by the Legislative Body. But the government rejected both restrictions. At most it would offer an annual report to the Legislative Body on the total of bonds actually issued and on the use of the proceeds. The committee finally gave in and sanctioned the bond issue as requested, but the government's recalcitrance strengthened the suspicion that the city intended to use the fund to speed up construction of the Second Network contrary to the wishes of the Legislative Body and to finance unauthorized works.[28]

Haussmann used the fund just as the deputies feared. From it he obtained capital for the acceleration and extension of the

[27] *Moniteur*, Nov. 18, 1858; Jan. 8, June 13, Dec. 31, 1859; Caisse des Travaux de Paris, *Compte moral et financier des opérations, 1859-1861*, pp. 1-8; Arch. nat., C 1059, Corps législatif, Session 1859, Dossier No. 19.

[28] Arch. nat., C 1059, Dossier No. 19, Fle III Seine 31, 1859, 1860.

191

public works program, and the fund escaped public control. The regulation fixing the maximum limit of bonds outstanding each year took the form of an article in the annual budget law, and it came up for discussion near the end of each session, when deputies were impatient for adjournment. The opposition used it as an occasion for protest, but the legislature had little choice but to accept the government's recommendation. The bonds were nominally secured by a 20,000,000 franc endowment provided by the city and by the real property in the fund's possession, but Haussmann was not always careful to keep obligations in balance with these assets. Its operations never figured in the municipal budget, and the annual report on its operations had only a limited circulation among officials.[29]

The fund did, nonetheless, fulfill a legitimate need for short-term credits, and it provided a means of using capital resources held by the city that might otherwise have lain idle. The public had confidence in its securities, and they became a favorite investment of retired Parisian merchants.[30] Had Haussmann been more open about its operations, and had it been his only extra-budgetary device for raising funds it might well have escaped serious criticism. But it did not provide enough capital for the execution of the Emperor's and Haussmann's plans, and in the 1860's when he accelerated the tempo of public building to a high pitch he turned to another method of financing that got him into serious trouble.

It began in contracts between the city and private construction companies. Before 1858 the city generally acted as its own contractor on public works, private builders being unwilling to assume the risks of uncertain costs, particularly the unpredictable indemnities for condemned property. But after watching the experience of the city and of a few venturesome entrepreneurs, others took heart, and by the late fifties the city could find contractors to undertake even its biggest projects. By the

29 Arch. nat., C 1065, Corps législatif, Session 1860, Dossier No. 22, C 1145, Corps législatif, Session 1869, Dossier No. 259-60; Caisse des Travaux, *Compte moral*, 1859-69, passim.; Léon Say, *Observations sur le système financier de M. le Préfet de la Seine* (Paris, 1865), pp. 32-37; Say, *Examen critique*, pp. 16, 19, 38-39; *J.O.*, Feb. 27, Nov. 28, 1869.

30 *Moniteur*, July 1, 1865; *Revue générale de l'architecture et des travaux publics* (Paris), XVI (1858), 233.

terms of the usual contract for a new street the builder agreed to dispossess property owners and tenants and pay indemnities, execute the actual construction, dispose of condemned property outside the right-of-way, and deliver the completed street to the city. Only after a street or a prescribed section of it was completed and formally accepted by the Prefect did the city begin to pay the agreed contract price, and payment was spread in annual installments over as many as eight years. In accepting deferred payments, the building companies were granting short-term credits to the city for the financing of public works, and the city paid interest on the sums owing to contractors just as on its public loans. But the companies ordinarily lacked sufficient capital to lend to the city and still carry on their businesses. Legally they might assign their credits against the city to a bank or any other third party for cash but only after the schedule of payments was definitely fixed following the completion of the project.[31]

In 1863 a sudden rise in the interest rate on the Paris money market put one of the municipal contractors, *Ardoin, Ricardo et Cie.*, in financial difficulties embarrassing to the city. The company had contracted in 1861 and 1862 to build two portions of the new Rue Lafayette, and it agreed to accept payment on the first contract in three annual installments, the first falling due two years after completion and acceptance of the first section of the street. Until that time the company had to finance the entire operation, and when the tightening of the money market limited its ability to borrow it was unable to pay indemnities of 12,000,000 francs that fell due about the same time. The unhappy creditors turned to the city, demanding that the municipal government pay them, and the city, lacking funds, asked the government mortgage bank, the *Crédit foncier*, for assistance.[32]

More than a year earlier in December, 1861, this bank had agreed with Ardoin, Ricardo to discount the initial payment on the Rue Lafayette contract when the first section of the street

[31] Arch. nat., C 1134, Corps législatif, Session 1869, Dossier No. 140, C 1145, Dossier No. 259-60; *Moniteur*, Dec. 11, 1867.
[32] Arch. nat., C 1134, Dossier No. 140, C 1145, Dossier No. 259-60.

should be completed, formally accepted by the Prefect, and the dates of payments specifically fixed. Once that section was delivered to the city the company had used this credit by delivering to the bank bills, called delegation bonds (*bons de délégation*), drawn on the city and payable to bearer. Each bill had to receive the Prefect's endorsement before it was negotiable but only to assure that the total issue did not exceed the city's obligation to the company. Legally the operation was simply a transfer of credit between the company and a third party. In 1862 the *Foncier's* directors had approved a similar credit on a section of the street covered by the company's second contract.[33]

Importuned by the city in 1863 the *Crédit foncier* agreed to discount immediately *all* the anticipated payments under the first of the two contracts even though work on the latter two sections of the street was not yet completed. The bank deposited to the credit of *Ardoin, Ricardo et Cie.* in the Public Works Fund a sum equal to the entire amount the company would receive under its first contract with the city, and the company delivered to the bank delegation bonds representing its future claims against the city. Haussmann made the transaction possible by considering the project "completed" as soon as the *Crédit foncier* made the deposit, an action he justified by maintaining that the deposit covered all anticipated costs and assured completion of the project. With the job nominally finished, the dates for all the payments on the contract could be fixed at once, and the bank simply discounted these payments. The innovation was the city's considering the project terminated while it was still in progress.[34]

This was an extraordinary procedure adopted to meet an emergency, but a similar instance of financial embarrassment the following year inspired the city to draw contracts thereafter in a way that permitted its routine use. In 1864 an exorbitant indemnity award ruined the builder of the new Rue Gay-Lussac, and the municipal treasury had to assume his obligations. When the city made its next major contract, with *Berlencourt et Cie.*, for the construction of the Boulevard de Magenta,

33 Arch. nat., C 1134, Dossier No. 140.
34 Arch. nat., C 1134, Dossier No. 140, C 1145, Dossier No. 259-60.

it sought to forestall such unexpected demands on the city should the company run short of funds. The contract committed the city to pay Berlencourt 1,000,000 francs when the boulevard was completed and a total of 20,000,000 francs in six annual installments starting in 1866, but it required the company to deposit 20,000,000 francs in the Fund for Public Works as a guarantee of payment of indemnities and other costs. Berlencourt could draw on this deposit to pay his creditors, including dispossessed property owners as well as his suppliers and subcontractors, as their bills became due. But 20,000,000 francs was a huge outlay of capital required at the outset of the operation, and until part of the job was finished and accepted the contractor had no claim against the city that could be negotiated for cash. To accommodate Berlencourt the city revived the extraordinary procedure of the Ardoin, Ricardo case in 1863; it agreed to consider the project "completed" as soon as the 20,000,000 franc deposit was in the Public Works Fund (even though no actual work had been accomplished), and the contract specifically authorized Berlencourt to draw delegation bonds against its credits with the city. The total might not exceed the amount of the company's deposit. The bonds, payable to bearer, were readily negotiable in the open market.[35]

Such a contract enabled a builder to raise capital on a municipal contract *before* the project was started. Payments spread over several years, so convenient for Haussmann, thereby became financially practical for contractors. The combination of deferred payments and delegation bonds also enabled the city to finance large public works without legislative sanction. Municipal borrowing required parliamentary approval, but under this arrangement the contractors, not the city, issued the bonds and incurred the debts. The city simply paid on its contracts, and payments spread over several years in the future could, Haussmann expected, be covered from growing budgetary surpluses. The Prefect was quick to appreciate the advantages of these arrangements, and he made increasing use of them. By 1868 delegation bonds worth nearly half a billion

[35] Arch. nat., C 1134, Dossier No. 140.

francs had been issued, endorsed, and discounted, and about 450,000,000 francs remained to be paid on them.[36]

The city had, in fact, contracted a loan of some half a billion francs, and until 1867 the Legislative Body knew of it only by rumor and indirect report. Deputies were aware that the city was raising money outside the municipal budget and approved loans, but they did not know from what sources, and until 1867 Haussmann offered them no enlightenment. Payments under most of the contracts would begin only in 1869, and until then they put no burden on the municipal budget except a modest interest charge, and the Prefect's public reports never mentioned either the contracts or the heavy load they would shortly place upon the city's resources.

The *Crédit foncier* took most of the delegation bonds either directly or by re-discount. At the end of 1867 it had 398,000,000 francs invested in them. It raised the necessary capital by issuing communal bonds, an operation of dubious legality, and its public reports never mentioned that the city of Paris was the ultimate recipient of the proceeds.[37]

The exposure of the term contracts and delegation bonds came not from Haussmann's usual critics, the republican deputies in the Legislative Body, but from the other end of the political spectrum. In January and February, 1865, the Orleanist newspaper, the *Journal des Débats*, published three articles charging Haussmann with contracting large loans for which the municipality had obtained no authorization as required by law, and they described how he had done it surreptitiously through deferred payment contracts and delegation bonds. The articles were from the pen of the journal's editor, Léon Say, a friend of Alphonse de Rothschild and himself a director of the Northern Railway, a Rothschild enterprise, and they reflected the continuing hostility of the conservative financial community towards Haussmann and all the unorthodox finance of the Second

[36] Arch. nat., 45 AP 19, Table of delegation bonds issued, 1865-68, C 1134, Dossier No. 140.

[37] Arch. nat. C 1134, Dossier No. 140; *Moniteur*, May 6, 1863, May 2, 1864, May 3, 1865, May 6, 1866, Apr. 28, 1867; Léon Say, *La Ville de Paris et le Crédit foncier; lettre à MM. les membres de la Commission du Corps législatif* (Paris, 1868), pp. 7-8.

Empire. But the articles were also the first competent analysis of Haussmann's financial methods available to the public, and it was not long before Say's charges reached the floor of the Legislative Body.[38]

In April, 1865, the delegation bonds were mentioned for the first time in the parliamentary debates when Ernest Picard denounced them and the contracts that permitted their creation, but it was obvious that he did not fully understand the operations involved, and he only hinted at the role of the *Crédit foncier*. The following year he was better informed. In the debate on the bond issue of the Public Works Fund in June, 1866, Picard gave an accurate description of the process of borrowing by contracts and delegation bonds, and he charged that Haussmann had by these means contracted unauthorized debts with the *Crédit foncier* totaling more than 400,000,000 francs. The Minister of State Rouher, though he had no love for Haussmann, came to the Prefect's defense. He freely admitted that the city had arranged to pay its contractors over a period of years, but this was a common administrative practice among municipalities. It was perfectly legal, and the municipal administration in Paris had used it openly and without any attempt at concealment. The contracts had all been approved by imperial decree, their terms were open to public scrutiny. About the delegation bonds he said nothing, leaving the impression that they were less defensible.[39]

In the session of 1867 debate on the finances of Paris occupied most of three days' meetings. Picard and Jules Favre charged the municipal administration with contracting illegal loans. "The Prefect of the Seine," exclaimed Favre, "puts himself above the law. . . ." There was no limit on what Paris or any other commune might borrow by Haussmann's methods if the Legislative Body failed to put effective controls on the Prefect. From the other side of the assembly Berryer, a legitimist, reiterating a demand by the Orleanist *Revue des deux mondes,* insisted that the government reveal the names of the communes

[38] Say, *Observations*, pp. 7, 36, 44-49; Georges Michel, *Léon Say* (2d edit., Paris, 1899), pp. 42, 44-45.
[39] *Moniteur*, Apr. 7, 1865, June 27, 1866.

that had borrowed from the *Crédit foncier* since the beginning of the year. The Legislative Body, he said, had authorized only 35,000,000 francs of communal borrowing in that period, and the *Crédit foncier* had placed 291,000,000 francs in what it designated as "communal loans." He suspected that most of it had been used to discount delegation bonds of Parisian contractors and that the *Foncier* was a party to Haussmann's "illegal" financing. Rouher again stood firmly in Haussmann's defense. He dismissed the delegation bonds as simple transfers of credit between a contractor and a third party, involving no new obligations for the city. In making short-term commitments of future revenues in term contracts Haussmann had followed accepted practice, and as long as the obligations could be met from ordinary revenues (as he claimed they could), no loan requiring legislative approval was involved. At the conclusion of the debate the Legislative Body rejected an amendment proposed by Picard and others to establish an elected municipal council in Paris. Haussmann claimed the vote was an endorsement of his financial policies, certainly a gratuitous assumption. He should have seen in the debate a warning that the Legislative Body, or a dangerously large minority within it, meant to know the truth of his spending and borrowing and to place a check upon them both.[40]

The growing recalcitrance of the Legislative Body reflected widespread dissatisfaction with the Imperial regime. In the preceding three or four years it had suffered dangerous reverses in Mexico and Germany, and in 1867 it was offering no reassuring leadership at home. The Emperor's ill health, the fear of war, and the uncertainty over further changes in the constitution were unsettling in both politics and business. The reserves of the Bank of France rose to 1,000,000,000 francs in 1867 as investors refused to venture their capital. The conservative bankers had never accepted the inflationary financial policies of the government, and since 1861 they had been attempting, particularly through the Minister of Finance Fould, who shared their views, to put a brake on government spending and borrowing and to limit the Saint-Simonians' headlong creation of

40 *Moniteur*, Apr. 1, 12, 13, Dec. 11, 1867.

credit. Their influence and the growing independence of the Legislative Body combined to bring the finances of the state under closer parliamentary control, and in 1867 they forced the Pereires out of the *Crédit mobilier* and virtually broke their power. But Haussmann continued to borrow and spend without hindrance, and the campaign against the national government's spending would be meaningless if the Prefect of the Seine could continue to float hidden municipal loans as large as national loans at his own pleasure.[41]

Rouher replaced Fould in the Ministry of Finance in January 1867, and the change appeared to be a victory for inflationary policies, but Rouher understood the warnings that came in the session of 1867. He insisted that the city and the *Crédit foncier* put their dealings above reproach. Haussmann was aware that the persistent charges of illegal financial operations imperiled the city's credit, and Frémy, the Governor of the *Crédit foncier*, must have feared for the *Foncier's* investment in delegation bonds while their legality was in question. On November 8, 1867, Haussmann and Frémy signed an agreement consolidating the city's obligations in delegation bonds held by the *Crédit foncier* into a single long-term debt of 398,000,000 francs, which the city undertook to repay in semi-annual installments over the next sixty years. The Municipal Council gave its approval on December 2.[42]

In a report to the council published on December 11, 1867, and in a report to the Emperor six months later Haussmann openly described for the first time the city's dealings with contractors and with the *Crédit foncier*, but he admitted no illegal or irregular actions. The deferred payment contracts and the conversion of the obligations into a long-term debt by the agreement of November 8 were, he claimed, parts of a well conceived and irreproachable policy. Until the costs of the Second and Third Networks were known a long-term loan was impractical because no one could know how large it should be. By the latter months of 1867 the final contracts for the two

41 Girard, *Politique*, pp. 269-75, 361-72; *Revue des deux mondes*, 37th Year (1867), LXVII, 1002-04, LXVIII, 1042-45; LXXI, 78-82, 1040-41, LXXII, 1027-28.
42 *J.O.*, Feb. 27, 1869; Arch. nat., C 1134, Dossier No. 140.

networks had been let, and Haussmann recommended that no further works be started. The total costs remaining to be paid were known, and the time had come to consolidate them into one long-term debt. In the interim period the city had financed the operations by contracting with builders who accepted payments in installments spread over several years, but the total obligation contracted in this way never exceeded the anticipated surplus in the municipal budget, and the city was able to meet all future installments as they came due. The term contracts had been negotiated under well-established administrative powers of the municipal government, and they required no legislative approval. Now that the obligations were being converted into a long-term debt, which, Haussmann agreed, did require specific legal sanction, he was immediately submitting the city's agreement with the *Crédit foncier* to the Legislative Body for approval. The conversion to a long-term loan was not essential for the city, he said, since it could meet all its obligations as they stood, but the operation would lighten the annual burden on the budget in the next decade and make funds available either for additional public works, if the public demanded them, or for tax reductions. As a pledge of his own good faith and to protect himself against irresponsible criticism in the legislature he urged that in the future the municipal budget of Paris be debated and approved each year by the Legislative Body.[43]

By his own account Haussmann was an injured innocent, but the role did not suit him, and not everyone accepted his explanations. A week after his report to the Municipal Council appeared in the *Moniteur* Jules Ferry published the first of his mocking articles on *The Fantastic Accounts of Haussmann*, and he continued them through the winter and spring while the Legislative Body awaited the government's bill on the Paris-*Crédit foncier* agreements.

What! [he exclaimed in the opening article] So many millions in the hands of a single man! But two billions in the budget of France, and the prefect, in fifteen years, has spent scarcely less than two billions! And that is the power that for fifteen years has been

---

[43] *Moniteur*, Dec. 11, 1867, June 18, 1868; Haussmann, *Mémoires*, II, 330-33.

exercised by an administration without control, by an irresponsible power, by a single man backed by an appointed municipal council.[44]

He accused Haussmann of lack of foresight in estimating costs, of juggling budget figures to conceal the true state of the municipal finances, and of falsifying his intention to undertake more public works. Through all the articles ran the refrain that Haussmann had flouted the law. "The prefect breaks the law with abandon; one can even say, with a kind of coquetishness."[45]

The Legislative Body, too, found Haussmann's explanations inadequate. In April, 1868, the government submitted the Paris-*Crédit foncier* agreement to the legislature and asked for passage of a single-article law sanctioning the long-term loan. The committee appointed to examine the proposal declined meekly to accept the government's recommendations. Through the spring and early summer it held hearings, pried into all the city's financial operations in the past decade and its plans for the future, and insisted that the *Crédit foncier* explain its role. The committee examined the records, quizzed cabinet ministers, and listened to oral testimony of Haussmann and Frémy. Then it demanded that the redemption period of the debt to the *Crédit foncier* be cut from sixty to forty years, that the remaining short-term debts of the city, amounting to 67,000,000 francs, be consolidated into a second long-term obligation to the *Foncier*, and that the city's spending on public works be brought under control of the legislature. The government accepted the first two demands and agreed to the third in principle, but the Council of State and the committee engaged in a long wrangle over the form of legislative control of the municipal public works budget, and they reached no agreement. In its report to the Legislative Body the committee submitted two articles intended to achieve this control: the government's, a complicated measure, which it regarded as ineffective, and its own, which would require the legislature's approval each year of the entire public works' budget of the city.[46]

The members of this committee were well-disposed toward

[44] *Temps*, Dec. 20, 1867.   [45] *Temps*, May 5, 1868.
[46] *Moniteur*, June 5, Aug. 8, 9, 1868; Arch. nat., C 1134, Dossier No. 140.

the government and even toward Haussmann, and their critical stand promised serious trouble ahead when the bill should come to the floor of the parliament. The prospect worried both the Emperor and Rouher, and in May, 1868, they decided to postpone the evil day to the end of the session after the vote on the annual budget law. As the time approached the prospect appeared no brighter and in July, after discussing the matter with Haussmann and the President of the Legislative Body, the Emperor ruled against risking an all-out debate that year. On July 23, as the budget discussions neared their end, Rouher informed the assembly that no time remained to take up the Paris-*Crédit foncier* agreements. They would be considered early in the session of 1869.[47]

The following February when the day fixed for the opening of the debate finally came the visitors' galleries were filled an hour before the session opened. An imposing array of ministers took their places on the government bench: the Minister of State, the Minister of Finance, the Minister of the Interior, the Minister of Foreign Affairs, the Minister of Justice, the Minister of Public Works, the Minister of Education, and the President and members of the Council of State. The government's strategy was to present a bold front, to defend the operations of Haussmann and the *Crédit foncier* as perfectly legal and regular, and to concede none of the opposition's charges.[48]

In the opening session on February 22 Picard and another republican, Garnier-Pagès, delivered sharp attacks on Haussmann and accused him of a whole catalogue of misdeeds, but they had been doing that for years, and the ministry expected a repeat performance. The following day Thiers, the respected spokesman of the moderate opposition, took the floor. He was a skillful speaker, and some of his jibes at Rouher and Haussmann were more telling than careful financial analyses. He taunted the Minister of State with the charge that Haussmann, not Rouher, was the real "Vice-Emperor," and he mocked Hauss-

47 Arch. nat., 45 AP 1, Rouher's notes on cabinet meetings, May 2, July 18, 1868; *Moniteur*, July 24, 1868, p. 1109.
48 *Moniteur*, Feb. 23, 1869; *J.O.*, Feb. 23, 1869.

mann for saying that his work in Paris was finished: "Your work is finished! Better say it is your resources that are finished. . . ."[49] To the substance of the case against Haussmann he added nothing, but he stated the case effectively, and the whole assembly, including the supposedly loyal imperialists, listened with careful attention. By the fourth day of debate it was clear that disaffection had spread into the ranks of the government's majority. The banker Calley de Saint-Paul, an imperialist, that day denounced the transactions of the *Crédit foncier* and the city of Paris as illegal, and accused the *Foncier* of making "monstrous profits." Rouher was now thoroughly alarmed. Should this trend continue, the government might lose its majority and suffer a damaging defeat on the pending bill. The Empire could not risk such a reverse on the eve of the parliamentary elections scheduled for the following May.[50]

That evening, the Paris correspondent of the London *Times* heard, Rouher went to Napoleon and told him that continued defense of Haussmann against all charges would imperil the Empire itself; the Prefect would have to be sacrificed to save the Emperor.[51] Napoleon gave his consent, though certainly with a heavy heart, for Haussmann had been an able and devoted public servant.

The next day Rouher rose in the Legislative Body and admitted that the Prefect in engaging nearly 500,000,000 francs of the city's future revenues had exceeded the proper limits of administrative authority. He should have obtained preliminary authorization from the legislature. Rouher refused to concede that any of the procedure had been illegal, but, he said, it was "irregular." He went on to admit that the municipal Public Works Fund had contracted debts in excess of the maximum fixed by the Legislative Body. He promised that in the future there would be no more delegation bonds, no more term contracts, no more "discount operations."[52] "Concessions rained down from the tribune as thick as hail," wrote

---

[49] *J.O.*, Feb. 24, 1869.
[50] *J.O.*, Feb. 23, 24, 25, 26, 1869; *Moniteur*, Feb. 28, 1869.
[51] *Times* (London), Mar. 2, 1869.
[52] *J.O.*, Feb. 27, 1869.

a columnist of the day. "The majority was lost in astonishment, the left was stunned, and the right rubbed its eyes."[53]

But the shock quieted the left only momentarily, and the right quickly opened its eyes. They had a new taste of power, and Rouher's retreat did not go far enough for them. In the next day of debate Thiers denounced the minister's use of the word "irregular" to describe Haussmann's borrowing. "It is not merely an irregularity," he shouted. "It is a flagrant violation of the law, and the most amazing violation ever committed!"[54]

In the succeeding days the attack shifted to the *Crédit foncier*. The bank had made large profits from delegation bonds and would make more from the long-term loan to the city. (Its annual dividend nearly doubled between 1861 and 1868.) Banker deputies from the government's majority who coveted these profits, joined the opposition in accusing the bank of both illegal borrowing and illegal lending in its dealings with the city and of charging excessive commissions.[55]

The first test vote in the long debate came March 2 on an amendment that would have scrapped the agreements and substituted a public loan. The opposition, which in the past had managed at best to garner about twenty-five anti-Haussmann votes, had a dangerously large ninety-seven to the government's 141. Rouher again feared for his majority, and he went through the corridors and lobbies buttonholing individual members and threatening to resign if the agreements were not approved. The revolt developed no further. Two days later in the ballot on Article 1 of the law the minority vote dropped to sixty-nine, and in the final vote on the entire law on March 6 it fell to forty-one.[56]

Rouher avoided defeat on a crucial issue, but he paid a heavy price. He was forced to accept the examining committee's proposal requiring legislative approval of the city's public works budget each year, and he promised a halt to extra-budgetary financing by term contracts and delegation bonds or

53 *Moniteur*, Feb. 27, 1869.   54 *J.O.*, Mar. 3, 1869.
55 *J.O.*, Mar. 3, 4, 1869; *Moniteur*, May 3, 1862.
56 *J.O.*, Mar. 3, 5, 7, 1869; *Moniteur*, Mar. 6, 1869; *Times*, March 8, 1869.

by the Public Works Fund. To mollify critics of the *Crédit foncier* he accepted a provision in the law authorizing the city to float a public loan to pay off the *Foncier* immediately.

The opposition, though it had failed to block passage of the law, had won a political victory. In forcing the government to public admission that one of its highest officials had been guilty of financial irregularities it had added appreciably to the mounting discredit of the regime and surely contributed to the surprising success of opposition candidates in the general elections a few weeks later.

After Rouher's admission of "irregularities" on February 26, rumor spread that Haussmann had resigned, but all who knew him recognized it as false, for he was not a man to surrender without a battle. When the Paris-*Crédit foncier* bill came before the Senate he could speak for himself, and there, as in his talk with Persigny back in 1853, he apologized for nothing. He slashed back at Thiers and chided Rouher, and in a long and surprisingly dispassionate review of his financing of the rebuilding of Paris he admitted no illegal actions nor any irregularities.[57] He closed with a peroration defying the critics of himself and the Municipal Council:

When we leave the City Hall we shall leave it as we entered, head high and heart firm, as men of virtue, as men of honor, as faithful servants, with courage and resolution, and with loyalty and devotion above reproach.[58]

Haussmann stayed on in the City Hall through 1869, head high as usual but with hands tied. He successfully floated a 250,000,000 franc loan in May, 1869, to pay part of the debt to the *Crédit foncier*. The Rothschilds, the Mallets, and other conservative banking houses participated in it, apparently glad to lend money to an administration they had so lately condemned. Perhaps by now they objected less to Haussmann's policies than to the loss of business those policies had caused them. The *Crédit foncier* had grown fat on lending to the city while the old banks were excluded. Now they were having

[57] *Times*, Mar. 2, 1869; *J.O.*, April 14, 1869.
[58] *J.O.*, Apr. 14, 1869.

their revenge on the *Crédit foncier* as they had on those other interlopers, the *Crédit mobilier* and the Pereires in 1867.[59]

Their expression of confidence in the city's credit must have been gratifying to Haussmann, but the loan, all earmarked for redemption of the debt owing to the *Crédit foncier*, did not give him the means to continue the rebuilding of Paris. For expenditure on public works he had only the budgetary surplus. The Public Works Fund was incompatible with parliamentary control of municipal spending, and by a decree of April 19, 1869, the Emperor ordered its dissolution. The government had pledged that term contracts and delegation bonds would not be used again, and Haussmann, deserted by the Emperor in the critical debates of February, 1869, could no longer defy both the ministers and the Legislative Body. At the same time Haussmann lost these weapons from his financial armory the full burden of the city's accumulated indebtedness fell for the first time on the municipal budget. The amortization of the Loan of 1865 began in 1869, and in the same year the city had to start the annual payments on its debt to the *Crédit foncier*. The budget of 1869 made provision for interest and amortization charges adding up to nearly 63,000,000 francs, more than a third of the city's ordinary revenues.[60] In his annual budget message delivered to the Municipal Council at the end of October, 1869, the unhappy Prefect, referring to public works, declared, "It will be possible to undertake only very modest projects."[61]

Throughout that same difficult year of 1869 the course of national politics made Haussmann's position increasingly tenuous. In the general elections at the end of May the opposition candidates won more votes than ever before, and they took nearly two-thirds of the seats in the new Legislative Body. The Emperor hesitated between concession and repression, but the liberal and impatient temper of the new legislature was unmistakable, and in July he decided for the way of concession.

---

59 *J.O.*, Nov. 28, 1869; Haussmann, *Mémoires*, II, 334-35; Girard, *Politique*, p. 378.
60 *J.O.*, Apr. 23, Nov. 28, 1869, Aug. 12, 1870; Haussmann, *Mémoires*, II, 403; Cadoux, *Finances*, pp. 72-73; Arch. nat., C 1034, Dossier No. 140.
61 Arch. nat., C 1145, Dossier No. 259-60.

On July 12, he told the deputies he would shortly propose to the Senate constitutional amendments substantially increasing the powers of the Legislative Body and making the Senate a second house of parliament. After the amendments were formally adopted and promulgated in September, 1869, the Emperor opened negotiations with Emile Ollivier, one of the original five opposition deputies elected in 1857, to enter the government. Ollivier insisted on conditions that would make him a veritable prime minister and the cabinet a parliamentary ministry. Napoleon was not prepared to go that far, but when the Legislative Body met for its regular session at the end of November, and a majority endorsed a demand for a responsible ministry, free elections, and a free press, he changed his mind. Without the support of this center, constitutional bloc in the assembly the Emperor could count on only a minority of about eighty votes. His choice was between satisfying the majority or dissolving the Legislative Body, and the latter course would solve his dilemma only if he used repressive measures to assure the election of favorable candidates. Again he chose concession, and on December 27 invited Ollivier to form a cabinet of his own choice. Ollivier accepted, took his ministers from the center bloc in the house, and announced that he would resign if he lost the support of the majority.

Haussmann watched these developments with grave misgivings. He had no sympathy with parliamentary government, and when the Emperor consented to the establishment of the Ollivier ministry Haussmann declined to remain as prefect even long enough to see the budget of 1870 through the Legislative Body, so determined was he to avoid even the appearance of being associated with the new parliamentary regime. Four days after the Emperor formally appointed the ministry the official journal carried a decree designating a new Prefect of the Seine, "replacing the Baron Haussmann, who is relieved of his duties."[62]

This terse decree would have been a colorless finale to a dramatic career, but Haussmann contrived to go out of office

[62] Haussmann, *Mémoires*, II, 536-37; Emile Ollivier, *L'Empire libéral* (Paris, 1895-1918), XII, 358-59; *J.O.*, Jan. 6, 1870.

with a flourish. On the morning of January 10, Haussmann's last day at the City Hall, the new Minister of the Interior held a reception for officials of his department. Haussmann assembled the members of the Prefectoral Council, the subprefects, and the heads of the various services in the municipal and departmental governments, and in the dress uniform of his office he led them to the city's ceremonial carriages drawn up before the City Hall. With an escort of the Paris Guard in full uniform the gilded carriages, each with liveried drivers and footmen, moved in procession across the city to the Ministry of the Interior on the Place Beauveau. Entering the ministry the Prefect, followed by his staff, strode through the first rooms "filled with a crowd that opened before me as it might before the ghost of Banquo." Ushered into the presence of the Minister, Haussmann ranged his staff in a semi-circle around him and in a few words presented them to the Minister and pledged their devotion to the Empire. The Minister replied sympathetically, expressing his admiration for the Prefect. Haussmann added a few words, then turned and led his party from the room, followed by the staff of the ministry, who crowded around to shake his hand and to express their admiration and respect.[63] "So it was," Haussmann wrote of the occasion, "that I retired from active duty, as I had promised my peers, the Senators of the Empire: head high and heart firm."[64]

The controversial prefect was gone, and all those who opposed him should have been well pleased, but the great building projects that had been the source of employment and prosperity in Paris were gone, too. The number of condemnations for public works, at a peak of 848 in 1866, fell to thirty-nine in 1869 and to eight in 1870. In the spring of 1870 the new Prefect of the Seine asked for authority to float a loan of 250,000,000 francs to be used in part to finance a modest program of public works over the next seven years. The ministry endorsed the request, and the Legislative Body's committee on the Parisian public works budget approved, but before the proposal was brought to the floor of the parliament, petitions for more public works rained down on both government and

63 Haussmann, *Mémoires*, II, 558-61.   64 *Ibid.*, p. 561.

legislature. Builders, construction workers, property owners, and business men by the hundreds urged immediate revival of the generous program of earlier years, and from every corner of the city residents protested the indispensability of completion of suspended projects in their districts. At the end of June the council of ministers took the initiative in proposing an additional municipal loan of 140,000,000 francs to finance completion of two of Haussmann's major projects, the Avenue de l'Opéra and the Boulevard Saint-Germain, and a few lesser projects. The legislative committee quickly gave its consent, but other events shortly ended all hopes for an early revival of public works.[65]

The day before the city's budget came before the Legislative Body France declared war on Prussia. Committee and ministry dropped the recommendations on loans and eliminated most of the appropriations for new public works, but even war did not still the popular demands. Deputies protested that the revised budget would throw 100,000 construction workers out of jobs, and the government agreed to restore some of the cuts. But within eight weeks after the approval of the budget Paris was besieged, its energies and resources concentrated on survival.[66]

[65] Halbwachs, *Expropriations*, p. 188; Arch. nat., C 1145, Dossier No. 259-60, C 1147, Corps législatif, Session 1870, Dossier No. 259-60; *J.O.*, Apr. 5, May 28, June 10, 1870.

[66] *J.O.*, July 20, 1870; Arch. nat., C 1145, Dossier No. 259-60.

IX · PARIS IN 1870 AND AFTER

WHEN the Second Empire fell in September, 1870, a few months after Haussmann's removal from office, Louis Napoleon had achieved his ambition to build a new Paris. In diplomacy and war he was one of the great failures of history, and he died in 1873 a disappointed and unhappy man, but from the old Paris to which he came in 1848 he had fashioned a monumental city that won acclaim in his own time, became a model for city designers throughout the world, and has continued to excite admiration for nearly a century.

In 1870 a few of the well-known streets of the present city remained to be finished—among them the Avenue de l'Opéra, the Boulevard Saint-Germain, the Boulevard Raspail, and the Rue du Louvre. Later administrations completed them as Napoleon and Haussmann had planned, but they added few streets that were neither started nor suggested by the Emperor or the Prefect. In the twentieth century relaxed building regulations permitted structures of varying heights with many-storied roofs that marred the harmony of imperial avenues, but except for a few landmarks like the Church of the Sacré-Coeur and the Eiffel Tower the new buildings erected since 1870 have not fundamentally altered the characteristic appearance of the city. The open spaces that today help make life tolerable in a city of apartment dwellers were all there by 1870, from the two great *bois* on east and west to the dozens of neighborhood parks scattered about the city. Below ground, succeeding prefects have installed more water mains, more sewer lines, and added sanitary sewers, but the essentials of the systems were established during the Empire, and the later regimes have only carried on the work of Haussmann and Belgrand. Tourists still flock to the sewers in the summer months, and the city still proudly displays to them Belgrand's great sewer gallery, the General Collector of Asnières under the Rue Royale.

Napoleon III's reputation rests largely on aspects of his career quite apart from his work in Paris, but in summing up the credits and debits of his entire record one must enter a large item of credit for the breadth of his conception of a new Paris, for his backing of Haussmann against a multitude of oppositions, and for his seeing the transformation of the city through almost to the end before he yielded under the heaviest pressure to sacrifice Haussmann. He can be condemned for failing to support the Prefect on some individual issues— the Somme-Soude water project and the Méry cemetery, for example,—and for his final consent to Rouher's attempt to shift the blame for operations in delegation bonds solely on to Haussmann's shoulders. But in an imperfect world his record is not bad. In some matters of detail, moreover, he demonstrated unusual foresight. His insistence on unconventional design for the pavilions of the Central Markets was both farsighted and courageous. His planning of new streets was sufficiently advanced that only a century later in a quite different situation did it appear seriously defective.

Haussmann's place in history depends on his work in Paris. But even though the field of judgment is narrowed he is not easily judged, for his career and his personality are obscured by clouds of partisan passion difficult to penetrate.

That he had many enemies is not surprising. He was high-handed and occasionally ruthless in dealing with opponents and even with his colleagues. "Haussmann had the impudent manner of a lackey of a rich household," wrote Napoleon's prime minister, Emile Ollivier. "But," Ollivier added, "he possessed the qualities of a first rate administrator."[1] His impatience and occasional petulance were perhaps only expressions of a vigor essential to his job. A mild and patient man could not have rebuilt Paris in seventeen years.

His financial methods were unwise in that they got him into political difficulties that obstructed his work, but no charge of illegal financial operations was successfully maintained against

[1] Emile Ollivier, *L'Empire libéral* (Paris, 1895-1918), III, 86.

him. At worst his use of deferred payment contracts and delegation bonds was irregular, and one may ask if he could have completed the Second and Third Networks had he clung to methods that everyone, including the conservative and unimaginative Orleanists, would have regarded as "regular" procedure. For him the ends he aspired to achieve justified his means so long as the means were legal; and an image of twentieth century Paris without Haussman's streets, parks, water supply, and sewers suggests that he was probably right. In 1882 Jules Simon, one of his implacable critics in the 1860's, declared, "It is of little importance to us today that the accounts of Haussmann were fantastic. He had undertaken to make Paris a magnificent city, and he completely succeeded."[2] Nothing less than what he did would have saved Paris from pestilence arising from antiquated sewers and contaminated water and from growing paralysis in the medieval street system. If New York City should continue to grow as at present in a manner so disproportionate to the capacity of its streets, its citizens may wish for a man with Haussmann's determination and his disregard of the orthodox rules.

The charges that Haussmann enriched himself personally by graft or by unethical speculation in Parisian real estate are without foundation. Léon Say in one of his pamphlets hinted that the Prefect was taking a quarter of a million francs annually from the municipal budget in addition to his salary and expense account, and Raspail in 1870 implied that Haussmann had made a "scandalous fortune" while in office, but neither offered any proofs, and the political motivation of their charges is obvious.[3] According to a much repeated story the Baroness Haussmann gave her husband away by a naive complaint that no sooner did he buy a house than it was condemned and demolished, twenty-seven houses being demolished just after he acquired them. Haussmann was using official information, his enemies concluded, to make huge profits from indemnities

---

[2] *Le Gaulois*, May 1882, quoted by G. E. Haussmann, *Mémoires* (Paris, 1890-93), II, ix.
[3] Léon Say, *Examen critique de la situation financière de la ville de Paris* (Paris, 1866), pp. 124-26; *Journal officiel de l'Empire français*, Jan. 11, 1870.

for his properties. The story owes its currency to Nassau Senior, the English economist, who published a book of interviews with "distinguished persons" of the Second Empire, and he got it from a disgruntled Orleanist.[4] The charge is no more credible than Say's or Raspail's. The Prefect did draw a large salary, and he had a generous expense account, but the expenses of his office were heavy, and there is nothing in his subsequent career, when he lived in modest retirement, to indicate that he had acquired a fortune in office.

By any standard his material accomplishment in Paris was impressive. The most telling criticisms that can be brought against it are of its shortcomings, but in his own time he had to fight chiefly those who thought he did too much, not too little. What he did, he accomplished over tremendous opposition, and he had only seventeen years. One may well wonder that he did so well.

The rebuilding of Paris was controversial when it was in progress, and though the political passions that colored judgments in the 1850's and 1860's have cooled, the controversy goes on. Today it is virtually impossible to arrive at a judgment of Napoleon III and Haussmann that will satisfy everyone, from adherents of the sociological point of view in city design, typified by Lewis Mumford, who deplore the "parade streets" and facade architecture of Second Empire Paris, to those, like Henry Hope Reed and Christopher Tunnard, who would rehabilitate the monumentalism of the Ecole des Beaux Arts embodied in Napoleon III's city.

Between one extreme and the other the Emperor and Haussmann are praised and condemned for what they did and for what they failed to do. Driving down the Avenue Foch on a spring morning or relaxing in the Bois de Boulogne on a hot summer's afternoon one can have for them only thoughts of gratitude and praise. Caught in a Parisian traffic jam one damns them for running so many streets into a single *place* and regrets that they did not build underpasses, express highways, and underground garages. Others condemn them, not for failing to

[4] N. W. Senior, *Conversations with Distinguished Persons during the Second Empire from 1860 to 1863* (London, 1880), I, 224.

foresee the future, but for failing to respect the past—for destroying monuments of French architecture and for substituting straight, impersonal avenues for the more intimate and variegated streets of the old city.[5] But Napoleon and Haussmann lived neither in the Middle Ages nor in the twentieth century, and their purposes differed from those of Philip Augustus in the thirteenth century as their purposes and specialized knowledge differed from those of Le Corbusier in the twentieth.

Their professed objectives were to facilitate the maintenance of public order, to provide for growing traffic, to improve living conditions, and to build a beautiful and monumental capital. At the Empire's close they might boast that each had been achieved, though in each case the shortcomings were sufficient to nourish conflicting judgments of their accomplishment.

Even on the success of their efforts to facilitate the maintenance of public order opinions differ. The strategic avenues and the barracks erected at key points did not prevent the Communards from sustaining a resistance against the regular army in 1871 more prolonged than the fight the desperate men of June, 1848, carried on in the maze of old streets in the center of the city. On the other hand, Haussmann's destruction of narrow and winding streets did make the raising of barricades much more difficult, and the wide military access avenues almost eliminated for barricade fighters any chance of ultimate success. The Third and Fourth Republics have been largely spared the recurrent street fighting that plagued the July Monarchy. Since 1870 no regime in France has been overthrown by insurrection in the streets of Paris.

To many contemporaries Napoleon's and Haussmann's new boulevards and avenues appeared to be extravagantly wide for any conceivable requirements of traffic, and some of them, whatever their width, seemed useless. Who would ever want to go from the Bourse to the Opera, critics asked, so why build the Rue du 4 Septembre? But Haussmann did build it, and his critics saw in it another example of imperial extravagance. Yet the selection of new avenues was not unreasonable, and the

[5] See, for example, Georges Pillement, *Destruction de Paris* (Paris, [c. 1941]).

decisions for generous dimensions certainly proved astute. The street system of 1870 served the city well for nearly a century, and only with the great influx of automobiles since World War II have streets become clogged. One may regret that the Emperor and Haussmann did not build for the automobile age, but to build for eighty years in the nineteenth and twentieth centuries is no mean achievement. When Napoleon was planning his new avenues and boulevards a traffic count of 12,000 vehicles a day (on a congested street leading to the Strasbourg Railway Station) was considered high. A century later in 1950, 79,000 cars a day were counted passing through the Place de l'Alma and 62,000 through the Place Saint-Augustin.[6] At a time when the internal combustion engine had not yet been invented and assembly lines were unheard of, no one could have foreseen such a revolutionary increase.

Some defects in the street system, however, are not owing solely to the unpredictable expansion of traffic. The great *places* with radiating avenues, the Place de l'Etoile and the Place de la République, for example, concentrate traffic, create centers of congestion, and slow down movement. Broad avenues terminating on monumental buildings provide majestic vistas, but the monuments interrupt the free flow of traffic. The main arterial streets, the Rue de Rivoli and the Boulevard de Sébastopol and its continuations on both sides of the river, were from the start burdened with a dual function: to carry the main streams of traffic across the city and to serve as major shopping and business streets, and as volume of traffic increased the two proved to be ill-compatible. Shoppers on foot or in carriages or automobiles obstructed through traffic, and through traffic made local movement nerve wracking and hazardous. Streets to carry cross-town traffic around business and residential districts would have been more desirable.

The two centers of maximum congestion in Paris today are the neighborhood of the Central Markets in the mornings and the approaches to the Saint-Lazare Station in the evenings. In a sense Napoleon and Haussmann are responsible for both— they built the markets on their present site in the heart of the

[6] *Vie urbaine* (Paris), No. 62 (Oct.-Dec. 1951), p. 310.

city, and they left the Saint-Lazare Station inadequately served with approach streets. Neither, however, had a decisive voice in the location of the markets. The first Napoleon made the original decision to build in the center of the city, and the Municipal Council reaffirmed his choice in 1846 and again in 1851. Work actually started before Haussmann became Prefect of the Seine and while Napoleon was President of the Republic, without personal authority over the municipal government. The site is now, however, so obviously unfortunate that one might condemn Napoleon and Haussmann for not moving it in 1853 before they started work on their iron and glass pavilions, but by that time the city, having acquired and cleared most of the land, had a heavy stake in the site. Only a few years earlier, moreover, the Municipal Council had weighed the advantages of a peripheral site and decided against a move. The location chosen had been the center of Parisian markets for centuries, and the forces of habit and vested interest opposing any change were strong. In 1853 the retention of the central site was probably the only practical course. It was probably the correct course, too, for any other might have seriously disrupted the provisioning of the city.

Napoleon's and Haussmann's failure to build a broad street approaching the Saint-Lazare Station, like the Boulevard de Strasbourg for the Eastern Station, is less readily explained. The Emperor's plan made no provision for it. Haussmann thought of the Rue Auber and the Rue du Havre as access streets, but by his usual standards the latter was narrow, and station bound traffic on it had to cross the Rue Saint-Lazare in front of the station at a point where half a dozen converging avenues poured vehicles into that street. It was a defect in planning that should have been apparent at the time. Napoleon and Haussmann, usually so concerned with the needs of traffic at the new railway stations, were strangely indifferent or niggardly in their solution here, and for their error Parisians now pay in traffic congestion. The Prefect of Police has recently proposed the drastic solution of moving the entire station westward to the peripheral quarter of Les Batignolles.[7]

[7] *Vie urbaine*, No. 62, p. 312.

Much of the criticism of the imperial transformation of the city has been directed at its artistic shortcomings, a development that puzzled and dismayed Haussmann. He was proud of his good taste and his artistic abilities, and his defense of his aesthetic judgment has a plaintive tone wholly lacking in his usual disdainful blasts at critics of other aspects of his work. But for him good city design was a relatively mechanical matter: one need only know the rules and apply them. From French official architecture of the two preceding centuries he took as his basic rule the classical prescription of a straight avenue, preferably lined with uniform facades, and terminating on a monumental building. Applying it he gave Paris many impressive vistas—the Avenue de l'Opéra terminating on the new opera house, the several avenues converging on the Arch of Triumph of the Etoile and on the column of the Place de la Nation, and many others. But more subtle aspects of design— the proportion of buildings to streets, the unity of site and structure, the effects of light and shade—eluded him. A little knowledge and a little taste are both dangerous things, and in Haussmann they produced for Paris some avenues that are dull and monotonous and some combinations of streets and monuments that cannot bear critical scrutiny. The western portion of the Boulevard Malesherbes is but little more inspired than a barracks street in a military camp. In Haussmann's time it and others like it where the city prescribed uniform facades were enlivened by gilded iron work on balconies and by colored awnings, but the monotonous uniformity could not be hidden. The Place de l'Etoile, in which Haussmann took great pride, is certainly not dull, but it is a mechanical conception, and it is out of all human proportion. From ground level the observer has no impression of architectural unity, partly because the curving surface obstructs the view across the vast *place* and also because the *place* is far too big to be encompassed in a single view. It is impressive by its size, but aesthetically it is much less satisfying than the more subtly designed Place Vendôme or the Place de la Concorde. The frequency with which it is shown in aerial views confirms its defects; one can see it properly only from the air.

217

The Tribunal de Commerce on the Ile de la Cité, which was Haussmann's terminus for the Boulevard de Sébastopol, has no functional relationship with the boulevard. The line of the thoroughfare cuts the site obliquely, and the building faces on another street. The dome, which the architect was instructed to build on the boulevard's axis, looks like an afterthought added on a building quite complete without it.[8] It is too small for the long vista and is usually lost in haze or hidden by leaves of the trees lining the street.

The Opera House, though certainly monumental, is poorly integrated with the Avenue de l'Opéra. It is too large for its site, and it runs over the sides of the frame provided by the buildings adjoining the avenue. In the opposite direction Haussmann aligned the street on the cupola of the Pavillon de la Bibliothèque of the new Louvre, but that pavilion actually faces on the Rue de Rivoli and lacks any functional connection with the Avenue de l'Opéra. The avenue is terminated by the Hôtel du Louvre, and as one moves southward along it the pavilion's cupola disappears behind the hotel building.

These deficiencies reflect both Haussmann's mechanical conception of design and his concern with traffic. He thought of the streets first as traffic arteries, then sought architectural embellishments that might be attached to them, and too often the embellishments, an American critic observed, looked like "ornaments pinned here and there on the breast of Paris."[9]

The architecture of these "ornaments," the official architecture of the Second Empire, has had its share of critics, too. In the eyes of many observers it is excessively bound to the classical forms of the French academic tradition as taught at the Ecole des Beaux Arts, and to others it is ostentatious. Both characteristics are unquestionably there, and both have roots in Napoleon III's France. Napoleon perhaps deliberately encouraged the revival of architectural forms associated with the great days of the monarchy before the Revolution in order to make up for the lack of legitimate tradition behind his own

8 *Revue générale de l'architecture et des travaux publics* (Paris), XXIII (1865), 248.

9 Joseph Hudnut, *Architecture and the Spirit of Man* (Cambridge, Mass., 1949), p. 172.

throne. Certainly these forms were revived in the new buildings of the Louvre, which he began immediately after his
seizure of power, and they established the official style of the
regime. The style differed from its models in its opulence and
over elaboration, but these new characteristics were honestly
expressive of the prosperous and materialistic decades of the
Second Empire. Charles Garnier is frequently condemned for
the artistic extravagances of the Opera House, but his rivals,
products of the same age and the same training, submitted
designs that were as lavish as his. In dealing with more purely
utilitarian problems, however, the same architects created
simple and functional buildings like the pavilions of the Central
Markets and the livestock markets in La Villette. For this fresh
development in the architecture of the Second Empire, Louis
Napoleon, together with Haussmann, is in part responsible,
because he helped force the architects from their academic
grooves.

Both the Emperor and the Prefect were anxious to improve
living conditions in Paris, and declining death rates and the
disappearance of cholera attest to a measure of success for their
efforts, although other factors, too, contributed to these happy
results. On the other hand, though they destroyed old slums,
they failed to take adequate precautions against the rise of new
ones, nor did they protect residence areas from the encroach-
ment of industry. If their accomplishment is measured against
Lewis Mumford's ideal environment for urban living—with
abundant housing space for growing families and accumulating
possessions and plenty of adjoining outdoor space for recreation
—it was certainly deficient. But their judgment of what urban
architecture and planning should accomplish differed from
Mumford's. Mumford tends to judge architecture and city
design on the basis of their social utility, insisting that the
aesthetic element be organically related to structure and to
social use. Haussmann and Napoleon were prone to treat architecture as an artistic overlay that would provide a fitting back-
drop for the imperial pageant. Mumford, moreover, has a
fundamental dislike of the big city and would remake it to
recapture some of the tranquillity and privacy of a small town.

Napoleon and Haussmann frankly accepted Paris and tried to make it beautiful and monumental as a city.

For guidance they turned to the classical tradition of city design that stemmed from the Italian Renaissance and seventeenth and eighteenth century France. Their critics claim that in applying the prescriptions of classical designers they revived conceptions of city planning that were already outmoded in their own time and perpetuated them in an age to which they were quite unsuited. By the middle of the nineteenth century the conditions that determined classical ideas of city design were disappearing, and industrialization and improved transportation were producing a new kind of city with other needs. Second Empire Paris, somewhat like the Chicago World's Fair of 1893 in American architecture, gave vogue to old ideas and discouraged the acceptance of new ideas more suitable to the industrial era.

Napoleon's and Haussmann's revival of classical city planning did, nonetheless, perform two valuable services. It demonstrated that a big city can be beautiful, even magnificent, and gave heart to all who rebelled against the drab ugliness of industrial cities and against the chaos of the spreading metropolises of the nineteenth and twentieth centuries. It also demonstrated to city planners of whatever persuasion that civic architecture must be conceived on a grand scale, that the relationship of buildings to each other is at least as important as the design of individual structures. The influence of this lesson can be seen in Brussels, Rome, Mexico City, Washington, and other cities where the Emperor's and Haussmann's work was copied, and in America Daniel Burnham, a leader in the City Beautiful movement, passed it on to his followers. "Make no little plans," he wrote. "They have no magic to stir men's blood and probably themselves will never be realized. Make big plans; aim high in hope and work. . . ."[10] These were words that Louis Napoleon might have used to admonish the Prefect Berger, or Haussmann to exhort the Municipal Council.

The classical tradition was, however, only a part of their con-

[10] Charles Moore, *Daniel H. Burnham, Architect, Planner of Cities* (Boston, 1921), II, 147.

ception of city planning. First among practical planners and
builders Napoleon and Haussmann thought not only of the
vistas and façades of a "parade city" but also of the needs of
traffic, of water supply and sewers, of slum clearance and open
space. Here they were concerned as no planners before them
with social utility, and particularly in their parks, the collector
sewers, and the new water supply they made to Paris and to
city planning sociological contributions of the first order.

One cannot deny that Paris falls short of being a model of
efficient urban design nor that it is less than an ideal environment for family life, but those are not the only criteria by
which a city must be judged. Beauty is important, too, and to
the great majority of men Paris is one of the two or three most
beautiful cities in the world. Its beauty has inspired much
creative activity, it has contributed beyond all measure to the
happiness of generations of residents and of thousands of
visitors, and most men find its beauty in the boulevards and
parks and monumental vistas that are in large part the work of
Napoleon III and Baron Haussmann.

BIBLIOGRAPHY

I. ARCHIVES

1. National Archives, Paris
   Series 45 AP: Boxes 1-3, 19, 24.
   Private papers of Rouher, Napoleon III's Minister of State.

   Series BB³⁰: 371 Amiens, (1859-64); 373 (Besançon), 1851-69; 378 (Limoges), 1851-68; 383, 384 (Paris), 1850-68; 386 (Rennes), 1851-68; 389 (Rennes), 1868-69; 390 (Rennes), 1869-70.
   Reports of procurers-general to the Minister of Justice.

   Series C: Boxes 993, 1042, 1054, 1058, 1059, 1063, 1065, 1067, 1070, 1072, 1077, 1088, 1102, 1133, 1134, 1145, 1146, 1147; 1852-70.
   Papers of the Legislative Body.

   Series F¹ᶜIII: Côtes-du-Nord 11 (1852-70); Creuse 8 (1852-70); Haute-Saône 9 (1851-70); Marne 9 (1858-60); Seine 30, 31 (1852-70); Seine-et-Marne 6, 7 (1850-70); Yonne 11 (1858-66).
   Reports of prefects to the Minister of the Interior.

II. PERIODICALS

1. NEWSPAPERS

a. Parisian
   Le Globe (Paris), April 1832.
   Le Journal officiel de l'Empire français (Paris), 1869-70.
   Le Moniteur universel (Paris), 1847-69.
   Le Siècle (Paris), 1852-70.
   Le Temps (Paris), December 1867-May 1868.
b. Provincial and foreign
   L'Abeille de la Creuse (Guéret), 1853-54.
   Le Conciliateur: journal des intérêts de la Creuse (Guéret), 1851-54, 1863, 1867-70.
   L'Echo de la Creuse (Guéret), 1851-54, 1867-68.
   Journal de la Haute-Saône (Vesoul), 1851-52, 1857, 1859-60.
   Journal de la Seine-et-Marne (Meaux), 1851-54, 1860.
   Journal de Vitré (Vitré, Ille-et-Vilaine), 1851-52, 1863, 1868-70.

Le Mémorial de la Creuse (Aubusson), 1850-52.
Le Mémorial de l'Arrondissement de Figeac (Figeac, Lot), 1851-56, 1859-63, 1867-68.
La Presse bretonne (Guingamp, Côtes-du-Nord), 1851-52, 1861-63, 1866-67.
La Presse gravloise (Gray, Haute-Saône), 1851-52, 1861, 1863.
The Times (London), 1868-69.

2. MAGAZINES

Annales des Ponts et Chaussées: mémoires et documents (Paris), 1831-81.
The Builder: An Illustrated Weekly Magazine for Architect, Engineer, Archeologist . . . (London), 1848-70.
L'Echo agricole (Paris), January-April 1860.
Revue des deux mondes (Paris), 1850-70.
Revue générale de l'architecture et des travaux publics (Paris), 1849-73.
Revue municipale et Gazette réunies (Paris), October 20, 1861-February 26, 1862.
La Vie urbaine (Paris), 1919-52. (Publication suspended 1940-50.)

III. MEMOIRS AND OTHER PUBLICATIONS OF CONTEMPORARIES

Alphand, Adolphe, *Les Promenades de Paris, histoire-description des embellissements-dépenses de création et d'entretien des Bois de Boulogne et de Vincennes, Champs-Elysées-parcs-squares-boulevards-places plantées*. Paris, 1867-73. 1 vol. text and atlas.
Arnault, Antoine, *Souvenirs d'un sexagénaire*. Paris, 1833. 4 vols.
Bailey, George H., *Report to the Newark Aqueduct Board upon the Subject of a Supply of Water*. Newark, N.J., 1861. 64 pp.
Baltard, V., and F. Callet, *Monographie des Halles centrales de Paris construites sous le règne de Napoléon III*. Paris, 1863. 36 pp. 36 plates.
Balzac, Honoré de, *La Cousine Bette (Oeuvres complètes de Honoré de Balzac, XVII)*. Paris, 1910-12.
Beaumont-Vassy E. F. de, *Histoire intime du Second Empire*. Paris, 1874. 413 pp.
Belgrand, Eugène, *Recherches statistiques sur les sources du bassin de la Seine qu'il est possible de conduire à Paris*. Paris, 1854. 86 pp.
———, *Les Travaux souterrains de Paris*. Paris, 1873-77. 5 vols. text. 5 atlases.

Bonaparte, Louis Napoléon, *Oeuvres de Louis Napoléon Bonaparte.* Paris, 1848. 3 vols.

Brame, J., *De l'émigration des campagnes.* Paris, 1859. 176 pp.

Caussidière, Marc, *Mémoires de Caussidière.* 3d ed., Paris, 1849. 2 vols.

Cochin, A., *La Ville de Paris et le Corps législatif.* Paris, 1869. 96 pp.

Dabot, Henri, *Lettres d'un lycéen et d'un étudiant de 1847 à 1854.* 2d ed., Péronne, [1900]. 110 pp.

Daly, César, *Architecture privée au XIXᵉ siècle: nouvelles maisons de Paris et de ses environs.* Paris, 1870. 2 vols.

Daubanton, L. J. M., *Du déplacement de la population de Paris.* Paris, 1843. 54 pp.

Davesiès, Lucien, *Paris tuera la France: necessité de déplacer le siège du gouvernement.* Paris, 1850. 70 pp.

Descauriet, Auguste, *Histoire de la transformation des grandes villes de l'Empire.* Paris, 1863. 467 pp.

Des Cilleuls, A., *Histoire de l'administration parisienne au XIXᵉ siècle,* Paris, 1900. 2 vols.

Du Camp, Maxime, *Paris: ses organes, ses fonctions et sa vie dans la seconde moitié du XIXᵉ siècle.* Paris, 1869-75.

Evans, T. W., *Memoirs of Thomas W. Evans.* New York, 1905. 527 pp.

Ferry, Jules, *Les Comptes fantastiques d'Haussmann.* Paris, 1868. 95 pp.

Fleury, Emile, *Souvenirs du Général Cte. Fleury.* Paris, 1897-98. 2 vols.

Fourier, Charles, *Oeuvres complètes.* Paris, 1841-48, Vol. v.

Fournel, Victor, *La Déportation des morts.* Paris, 1870. 96 pp.

Garnier, Charles, *Le Nouvel Opéra de Paris.* Paris, 1878-81. 2 vols. text. 5 atlases.

Gore, Catherine, *Paris in 1841.* London, 1842. 268 pp.

Granier de Cassagnac, Adolphe, *Souvenirs du Second Empire.* Paris, 1881-84. 3 vols.

Haussmann, G. E., *Mémoires du Baron Haussmann.* Paris, Vol. I, 3d edit., 1890; Vol. II, 1890; Vol. III, 4th edit., 1893.

Houssaye, Arsène, *Les Confessions: souvenirs d'un demi-siècle, 1830-1880.* Paris, 1885. 4 vols.

Hugo, Victor, *Les Misérables.* Vols. v-IX in *Oeuvres complètes, Romans.* Paris, [n.d.].

Husson, Armand, *Etude sur les hôpitaux.* Paris, 1862. 609 pp.

Jarves, J. J., *Parisian Sights and French Principles.* New York, 1852. 264 pp.

Lacour, Louis, *Annuaire général du Département de la Seine pour l'année 1860.* Paris, 1860. 493 pp.

Lavergne, L. D. G. de, *L'Agriculture et la population en 1855 et 1856.* Paris, 1857. 411 pp.

Lazare, Louis, *La France et Paris: études historiques et municipales.* Paris, 1872. 260 pp.

———, *Publications administratives.* Paris, 1862-68. 12 vols.

———, *Les Quartiers de l'Est de Paris et les communes suburbaines.* Paris, 1870. 240 pp.

———, *Les Quartiers pauvres de Paris.* Paris, [1869]. 160 pp.

———, *Les Quartiers pauvres de Paris: le XXᵉ arrondissement.* Paris, 1870. 234 pp.

Legoyt, A., *Du progrès des agglomérations urbaines et de l'émigration rurale en Europe et particulièrement en France.* Marseille, 1867. 280 pp.

Lytton, Edward Bulwer, *Night and Morning.* Philadelphia, 1879. 370 pp.

Merruau, Charles, *Souvenirs de l'Hôtel de Ville de Paris, 1848-1852.* Paris, 1875. 509 pp.

Millaud, Edouard, *Le Journal d'un parlementaire. (De l'Empire à la République, Mai 1864- Février 1875).* Paris, 1914.

Mille, A. A., *Rapport sur la mode d'assainissement des villes en Angleterre et en Ecosse.* Paris, 1854. 33 pp.

Nadaud, Martin, *Les Mémoires du Léonard, ancien garçon maçon.* Paris, [n.d.]. 240 pp.

Ollivier, Emile, *L'Empire libéral: études, récits, souvenirs.* Paris, 1895-1918. 18 vols.

Patte, Pierre, *Monumens érigés en France à la gloire de Louis XV.* Paris, 1765. 232 pp.

Persigny, Fialin, *Mémoires du Duc de Persigny.* Paris, 1896. 512 pp.

Quentin-Bauchart, Ernest, *Etudes et souvenirs sur la Deuxième République et le Second Empire (1848-1870).* Paris, 1901-02. 2 vols.

Rambuteau, Claude, *Memoirs of the Comte de Rambuteau.* New York, 1908. 324 pp.

Say, Léon, *Examen critique de la situation financière de la Ville de Paris.* Paris, 1866. 160 pp.

———, *Observations sur le système financier de M. le Préfet de la Seine.* Paris, 1865. 64 pp.

———, *La Ville de Paris et le Crédit foncier; lettre à MM. les membres de la Commission du Corps législatif.* Paris, 1868, 16 pp.

———, *La Ville de Paris et le Crédit foncier; 2ᵉ lettre . . . Paris,* 1868. 11 pp.

Senior, N. W. *Conversations with Distinguished Persons during the Second Empire from 1860 to 1863.* London, 1880. 2 vols.

Sue, Eugène, *Les Mystères de Paris.* New ed., Paris, [n.d.]. 4 vols.

Trollope, Frances, *Paris and the Parisians in 1835.* London, 1836. 2 vols.

Voltaire, *Oeuvres complètes.* Paris, 1876-78. Vols. v and x.

Zola, Emile, *L'Assommoir.* Paris, [n.d.]. 2 vols.; N.Y., 1924. 437 pp.

————, *La Curée.* Paris, 1922. 387 pp.

IV. MAPS AND GUIDEBOOKS

Atlas des anciens plans de Paris. Paris, 1880. 1 vol. text, 2 vols. plans.

Baedeker, Karl, *Paris und Ungebungen.* Coblenz, 1858. 328 pp.

————, *Paris et la France du Nord.* Coblenz, 1867. 334 pp.

————, *Paris and Northern France.* Leipsig, 1872. 320 pp.

————, *Paris and its Environs.* Leipsig, 1876. 370 pp.

————, *Paris and Environs.* Leipsig, 1884. 379 pp.

Chaix, N., *L'Indicateur des chemins de fer et de la navigation,* No. 595 (Dec. 30, 1860-Jan. 6, 1861), No. 613 (May 5-12, 1861).

————, *Recueil général des tarifs des chemins de fer,* No. 16 (Feb. 1860).

Delvau, A., *Les Plaisirs de Paris; guide pratique et illustré.* Paris, 1867. 299 pp.

Galignani, *New Paris Guide.* Paris, 1845. 548 pp.

————, *New Paris Guide for 1851.* Paris, [1851]. 626 pp.

————, *idem 1854.* Paris, [1854]. 632 pp.

————, *idem 1855.* Paris, [1855]. 632 pp.

————, *idem 1856.* Paris, [1856]. 612 pp.

————, *idem 1861.* Paris, [1861]. 612 pp.

————, *idem 1863.* Paris, [1863]. 612 pp.

————, *idem 1870.* Paris, [1870]. 612 pp.

————, *Illustrated Paris Guide for 1878.* 2d ed., Paris, [n.d.]. 306 pp.

Joanne, Adolphe, *Paris illustrée en 1870 et 1877.* 3d ed., Paris, [n.d.]. 1087 pp.

Joanne, Paul, *Paris.* Paris, 1913. 439 pp.

V. OFFICIAL PUBLICATIONS

Annuaire des eaux de la France pour 1851. Paris, 1851. 315 pp.

Bulletin des lois de la République française, 10th Series, Vol. 9 (1852), 12th Series, Vol. 5 (1872).

Devilleneuve, Carette, and P. Gilbert, *Recueil général des lois et les arrêts,* Années 1861, 1865, 1870.

Documents relatifs aux eaux de Paris. Paris, 1861. 461 pp.

France, Académie des Sciences, *Notice sur les travaux scientifiques de M. Belgrand.* Paris, 1871. 27 pp.

France, Bureau de la Statistique générale, *Annuaire statistique de la France,* IV (1881). Paris, 1881. 644 pp.

———, *Statistique annuelle*, I (1871). Paris, 1873. 461 pp. II (1872). Paris, 1875. 380 pp.

———, *Statistique de la France*. 2d series. Paris and Strasbourg, 1835-73. 21 vols.

France, Ministère de la Justice, *Compte général de l'administration de la justice criminelle en France*. Paris, 1840-71. 32 vols.

New York City, Department of Water Supply, Gas, and Electricity, *A Description of the Water Supply System of the City of New York*. N.Y., 1952. 63 pp.

New York City, Water Supply Board, *The Water Supply of the City of New York*. [N.Y.], 1950. 115 pp.

Paris, *Collection officielle des ordonnances de police*, Vols. V (1845-50), VI (1851-61), VII (1862-74). Paris, 1852, 1865, 1874.

Paris, Administration générale de l'Assistance publique, *Rapport à Monsieur le Préfet de la Seine sur le Service des enfants assistés en 1856*. Paris, 1857. 52 pp.

———, *idem, Année 1866*. Paris, 1867. 31 pp.

Paris, Caisse des Travaux de Paris, *Compte moral et financier des opérations*, Années 1859-69. Paris, 1862-70. 9 vols.

Paris Chambre de Commerce, *Statistique de l'industrie à Paris . . . pour les années 1847-1848*. Paris, 1851. 1209 pp.

———, *Statistique de l'industrie à Paris . . . pour l'année 1860*. Paris, 1864. 1088 pp.

Paris, Commission on Cholera-Morbus, *Report on the Cholera in Paris . . . printed by recommendation of the Board of Health and the Academy of Medicine of the City of New York*. New York, 1849. 198 pp.

Paris, Direction des Affaires municipales, *Bulletin de statistique municipale*, 1865-1872.

Recueil général des lois, décrets et arrêtés depuis le 24 février 1848, Series X, Vols. III-V (1850-1852).

Recueil général des Senatus-consultes, décrets et arrêtés depuis le 2 décembre 1852, Series XI, Vols. I-XVI, 1852-1868.

Seine, Département de la, *Annuaire statistique de la ville de Paris*, I (1880). Paris, 1881. 622 pp.

———, *Extension des limites de Paris*. Paris, 1859. 129 pp.

Seine, Département de la, Bureau des Eaux, Canaux, et Egouts, *Dérivation des sources de la vallée de la Vanne*. Paris, 1871. 86 pp.

Seine, Département de la, Commission d'Extension de Paris, *Aperçu historique*. Paris, 1913. 243 pp.

———, *Considérations techniques préliminaires (la circulation-les espaces libres)*. Paris, 1913. 103 pp. 25 plates.

Seine, Département de la, Direction des Travaux de Paris, *Les Travaux de Paris, 1789-1889: atlas*. Paris, 1889. 8 pp. 16 plates.

Seine Département de la Préfet de Police, *Rapport général sur les travaux du Conseil d'Hygiène et du Salubrité du Département de la Seine*, 1849-58, Paris, 1861, 626 pp.; 1862-66, Paris, 1870, 340 pp.; 1867-71, Paris, 1878, 359 pp.

Seine, Département de la, Service de la Statistique municipale, *Recherches statistiques sur la ville de Paris et le département de la Seine*. Paris, 1826-60. 6 vols.

————, *Résultats statistiques du dénombrement de 1896 pour la ville de Paris et le département de la Seine*. Paris, 1899. 667 pp.

Seine, Préfecture de la, *Documents relatifs aux travaux du Palais de Justice et la reconstruction de la Préfecture de Police*. Paris, 1858. 327 pp. text. atlas.

VI. BOOKS

Aulanier, Christiane, *Le Nouveau Louvre de Napoléon III* (*Histoire du Palais et du Musée du Louvre*, IV). Paris, [1953]. 93 pp. text, 87 illustrations.

Babeau, Albert, *Le Louvre et son histoire*. Paris, 1895. 351 pp.

Bidou, Henry, *Paris*. 5th ed.; Paris, [c. 1937]. 414 pp.

Boon, H. N., *Rêve et réalité dans l'oeuvre économique et sociale de Napoléon III*. The Hague, 1936. 176 pp.

Cadoux, Gaston, *Les Finances de la ville de Paris de 1798 à 1900*. Paris, 1900. 823 pp.

Chapman, J. M. and Brian, *The Life and Times of Baron Haussmann; Paris in the Second Empire*. London, [1957]. 262 pp.

Cheronnet, Louis, *Paris tel qu'il fut; 104 photographies ançiens*. [Paris, c. 1951]. 100 pp.

Chevalier, Louis, *La Formation de la population parisienne au XIXᵉ siècle* (Institut national d'Etudes démographiques, *Travaux et documents*, Cahier No. 10). Paris, 1950. 312 pp.

Christ, Yvan, *Le Louvre et les Tuileries: histoire architecturale d'un double palais*. [Paris, 1949]. 156 pp.

Dans les rue de Paris au temps des fiacres. Paris, 1950. 184 pp.

Dubech, Lucien, and Pierre d'Espezel, *Histoire de Paris*. Paris, 1926. 511 pp.

Dupont-Ferrier, Pierre, *Marché financier de Paris sous le Second Empire*. (Paris, 1925). 245 pp.

Duveau, Georges, *La Vie ouvrière en France sous le Second Empire*. Paris 1946. 605 pp.

Finer, S. E., *The Life and Times of Sir Edwin Chadwick*. London, [1952]. 540 pp.

Gerards, Emile, *Paris souterrain*. Paris, [1908]. 667 pp.

Giedion, Siegfried, *Space, Time and Architecture*. Cambridge, Mass., 1941. 601 pp.

Girard, Louis, *La Politique des travaux publics du Second Empire*. [Paris, 1951]. 415 pp.

Guest, Ivor, *Napoleon III in England*. London, [1952]. 212 pp.

Halbwachs, Maurice, *Les Expropriations et le prix des terrains a Paris (1860-1900)*. Paris, 1909. 416 pp.

Hanmer, L., *Public recreation (Regional survey of New York and its Environs*, Vol. v). New York, 1928. 256 pp.

Hautecoeur, Louis, *Histoire du Louvre*. Paris, [n.d.]. 119 pp.

Hudnut, Joseph, *Architecture and the Spirit of Man*. Cambridge, Mass., 1949. 310 pp.

Lambeau, Lucien, *Histoire des communes annexées à Paris en 1859: Bercy* (Paris, 1910), 505 pp.; *Charonne* (Paris, 1916, 1921), 2 vols.; *Grenelle* (Paris, 1914), 485 pp.; *Vaugirard* (Paris, 1912), 538 pp.

Lavedan, Pierre, *Architecture française*. Paris, [c. 1944]. 256 pp.

———, *Histoire de l'urbanisme*. Paris, 1926-52. 3 vols.

Lesage, Léon, *Les Expropriations de Paris (1866-1890); 1er série, 1866-1870*. Paris, 1913. 622 pp.

Lortsch, Charles, *Le Beauté de Paris et la loi*. Paris, 1912. 297 pp.

Martin, Alfred, *Etudes historiques et statistiques sur les moyens de transport dans Paris*. Paris, 1894. 462 pp.

Mathieu, Mae, *Pierre Patte, sa vie et son oeuvre*. Paris, 1940. 423 pp.

Maurain, Jean, *Baroche, ministre de Napoléon III*. Paris, 1936. 526 pp.

Mondain-Monval, Jean, *Soufflot: sa vie, son oeuvre, son esthétique (1713-1780)*. Paris, 1918. 553 pp.

Moore, Charles, *Daniel H. Burnham, Architect, Planner of Cities*. Boston, 1921. 2 vols.

Morizet, André, *Du vieux Paris au Paris moderne*. Paris, [c. 1932]. 399 pp.

Mumford, Lewis, *City development: Studies in Disintegration and Renewal*. New York, [c. 1945]. 248 pp.

———, *The Culture of Cities*. New York, [c. 1938]. 586 pp.

Pillement, Georges, *Destruction de Paris*. Paris, [c. 1941]. 324 pp.

Raval, Marcel, *Histoire de Paris*. Paris, 1948. 125 pp.

Réau, Louis; Pierre Lavedan et al., *L'Oeuvre du Baron Haussmann, Préfet de la Seine (1853-1870)*. Paris, 1954. 159 pp.

Schmidt, Charles, *Les Journées de Juin 1848* [Paris, c. 1926]. 126 pp.

Schnerb, Robert, *Rouher et le Second Empire*. Paris, 1949. 351 pp.

Simond, Charles, *La Vie parisienne à travers le XIXe siècle: Paris de 1800 à 1900 d'après les estampes et les mémoires du temps*. Paris, 1900-01. 3 vols.

Simpson, F. A., *The Rise of Louis Napoleon.* 3d ed.; London, 1951. 400 pp.

Thomas, E. F., *The Paris We Remember.* New York, 1942. 478 pp.

Tunnard, Christopher, *The City of Man.* New York, 1953. 424 pp.

Tunnard, Christopher; and Henry H. Reed, *American Skyline: the Growth and Form of our Cities and Towns.* Boston, 1955. 302 pp.

Wegmann, Edward, *The Water Supply of the City of New York, 1658-1895.* New York, 1896. 316 pp.

Young, G. M., *Victorian England: Portrait of an Age.* London, 1936. 213 pp.

VII. ARTICLES

(Articles in periodicals listed in Part III of the Bibliography are not listed separately here.)

Ackerknecht, E. H., "Anti-contagionism between 1821 and 1867," *Bulletin of the History of Medicine,* xxii (1948), 562-93.

———, "Hygiene in France, 1815-1848," *Bulletin of History of Medicine,* xxii (1948), 117-48.

Clement, Henry, "Emigrants du Centre de France" *Reforme sociale,* 1st Series, x (1885), 481-490; 2d Series, i (1886) 200-206, 285-291, 354-361.

Foncin, Myriem, "La Cité," *Annales de géographie,* xle Année (1931), 479-503.

———, "Versailles, étude de géographie historique," *Annales de géographie,* xxviiie Année (1919), 321-341.

Harrison, Frederic, "Paris in 1851 and in 1907," *Nineteenth century,* lxii (1907), 282-292.

Kennison, Karl R., "The Development of the Delaware Projects," *Delaware Water Supply News,* xvii (1955), 846-851.

Mille, A. A., "M. Belgrand," *Revue scientifique de la France et de l'étranger,* 2d Series, xiv (1878), 1190-1194.

Musset, R., "La Population et l'émigration bretonne," *Annales de géographie,* xxxiie Année (1923), 185-188.

Pinkney, David H., "Migrations to Paris during the Second Empire," *Journal of Modern History,* xxv (1953), 1-12.

———, "Money and Politics in the Rebuilding of Paris, 1860-1870," *Journal of Economic History,* xvii (1957), 45-60.

———, "Napoleon III's Transformation of Paris: The Origins and Development of the Idea," *Journal of Modern History,* xxvii (1955), 125-34.

Vossen, Franz, "Du Paris de Quasimodo au Paris d'Haussmann," *Annales: économies-sociétés-civilisations,* 2e Année (1947), 385-396.

INDEX

Academy of Fine Arts, 47; of Moral and Political Sciences, 153; of Music, 83

Allée de la Reine Marguerite, 96; de Longchamps, 96

Alphand, Adolphe, rôle in rebuilding of Paris, 45, 46-47; comment on Haussmann, 45; his *Promenades de Paris*, 47; Haussmann brings to Paris, 96; work on parks, 96-97, 100-02, 115

annexation of suburbs, 1860, effect on water needs, 114, 119; and sewer construction, 132; effect on cemetery problem, 145; adds to population of Paris, 152; costs, 166, 184-87 *passim*; law and hearings on, 169, 171-73; preliminary consideration of, 170, 171, 186; mentioned, 99

apartment buildings, residents in, 7, 8-9; typical design of, 91-92

aqueduct, Louis XIV's, 108; of the Somme-Soude, 109, 112-15 *passim*; Roman, 110; of the Vanne, 112, 123-24; of the Dhuis, 119, 121

Architecture polychrome chez les Grècs, L', 25

architecture, of new buildings in Paris, 77-92 *passim*, 218; suburban, 169; official, 218

Arch of Triumph of the Etoile, 62, 217

Arcis quarter, 165

Ardoin, Ricardo et Cie., contracts with city, 193-94, 195

Arrondissements of Paris, Sixth, 10; Eighth, 10; Sixteenth, 11; Twelfth, 50-51, 66

Asnières, Seine, 133. *See also* Collector of Asnières

asphalt, used for paving, 71, 72

Assommoir, L', Zola's novel, 17

attraction of Paris, in provinces, 154-65

Aube, Department of, aqueduct from, 123

Augustus, Emperor, 3, 31, 127

Avenue Daumesnil, 64; de Friedland, 28, 62, 79; de la République, 65, 66, 70; de l'Empereur, 63, 64; de l'Impératrice, 4, 62, 64, 98. *See also* Avenue Foch; de l'Italie, 67; de l'Observatoire, 57, 67

Avenue de l'Opéra, plans and construction of, 28, 60, 70, 84; plans to complete, 209, 210; relation to Opera House, 60, 84, 217, 218; mentioned, 10, 14

Avenue d'Iéna, 188; des Amandiers, 66; des Champs Elysées, 52, 62, 63, 84, 91; des Gobelins, 67; des Villiers, 61; de Wagram, 61, 62, 63; Foch, 62, 98, 213; George V, 63; Georges Mandel, 64; Henri Martin, 64; Kléber, 62, 63; Napoléon, 28, 60. *See also* Avenue de l'Opéra; Victoria, 89; Victor-Hugo, 62

Baltard, Victor, architect of Central Markets, 77-79; of La Villette livestock market, 79; of Church of Saint-Augustin, 79-80

Balzac, Honoré de, 11, 17, 80

Bank of France, loan to Paris, 51, 176; reserves of, 198

banks, opinions on Haussmann's financial methods, 5, 182, 196, 198, 205; opinions on government spending, 175-76, 177-78, 179

Baroche, Pierre Jules, 44

barracks, location of, 36, 75, 88, 214

barricades, insurrectionary in streets, 36, 72, 214

Barillet-Deschamps, chief gardener of Bois de Boulogne, 96

Bastille. *See* Place de la Bastille

Batignolles, Les, Seine, 61, 166, 170, 216

Beauharnais, Prince Eugène de, 41, 43

Beaux Arts. *See* Ecole des Beaux Arts

Belgrand, Eugène, rôle in rebuilding of Paris, 45-46; his *Travaux souterrains de Paris*, 46; Haussmann brings to Paris, 107-08, 112; work on water supply, 108-09, 110, 112-15, 118-22 *passim*; work on sewers, 127-29 *passim*, 131, 133-39, 141-42, 145; recommendation on cemeteries, 146-47; Continuation of his work by successors, 210

Belgian Railway Station, 39. *See also* Northern Railway Station

Belleville, Seine, 20, 101, 114, 116, 166

Belt Railway, 178

Bercy, Seine, 69, 172

Berle River, 113

Berlencourt et Cie., contract with city, 194-95

Berger, Jean Jacques, Prefect of Seine, opposition to Napoleon III's plans, 40-41, 49-50, 53-54, 75, 176; views on public finance, 49-50, 53-54, 176, 180, 181; and Central Markets, 51, 76, 77, 176; and Rue de Rivoli, 51; support in Municipal Council, 54-55, 181; proposes new reservoirs, 105; and sewer construction, 128; floats loan, 176, 177; mentioned, 55, 69, 220

Berryer, Antoine, 197

Bibliothèque Nationale, 14, 25, 75

Bièvre River, and sewer system, 19, 138, 142; aqueduct over, 124. *See also* Collector of the Bièvre

boats, passenger service on Seine, 168

Bois de Boulogne, Napoleon III's plans for, 25, 29, 30, 39; access streets, 27, 62, 64, 98-99; Alphand put in charge of, 27; transformation into municipal park, 52, 94-99, 100, 178; cost of, 99, 100, 101; popularity of, 99, 213; de Vincennes, access streets, 64; transformation into municipal park, 99-100, cost of, 100; suburbs around, 169

Bonaparte, Louis Napoleon. *See* Napoleon III

Bonaparte, Napoleon. *See* Napoleon I

Bondy, Forest of, 21

Bons de délégation. See Delegation bonds

Bordeaux, Gironde, Haussmann in, 41, 42, 43, 47

Boulevard Arago, 67; Auguste Blanqui, 12; Clichy, 69; Denain, 65; de Beaujon, 62; de la Chapelle, 17, 89; de la Madeleine, 61; de l'Hôpital, 12; de Magenta, 39, 64, 65; d'Enfer, 67

Boulevard des Capucines, on line of old city wall, 7; and streets of Second Network, 60; traffic on, 71; Opera House on, 60, 83, 84-85; Grand Hôtel on, 91

Boulevard de Sébastopol, plans and construction of, 27, 57, 58; vistas on, 58, 218; sewer under, 136; traffic on, 215; mentioned, 64; des Italiens, 7; de Strasbourg: plans and construction of, 27, 52, 57, 75, 178; access to railway stations, 39, 65, 216; vistas on, 58; sewer under, 136; du Centre, plans and construction of, 27, 57, 67, 68, 183; du Montparnasse, 27, 39, 138; du Palais, 27, 57; du Prince Eugène, 65, 66, 91, 136. *See also* Boulevard Voltaire; Haussmann, plans and construction of, 28, 62, 188; mentioned, 69, 136; Henri IV, 29; Jules Ferry, 66; Malesherbes, plans and construction of, 61, 101, 217; Pereires build on, 91; collector sewer under, 135, 136; mentioned, 62, 79; Mazas, 36; Montmartre, 28, 62; Ornano, 65, 69; Port Royal, 67; Raspail, 28, 69, 70, 210; Richard Lenoir, 65; Saint-Denis, 52; Saint-Germain, plans and construction of, 26, 28-29, 68, 70; proposals to complete, 209, 210; mentioned, 67; Saint-Marcel, 67; Saint-Michel, 27, 33, 57, 58; Voltaire, plans and construction of, 28, 64, 65; as a military street, 36; mentioned, 136. *See also* Boulevard du Prince Eugène

boulevards, Parisian copied in Mexico City, 4; inner ring of, 6-7, 15, 31, 39, 59; second ring of, 7, 173; proposed new, 28; military purposes of, 35, 36

Boulogne, Seine, 133, 167, 168, 169

Bourbons, ruling house of France, 31

Bourse, 214

bridges, proposed, 28, 29, 69, 190; new, 33. *See also* names of particular bridges under "Pont"

Brodick Castle, Scotland, 25

Buci, Carrefour de, 15

Budget, Municipal of Paris, 174, 180-91 *passim*, 195, 200, 206, 208, 209

Budget Committee of Legislative Body, 83-84, 191

building trades, employment in, 6, 157-63; importance in Parisian economy, 37; depression in, 175, 176, 179

building, private, 56, 75, 90-92, 178

Burnham, Daniel, 2, 220
buses, public, 17-18, 167-68
Buttes-Chaumont, 69, 100-01. *See also* Park of the Buttes-Chaumont

Cabet, Etienne, 30
Caisse des Travaux de Paris. See Public Works Fund
Callet, F., architect of Central Markets, 77, 78
Calley de Saint-Paul, deputy, 203
Canal de l'Ourcq. *See* Ourcq Canal; Saint-Denis, 121; Saint-Martin, 15, 65, 121, 136
Cantal, Department of, 156, 164
Carpeaux, Jean Baptiste, 87
cascades, in parks, 86, 97, 101, 102
cathedral, proposal for new, 32. *See also* Nôtre-Dame, Cathedral of
Ceinture Sewer, 19
cemeteries, proposals for new, 32, 145, 146-48; proposed bridge over Montmartre Cemetery, 69, 190; contaminate wells, 105; situation of, 145-46. *See also* names of particular cemeteries
Central Markets, plans for, 29, 33, 34, 75-76; access streets and traffic around, 28, 39, 56, 64-65, 215; construction of, 38, 51, 77-79, 80; Napoleon III urges start of, 49, 176; financing of, 51, 54, 153, 181; design of, 77-78, 211, 219; dispute over location of, 76-77, 216; mentioned, 56, 84, 165
cesspools, use of in sewage disposal, 19, 20-21, 129, 130, 131, 144, 145; contaminate wells, 105
Chadwick, Edwin, 31, 40, 127, 140
Chaillot water pumps of, 22, 105, 115, 121, 124; and sewer system, 19, 129, 134
Chalons, Marne, 108, 109
Champagne, France, 108, 111, 117
Champs de Mars, 64, 138
Champs Elysées, 8, 93
Chapelle, La, Seine, 166
Chartres, Eure-et-Loir, 108
Chatelet Theater, 76
Chaumont, hill of, 114, 115
cholera, centers of, 9-10, 12-13; epidemics, 23, 89, 123; causes of, 23; Saint-Simonians and, 30; disappearance of, 219
churches, new buildings, 75

City Beautiful movement, 2, 220
City Hall, new streets near, 27, 49, 51, 56, 89, 176; barracks near, 36; construction workers settle near, 157; Haussmann leaves, 205, 208; mentioned, 74, 182
city planning, influence of Napoleon III and Haussmann on, 3-5, 220-21; before Napoleon III, 4-5, 31-32, 220; Haussmann's ideas on, 92-93; judgment of Napoleon III's and Haussmann's, 213-21
Civil List, 99, 101
cleaning, of building exteriors, 93; of sewers, 129, 130, 141-43
Clichy, Seine, 140, 143
Cloaca Maxima, 134
Collector Bosquet, 138; of Asnières, plans and construction of, 133-36, 138, 144, 211; closed to invaders, 140; cleaning of, 142; of the Bièvre, 138, 139, 142; of the Hills, 136; of the Quais, 36, 142; of the Rue de Rivoli, design of, 128-29, 130, 134; plans and construction of, 128-29, 134, 141; mentioned, 135, 136
collector of sewers, in 1850, 19; plans and construction of, 127, 128-29, 133-39, 221; visitors to, 143, 210-11
Comédie Française, 84
Commission of Artists, plan for Paris, 32-33, 34
communards, 214
Commune of Paris, 1871, 151
Compagnie des Immeubles et de l'Hôtel de la Rue de Rivoli, 90-91, 92
Compagnie générale des Omnibus, 167, 168
Comptes fantastiques d'Haussmann, Les, 66, 174, 200-201
Contes fantastiques d'Hoffmann, 174
condemnations for public works, numbers of, 188, 208
condemned property, purchase and resale of, 5, 45, 183, 184, 185, 192, 193
Conservatoire des Arts et Métiers, 36, 58, 65
contractors, private, and construction of Collector of Asnières, 135; contracts for street construction, 192-200 *passim*
contracts, imposing restrictions on purchasers of land, 92-93; for street construction, 192-200 *passim*, 203, 204,

206; deferred payment, 193-200, 203, 204, 206, 212
Corbusier, Le, 214
Corps des Ponts et Chaussées, Alphand and Belgrand in, 46, 96, 107; General Council of, on water supply, 114, 116, 117
Costs of rebuilding Paris, 5, 174
Council of Ministers, Haussmann's relations with, 43, 45; and finances of Paris, 175, 186, 208, 209
Council of State, Haussmann on, 43; in disputes over Haussmann's projects, 60, 83, 118, 201; limits power to condemn property, 185; at debate on Paris-*Crédit foncier agreement*, 202
Coup d'Etat of December 2, 1851, Haussmann appointed to Bordeaux to aid, 42; acceleration of public works after, 51-52, 75; stimulus to business, 177-78; mentioned, 152
Cours la Reine, 52, 168
Court of Accounts, 188
Crédit foncier, rôle in financing rebuilding of Paris, 193-94, 196-206 *passim*; attacks on, 197-98, 204-05; agreement with city of Paris, 1867, 199-205 *passim*
Crédit mobilier, Société générale du, founding of, 179, 180, 181; Pereires lose control of, 199, 206; assistance on municipal loans, 187, 188
Creuse, Department of: contribution to population of Paris, 156, 157-61, 164; Prefect of, 158, 160
crime, in slum areas, 9, 10, 12

Daumier, Honoré, 65
death rate, 24, 219
debt, floating, Public Works Fund creates, 191
Delangle, Claude Alphonse, President of Municipal Council, 54-55
Delegation bonds, 194-99 *passim*; 203, 204, 211, 212
demolitions, displace population, 6, 8, 165; and housing shortage, 165; of *octroi* wall, 173
depopulation, of provincial areas: 153-65
depression, of 1847-1851, 175-77, 178; after 1856, 183

Deschamps, head of Service of the Plan of Paris, 47-48, 56
Des Idées napoléoniennes, 33-34, 50
Devinck, imperialist deputy, 188
Dhuis Aqueduct, 120, 121
Dhuis River, 113, 114, 119-23 *passim*
Dhuis-Surmelin water supply project, 119-23 *passim*
Director of Public Works, 106, 115
Director of Streets and Parks, 47
disease, 9. *See also* Cholera
drought, effect on water supply, 112-13, 120, 121-22, 139
dry goods stores, 164
Duc, Joseph Louis, 88
Dupuit, Director of Public Works, 115, 128, 141

Eastern Railway Station, 58, 65, 69, 216. *See also* Strasbourg Railway Station
Ecole des Beaux Arts, 47, 79, 213, 219; des Mines, 68; Militaire, 64
Eiffel Tower, 3, 210
election of 1852, 50, 177; of 1869, 203, 205, 206
electricity, use in street lighting, 72, 74; wires in sewer galleries, 133
Elysée Palace, 25
emigration, from provinces, 153-65
Epernay, Marne, 109, 118
Eugénie, Empress of the French, 82, 83, 86, 102
Eure River, 108
Europe, Quartier de l', 11
Exposition of 1867, 26, 85, 143, 187
expropriation of property, resistance to, 121

façades, requirement of uniformity in, 63, 92-93
Fantastic Accounts of Haussmann, The, 66, 174, 200-01
Faubourg Saint-Antoine, 36, 66; Saint-Germain, 16
Favre, Jules, 197
"Fermiers généraux, Wall of the," 7
Ferry, Jules, 66, 174, 200-01
fertilizers, in sewage, 140-41, 143-44
filtering, 106-07, 116-17, 118
finance, public, Haussmann's methods of, 6, 54, 148, 174, 180-206 *passim*, 211-12; Napoleon III's views on, 35; Persigny's views on, 45, 54; Berger's

views on, 49-50, 53-54, 176, 180, 181;
of Rue de Rivoli and Central Markets projects, 51, 54, 77, 153; of
Louvre, 52; of street networks, 58-
59; of parks, 99, 100, 101; of water
supply, 110-11, 117, 121, 123, 124; of
national public works, 175
flooding, of streets, 20; of sewers, 20,
129, 139-40, 148
"Fort de la Halle," 77, 79
fortifications, before nineteenth century,
6-7, 169; built in 1840's, 169-70, 172;
and location of collector sewers, 129,
135, 136; shift of population to, 166
Fould, Achille, and new buildings, 82,
85; opposes Haussmann, 187, 188,
198, 199
Fountain of the Innocents, 76
fountains, public, 22-23
Fourier, Francois M. C., 30
Franco-Prussian War, 123, 140, 151
Frémy, Louis, 42-43, 199, 201

Garnier-Pagès, Louis, 202
garbage removal, 19, 130, 131
gardens, private, 7-8; English, in Paris,
94, 103. See also Luxembourg Gar-
den; Tuileries, Garden of
Gare de l'Est. See Strasbourg Railway
Station, Eastern Railway Station; du
Nord. See Belgian Railway Station,
Northern Railway Station; Mont-
parnasse, 28; Saint-Lazare. See Saint-
Lazare Railway Station, Western
Railway Station
Garnier, Charles, 82, 85-87, 219
gas, pipes in sewer galleries, 130
Gennevilliers, Seine, 140, 142
Gironde, Department of, Haussmann
in, 41, 42, 47, 96; Prefect of, 42, 47,
96
Globe, Le (Paris), 30
Gobelins, 67
Goujon, Jean, 76, 82
Grand Hôtel, 91
Great Britain, Napoleon III in, 25;
water supply and sewers in, 109, 143;
mentioned, 127
"Great Crossing" of Paris, 27, 57-58,
183
Grenelle, Seine, 111
Gros-Caillou, 124
Grottoes, 97, 100, 101, 102

Halle aux Blés, 75, 76
Halles Centrales. See Central Markets
Haussmann, Georges Eugène, and city-
planning, 3-5, 26, 29, 58, 61-62, 66,
92, 213-21; opposition to, 5-6, 44, 154,
155, 172, 183, 184, 187-92 passim,
196-205, 211; financial methods of, 6,
54, 148, 174, 180-206 passim, 211-12;
and slums, 8, 32, 33, 93; on Paris of
his youth, 16-17; relations with Napoleon III, 25, 26, 29, 39, 40, 43, 44,
55, 188-90, 203, 206; street planning
and construction, 28-29, 55-59, 60-68,
70, 98, 183, 184, 192; motives of, 35-
36, 59, 66, 67, 214, 219, 221; family
and early career of, 41-42, 53; appointed Prefect of Seine, 41, 43; character and personality of, 45-48, 205,
211; associates of, 46-48; relations
with Municipal Council, 54-55; and
cemeteries, 69-70, 145, 146-48; dismissal of, 70, 207, 210; and street paving, 70-72; and street lighting, 72, 74;
plans and construction of public
buildings, 75, 82-84, 87; rôle in design of Central Markets, 77-79, 219;
creation of parks, 94, 95-99, 101, 104;
personal finances of, 97, 212-13; work
on water supply, 105, 106-22, 130,
131, 133, 136, 144; work on sewers,
127-39 passim, 143-44, 148, 150; and
increasing population, 146, 151, 152,
153-55; and constitutional reforms,
206-07; incomplete projects of, 209;
judgment of, 211-21; artistic taste of,
217-19
Haussmann, Baroness, 212
Haute-Banque, 175
Haute-Saône, Department of, migrations from, 161-62, 164; Prefect of,
161
Hautpoul, Marquis d', 68
highways, relation to Parisian streets,
15, 59, 67, 69
Hittorf, Jacques, 25, 98
Horeau, architect, project for Central
Markets, 76-77
hospitals, 75, 89-90. See also Hôtel Dieu
Hôtel Crillon, 84; des Invalides, 22,
138; Dieu, plans and construction of,
89-90; dispute over size and location
of, 90, 190; mentioned, 75; du Louvre,
91, 218
hotels, 62, 91, 164, 218

horses, 19, 71, 173
housing shortage, 155
Hyde Park, London, 30, 94, 95
Hydrometric Service of the Seine River Basin, 107

idea of rebuilding Paris, origins of, 29-34
Ile de la Cité, description of, 10-16; plans for, 30, 32, 87; new streets on, 57-58, 90; new buildings on, 58, 88-90, 218
Ile Saint-Louis, 32
immigration, into Paris, 152, 153-65
Impasse du Doyenne, 11
indemnities, for property condemned for streets, 6, 57, 185, 192-95 passim; Deschamps and, 48; Pereires ask none for Monceau lands, 61; to proprietors in Dhuis valley, 120-21
industrial districts, 9, 12, 101, 166
Institut de France, L', 15, 16
interest rates, 176, 178, 187
Invalides, Hôtel des, 22, 138
iron, use of in construction, 77-80 passim, 91-92
Ivry, Seine, 146, 166

Jardin des Plantes, as a public park, 8, 93, 102; obstacle to traffic, 15; mentioned, 12, 33, 138
Joanne, Adolphe, 104
Journal des Débats (Paris), 196
June Days of 1848, 37, 214
July Monarchy, improvements in Paris during, 18, 27, 88; Park of Monceau during, 101, 102; construction of new fortifications during, 169-70; economic philosophy of, 179; mentioned, 41, 214

Laffitte, Charles, 106, 128
lakes, in parks, 95-102 passim
Latin Quarter, 15, 16, 27
Lazare, Louis, 154, 155
Left Bank, complains of neglect, 13, 50-51, 52, 82, 85, 102
Legislative Body: opposition to Haussmann, 5, 61, 148, 186, 188-92 passim, 196-206; and Second Network, 59, 162, 183-86 passim, 190; concern over projected opera house, 60, 83; in Luxembourg Garden dispute, 103, 104;

asked to stop Vanne water supply project, 123; and Méry cemetery project, 148; approves annexation of suburbs, 172; and Third Network, 184; approves municipal loans, 182, 186, 187; debate on Paris-Crédit foncier agreement in, 200-04; forces constitutional reform, 206-07; and proposals for public works in 1870, 207, 209; mentioned, 38, 44, 45, 175
Lemercier, Jacques, 82
Lescot, Pierre, 82
lighting, of streets, 18, 32, 72-74; in Central Markets, 79
lighting service, 47, 72
loans, Persigny's views on, 45; municipal loan of 1849, 49; municipal loan of 1851 and 1852, 51, 53, 54, 77, 153, 176, 177-78, 181, 182; municipal loan of 1855, 181-82; municipal loan of 1860, 186-87, 188, 190; municipal loan of 1865, 186, 187-88, 190, 206; of national government, 186; "hidden," 188, 199; municipal of 1869, 205; mentioned, 5, 54
Loire River, 117, 125, 156
London, England, class quarters in, 8; water supply of, 22, 109, 118; influence on Napoleon's plans, 30-31, 39, 52, 94; Great Fire of, 39; Albert Memorial in, 82
Longchamps, Plain of, 95, 96, 98; Cascade of, 97; Villa of, 97; racetrack of, 98, 99
Loubat, tramway engineer, 167-68
Louis Philippe, King of the French, 14, 36
Louis XIV, King of France, demolishes fortifications, 7, 169; authorizes shops on Pont Neuf, 13; and city planning and building, 27, 31; and water supply, 108, 124
Louis XV, King of France, 31
Louis XVI, King of France, 169
Louvre, Palace of, slum adjoining, 10-11; obstacle to traffic, 14, 15; and Rue de Rivoli, 30, 32, 49, 51, 52, 176; plans for completion of, 34, 75, 80-81, 178; clearing of adjoining slum, 52, 178; construction of new buildings of, 80-82; official architecture of, 219; mentioned, 17, 72, 85, 218
Luxembourg Garden, as a public park,

8, 93, 102; obstacle to traffic, 15, 16; reduction in size of, 68, 102-04, 190; mentioned, 33
Luxembourg Palace, 16
Lycée Saint-Louis, 58
Lytton, Edward Bulwer, 9

Macadam paving, 71, 122, 140
Madeleine, Church of, 61
maintenance, of private buildings, 93
Mairie of First Arrondissement, 83
Mallets, bankers, 205
Manhattan Company, 106
maps of Paris, need for, 5; prepared, 56
Market of the Innocents, 76
markets, new buildings, 75. *See also* Central Markets
Markets Quarter, 165
Marne, Department of, 108, 118, 119
Marne River, springs in valley of, 109, 119; aqueduct in valley of, 114, 121; source of water supply, 124, 125
McKim, Charles, 4
Ménilmontant, stream of, 19; reservoir of, 121
Merruau, Charles, 26-27, 29
Méry cemetery, 146-48, 190, 211
Méry-sur-Oise, site of proposed cemetery, 146-47, 190
metal trades, 163
metropolitan area of Paris, 166
Mille, A. A., reports on British water supply and sewers, 109, 143; experiments with sewage as fertilizers, 140-41, 143-44; recommendations on sanitary sewage disposal, 143, 144
Minister of Finance, opposes Haussmann, 187, 188, 198, 199
Minister of Interior, in disputes over public works projects, 76, 102, 118; proposals on public finance, 179; Haussmann's final audience with, 208; mentioned, 161, 202
Minister of Public Works, 112, 118, 202
Minister of State, 81, 82, 197, 202
Ministry of Paris, 43
Misérables, Les, 12, 143
Monceau, Barrière de, 61; Plain of, 61; hill of, 133, 135. *See also* Park of Monceau
Moniteur, Le (Paris), 170, 171, 189, 200
Montfaucon, 100
Montmartre, Seine, 20, 114, 116, 170

Montmartre Cemetery, 69, 145, 190
Montmartre, hill of, 65, 69
Montparnasse Cemetery, 145
Montparnasse Railway Station, 52
Montrouge, Seine, 123, 166
Montrouge reservoir, 123, 124
Montsouris, hill of, 102
Morizet, André, 26
Morny, Duke de, 97-98
Moses, Robert, 40
Mumford, Lewis, 213, 219
motives for rebuilding Paris, political, 34, 37-38, 50, 179; military, 35, 36, 59, 66, 67, 183, 214; embellishment, 38, 214, 218; humanitarian, 38-39, 40, 219; facilitate movement of traffic, 39, 40, 214-16, 218; summary of, 214
Municipal Council of Paris, approves public works program in 1847, 34; relations with Haussmann, 43, 54-55, 181, 182, 187, 205, 206, 220; and fixing indemnities, 48; opposition to public works, 50, 53; pushes Rue de Rivoli project, 51; and location of Central Markets, 76-77, 216; approves site for new Opera House, 84; and water supply, 105, 106, 107, 109, 111, 113, 115-22 *passim*; and sewers, 130, 131, 133, 135, 136, 144; approves purchase of land for Méry cemetery, 147; and annexation of suburbs, 171; approves Second Network project, 183, 184, 185; and Third Network, 184; approves *Crédit foncier* agreement, 199

Nadaud, Martin, 37, 157-58, 160, 166
Napoleon I, Emperor of the French, project for Central Markets, 29, 50, 75, 76, 77, 216; plans and construction of Rue de Rivoli, 14, 27, 49, 50; additions to water supply, 21; neglect of north-south axis, 27; public works in Paris, 33; influence on Napoleon III, 33-34; plans and construction of new Louvre, 80; regulations on cemeteries, 145; mentioned, 41, 85
Napoleon III, Emperor of the French, ambitions for Paris, 3; and city-planning, 3-5, 92, 213-20; slums and slum clearance, 8, 32, 93, 221; as a landscape architect, 25, 94, 100; plans for Paris, 25-29 *passim*, 34-35, 40, 44, 56, 61, 67, 75, 183, 184, 192; relations

with Haussmann, 29, 39, 41, 42, 43, 47, 55, 189; and Central Markets, 29, 51, 75-78, 219; origins of idea of rebuilding Paris, 29-34; influenced by Napoleon I, 33-34; opposition to, 35, 154, 172, 189-90, 198, 206-07; views on rôle of government, 38, 179; motives for rebuilding Paris, 34-40, 50, 66, 95, 179, 183, 214, 219, 221; and presidential election of 1848, 41; conflict with Berger, 49-54 *passim*, 75, 176; revival of public works after *Coup d'Etat*, 52-53, 158, 175, 177, 178; attempted assassination of, 60, 83, 86; surrender at Sedan, 70; and street lighting, 72; and public buildings, 80-82, 86, 90; planning and construction of parks, 94-100, 102, 104; and water supply, 106, 118-19, 123; Chadwick's remark to, 127, 150; limited interest in sewers, 127-28; wishes on cemeteries, 146, 147-48; plans complicated by growing population, 151, 152; and annexation of suburbs, 169, 170, 172; and financing of rebuilding of Paris, 174-80, 188, 189, 190-91, 199, 202; advised by Saint-Simonians, 175, 179; needs to sustain economic boom, 178; asks early completion of Second Network, 187; authorizes addition to Loan of 1865, 187; and opposition to Haussmann, 188-90, 198, 199, 202, 203, 206, 211; poor health of, 198; constitutional reforms of 1869, 206-07; judgment of, 210-11, 213-21, his use of architecture, 219

National Assembly, Napoleon III proposes public works program to, 37; approves continuation of Rue de Rivoli, 49; approves Loan of 1851, 51, 77, 176; end of term and election, 50, 177; and financing of public works, 51, 175, 181; mentioned, 36, 80

National Constituent Assembly, 153

Network, First, 56-58, 59; Second, defined, 58-59, construction of, 60-68, 183, 188, 191; debate on, 162; financing of, 59, 183, 184, 185, 190, 199-200, 212; Third, defined, 59; construction of, 63, 66, 67, 68-70; financing of, 184-85, 199-200, 212

Neuilly, Seine, 61, 168

New York, N.Y., budget of, 5; population densities in, 7; water supply, 21, 106, 107, 116; Napoleon III in, 29-30; urban reform in, 40, 212; parks, 104

Northern Railway, 196

Northern Railway Station, 65, 69. *See also* Belgian Railway Station

Nôtre-Dame, Cathedral of, 10, 87, 88, 89 n., 90

Observatory, Square of, 104

Octroi, yield from, 50; wall, 7, 166, 169, 172, 173

Odéon, quarter of, 68

Odéon Theater, 16, 102, 174

odors, 18-21, 127-30 *passim*, 145

Ollivier, Emile, 207, 211

Olmsted, Frederick Law, 4

omnibus boats, 168

Opera House, new, selection of site for, 60, 83, 84-85, 190; construction authorized, 60; construction of, 62, 84-86; plans for, 83-85; selection of architect for, 85; criticism of, 86-87, 218; buildings around, 86, 87, 91; cost of, 190; terminates vista, 217, 218; official architecture of, 82, 219; mentioned, 75, 214

Opera House, old, 60, 83

Orléanists, 6, 196, 197, 212

Ourcq Canal, 21, 22, 101, 111, 121, 136

Ourcq River, 21, 33, 114, 121

Palace of Industry, 52

Palace of Justice, 10, 16, 87, 88

Palais Royal, garden of, 8, 93; obstacle to traffic, 14; mentioned, 33, 84

Panthéon, 29, 33, 67

parking, area proposed under Central Markets, 76

Park of the Buttes-Chaumont: 97, 101, 115; of Madrid, added to Bois de Boulogne, 96; of Monceau: 11, 61, 92-93, 97, 101; of Montsouris: 102, 115

parks, in 1850, 7-8, 93-94, 104; proposal of Saint-Simonians on, 30; in Napoleon III's plans, 39; creation of new, 47, 66, 94-102, 104, 210, 211. *See also* names of individual parks

Park Service, 47

Passy, Seine, 11, 115

Patrie, La (Paris), 115

Patte, Pierre, 32

Pavillon de la Bibliothèque, 218

paving, 18, 71-72
peddlers, 164
pedestrians, 70, 71, 96
Pereire brothers, building enterprises of, 90-91; and *Crédit mobilier*, 179, 181, 199, 206
Pereire, Emile, 61
Père Lachaise, Cemetery of, 66, 145
Perrault, Claude, 32, 82
Persigny, Fialin, Count de, on motives for rebuilding Paris, 36; selection of Haussmann, 42, 43, 44-45, 180, 205; on financing of public works, 45, 54, 179-80, 181, 182; urges public works on Berger, 54
Philip Augustus, King of France, 6, 12
Picard, Ernest, 188, 190, 197, 198, 202
Place Beauveau, 208; Dauphine, 88; de Grève, 157. See also Place de l'Hôtel de Ville; de la Bastille, and new streets, 27, 29, 30, 32-33, 64, 65; barracks near, 36; mentioned, 7, 15; de Laborde, 10, 11
Place de la Concorde, and Rue de Rivoli, 14, 32, 33; construction of, 31; proposed site for Opera House on, 84; its relation to sewer system, 133, 136; terminus of tramway, 167, 168; mentioned, 15, 217
Place de l'Alma, 64, 215; de la Madeleine, 133; de la Nation, 65, 217. See also Place du Trône; de la République, 36, 64, 66, 216. See also Place du Chateau d'Eau
Place de l'Etoile, and new streets, 28, 62-63, 98; design of, 63, 92, 217; traffic in, 215; mentioned, 138
Place de l'Hôtel de Ville, 15, 56. See also Place de Grève; de l'Odéon, 16; de l'Opéra, 16, 91, 92; de l'Oratoire, 51, 52; des Malesherbes, 61; des Victoires, 14; des Vosges, 8, 31, 93; du Chateau d'Eau, 28, 64, 65, 66. See also Place de la République; du Chatelet, 56, 57, 94; du Louvre, 83, 94; Maubert, 12, 33; du Palais Royal, 168; du Panthéon, 16; du Parvis Nôtre-Dame, 88, 89, 90; Saint-Augustin, 215; Saint-Michel, 12, 16; du Trocadéro, 64; du Trône, 28, 65. See also Place de la Nation; Vendôme, 84, 217
"Plan of the Artists," 32-33
Plan of Paris, Napoleon III's, 25, 26-27,

40, 128, 183, 216; Keeper of, 47; Service of, 48
planning commission, 26
pneumatic tubes, 133
police, 171
pollution, of rivers and wells, 19, 127, 128, 140, 145
Pont au Change: 16, 27, 57; Carrousel, 11; d'Arcole, 15; d'Austerlitz, 12, 15, 105; de la Concorde, 13, 19, 29, 68; de l'Alma, 63-64, 124, 137-138; de la Tournelle, 77, 113; Neuf, 13-14, 15, 19, 88; Nôtre-Dame, 13, 22, 124; Royal, 13, 19; Saint-Michel, 16, 57, 88; Sully, 29
population, of London, 31; of France, 153; of suburbs, 169, 170
population of Paris, increase of, 5, 146, 151-54, 165, 180, 183; sources of increase of, 5, 152-65; shifts of, 6, 8, 165-67, 168-69; concentrations of, 7, 10, 12, 13, 87; structure of, 152-53
Porte Dauphine, 98; de Clignancourt, 65; de Picpus, 64; Saint-Denis, 57
Prefect of Police, 72, 141, 216
Prefecture of Police, 88
Prefecture of Department of Seine, 72. See also Seine, Prefect of Department of
Prefectorial Council, 208
President of the Republic, 176-77. See also Napoleon III
Pré Saint-Gervais, 116
"private service" water supply, 111
procurers-general, on provincial emigration, 158, 159, 163
Promenades de Paris, Les, 47
property values, increase of, 61, 175, 180, 183, 185
Provisional Government, 1848, 27, 34
public health, concern with, 23-24; Napoleon III's interest in, 31, 39-40; threat to, in suburban zone, 171
public works, for unemployment relief, 37, 38
Public Works Fund, establishment and operation of, 190-92, 194, 195, 197, 203, 205; dissolved, 206
pump-priming, 175, 179
pumping stations, for water supply, 22, 105, 124
Public Relief Administration, 87, 89-90
"public service" water supply, 11, 124, 125

Quai aux Fleurs, 90; d'Austerlitz, 124; de Conti, 28; de la Cité, 88; des Orfèvres, 88
Quais, 15, 34

race tracks, 98, 99, 100
railroads, proposed for Central Markets, 79; proposed for Méry cemetery, 146-47; effect on growth of Paris, 154-55, 160, 162, 163, 164, 166, 168-69; suburban, 168-69; construction of, 175, 177
railway stations, access to, 39, 58, 59, 60, 65, 69. *See also* names of individual stations
Rambuteau, Claude, Count de, 34
Raspail, François, 212, 213
Reed, Henry Hope, 213
regulations, building, 63, 92-93, 210
Renaissance, city planning in, 31
rents, increase of, 4, 6, 155, 165; Parisian and provincial compared, 156
Republicans, their opposition to Haussmann, 6, 188, 190, 196; and spring water, 124; in Department of War, 41
Reservoirs, 105, 113, 115, 117, 121, 123, 124
residential districts, 10, 11, 101, 168-69
revolution, fear of, 5, 37, 153-54, 176, 177, 183-84; centers of, 10, 58, 65, 67
Revolution, French (1789), 32-33
Revolution of 1848, disrupts construction work, 34, 37, 158; mentioned, 41, 175
Revue des deux mondes, 197
Revue municipale, 155
Right Bank, 9, 10, 11, 14-15
Riis, Jacob, 40
river water, in water supply, 105-10 *passim*, 115-17, 118
Rohault de Fleury, Charles, 85, 87
Rome, Italy, influence on Napoleon III, 3, 127; influence of Paris on, 4, 220; water supply of, 106, 110, 113; sewers of, 134
Rond Point des Champs Elysées, 11, 92
Rothschild, banking house of, 175, 179, 196, 205
Rothschild, Alphonse de, 196
Rouher, Eugène, and Méry cemetery project, 148; defends Haussmann, 197, 198; becomes Minister of Finance, 199; puts check on Haussmann, 199, 202, 203-05; mentioned, 188
Rue Auber, 60, 61, 216; Auguste Comte, 103; Baltard, 79; Boissy d'Anglas, 84; Bonaparte, 28; Caulaincourt, 69, 70; Claude Bernard, 36, 67; Croix des Petits-Champs, 72; d'Arcole, 90; Dauphine, 12, 15; de Castiglione, 33; de la Chaussée d'Antin, 10; de la Cité, 90; de la Harpe, 16; de la Musée, 11; de la Paix, 10, 14, 33; de la Pépinière, 135; de Lyon, 34; de Médicis, 68; de Rennes, proposed, 26, 28, 39; authorization and construction of, 52, 68, 178; mentioned, 67; de Richelieu, 10
Rue de Rivoli, plans for, 14, 26, 27, 30, 32-33; construction begun by Napoleon I, 33; Provisional Government (1848) and, 34; as a military street, 36; Napoleon III presses for construction of, 49, 50, 75, 76; construction of, 51, 52-53, 56-57, 178, 183; financing of, 51, 53, 54, 153, 181; and new Louvre, 52, 80, 81, 218; private building on, 56, 91, 92; traffic on, 71, 215; proposal for lighting of, 72, 74; demolitions for displace population, 165; mentioned, 58, 72, 136
Rue de Rohan, 27, 80; de Rome, 61; Descartes, 67; de Seine, 16; des Ecoles, plans for, 28; authorization and construction of, 50-51, 52, 75, 178; mentioned, 58, 67; des Petits-Champs, 14; des Pyrenées, 69; de Tournon, 15-16; de Turbigo, 28, 36, 64; de Vaugirard, 16, 68; du Faubourg du Temple, 66; du Faubourg Poissonnière, 69; du Havre, 216; de Louvre, 210; de Pont Neuf, 28, 56, 188; du Temple, 15; Gay-Lussac, 36, 67, 194; Gluck, 60; Halévy, 60; Lafayette, 34, 91, 188, 193; Le Peletier, 60, 83; Meyerbeer, 60; Monge, 36, 67; Montmartre, 9, 16; Mouffetard, 36, 67; Neuve de Chabrol, 39; Rambuteau, 14; Royale, 6-7, 72, 84, 135, 211; Saint-Antoine, 27, 57; Saint-Denis, 9, 10, 15, 16, 57, 76; Saint-Dominique, 68; Saint-Honoré, 10, 14, 16, 84; Saint-Jacques, 12, 138; Saint-Lazare, 60, 216; Saint-Martin, 15;

Scribe, 60; Soufflot, 33, 57, 67, 68; Transnonain, 65

Sacré-Coeur, Church of, 3, 210
Saint-Arnaud, LeRoy de, 69
Saint-Augustin, Church of, 62, 79-80, 135
Saint Bartholomew's Massacre, 82-83
Saint-Cloud, 94, 121, 168, 189
Saint-Germain des Prés, Church of, 28, 39, 68
Saint-Germain l'Auxerrois, Church of, 82-83
Saint-Honoré quarter, 165
Saint-Jacques la Boucherie, hillock of, 53, 56
Saint-Julien le Pauvre, Church of, 89
Saint-Lazare Railway Station, area around, 10, 11; access to, 60, 216; traffic on access streets, 215
Saint-Paul, Church of, 56-57
Saint-Simon, Claude Henri, Count de, 175
Saint-Simonians, plans for Paris, 30; urge expenditures on public works, 37, 175, 179, 180, 198
Sainte-Chapelle, 58
Sainte-Eustache, Church of, 9, 14
Sainte-Eustache, Pointe, 16
Sainte-Geneviève, hill of, 15, 16, 33, 36, 52, 67
sanitary engineering, 128
sanitary sewage, disposal of, 19, 20-21, 130-31, 136, 143-45, 210
Say, Léon, attacks on Haussmann, 196-97, 212, 213
schools, new buildings, 75; attraction of, 165
Seine, Department of, Council of, 43; hearings on Méry cemetery in, 147; attraction of rural population, 153, 158; population of, 156, 166; Commission of, 171, 186
Seine, Prefect of Department of, office and duties of, 40, 42, 43; appointment of, 43, 207, 208; in charge of street lighting, 72; in charge of sewer cleaning, 141, 142; said to be out of control, 189, 197; mentioned, 170, 176, 180
Seine-et-Marne, Department of, migrations from, 162-63, 164; Prefect of, 163
Seine-et-Oise, Department of, hearings

on Méry cemetery in, 147; population of, 166
Seine River, use as a sewer, 19, 127-130 passim, 133-38 passim, 148; as source of water supply, 21, 22, 23, 96, 105-11 passim, 116, 117, 125; low water in, 112, 113, 121, 139; pollution of, 127, 128, 140, 145; suburbs bordering, 168, 169; boat service on, 168; mentioned, 12, 15-16, 39, 167
Seine River Basin, study of springs in, 112
Senate, Haussmann appointed to, 43; and opposition to Haussmann, 68, 69-70, 103, 147; approves annexation of suburbs, 172; Paris-Crédit foncier agreement before, 205; reform of, 207
Sens, Yonne, 123
sewage disposal, description of, 19-21, 127; British methods, 109, 143; mentioned, 101. See also Sanitary sewage
sewers, before Haussmann's time, 9, 19-21, 127, 128, 129; cleaning of, 20, 129, 130, 141-43; Haussmann's work on, 44, 127-45 passim, 148, 150, 221; Belgrand's work on, 46, 127, 131, 134-35, 137-39, 141-43, 145; construction of, 127, 128, 131-32, 134-39; design of, 129, 130, 132-36 passim, 139; private, 132, 144-45; costs of, 132, 184; after Haussmann's time, 210. See also Collector sewers
Shaftesbury, Anthony Ashley Cooper, Earl of, 40
sidewalks, lack of, 9, 18; construction of, 70
Siege of Paris, 1870-1871, 140, 151, 209
Simon, Jules, 212
Siphon, of Collector of the Bièvre, 138-39, 142
slum clearance, Saint Simonians' proposals on, 30; Napoleon III's and Haussmann's concern with, 33, 35, 39, 40, 219, 221; in particular areas, 57, 58 59, 65, 67, 88; mentioned, 126
slums, location of, 7, 9, 10-11, 12, 16, 80, 88; development of new, 93, 166, 171, 219; Napoleon III and Haussmann blamed for creation of, 8; need for clearing, 24. See also Slum clearance
Somme River, springs of as a source of water supply, 109, 110, 113-15 passim, 122

Somme-Soude water supply project, 110-20 *passim*, 211

Soude River, springs of as a source of water supply, 109, 110, 113-15 *passim*, 122

Sorbonne, Chapel of, 58

Sourdon River, 113, 114

spring water, in water supply, 106-16 *passim*, 120-22 *passim*, 124; dispute over merits of, 106-07, 109, 115-16, 118, 124

Strasbourg Railway Station, access to, 27, 39, 52, 215; design of, 77. *See also* Eastern Railway Station

street construction, mileage completed 70. *See also* names of individual streets, avenues, and boulevards

subsidies, for Central Markets, 51, 76, 176, 183; for Rue de Rivoli, 51, 53, 176, 183; for Boulevard de Strasbourg, 52; for Second Network, 59, 183, 186, 190; Haussmann's use of, 181, 184; mentioned, 5

suburbs, growth of, 165-71 *passim*. *See also* Annexation of suburbs

Surmelin River, springs as a source of water supply, 119, 120, 122, 123

surplus, budgetary, for financing public works, 181, 183, 186

synagogues, new buildings, 75

Tale of Two Cities, A, 6

taste, artistic, of Second Empire, 82, 87, 218-19; Haussmann's, 217-19

tax exemptions, to stimulate building, 51, 92, 176

taxes, municipal, to finance public works, 5, 45, 51, 176, 180, 182, 183; extended to suburbs, 172; reduction of, 200

telegraph, wires in sewer galleries, 133

telephone, wires in sewer galleries, 133

Temps, Le (Paris), 174

tenements, 9, 93

Thiers, Louis Adolphe, built anti-rot streets, 36; attack on Haussmann, 202-03, 204, 205

Third Republic, continuation of rebuilding of Paris, 29, 60, 124; spared street fighting, 214

toll bridges, 13, 49

traffic, obstacles to, 14-16, 58, 66; Napoleon III's and Haussmann's concern with, 30-31, 35, 39, 40, 214; Patte's proposals on, 32; relief of, 62, 65, 67, 214-16; increase of, 65, 213

tramway, 167, 168

transportation, public services, 17-18, 167-68

Travaux souterrains de Paris, Les, 46

trees, on streets, 8, 70

triangulation, 5, 56

Tribunal de Commerce, 58, 88, 218

Trollope, Mrs. Frances, 128

Tuileries, Garden of, 8, 15, 84, 93, 103

Tuileries, Palace of, slum adjoining, 10-11; clearing of adjoining slum, 52, 80, 180; junction with Louvre, 52, 80-82; mentioned, 118

Tunnard, Christopher, 213

unemployment, in Paris, 37, 175, 209; in Haute-Saône, 162

United States of America, influence of Napoleon III and Haussmann in, 4, 220; tramway in, 167

values, property, increase of, 61, 175, 180, 183, 185

Vanne Aqueduct, plans and construction of, 122, 124

Vanne River valley, source of water supply for Paris, 46, 112, 114, 122

Vanne water supply project, 119, 122-25

Vaugirard, Seine, 166

Versailles, Seine-et-Oise, planned city, 4-5, 31; growth of, 168, 169; mentioned, 108

Villette, La Seine, sewage disposal in, 20, 143; livestock market, 79, 219; opposes annexation to Paris, 171-72; mentioned, 101

Vincennes, Seine, access to, 27, 167. *See also* Bois de Vincennes

Viollet-le-Duc, Eugène Emmanuel, 88, 89n.

Visconti, Ludovico, architect of new Louvre, 80, 81, 82

visitors, to Exposition of 1867, 84, 143; to collector sewers, 143, 210-11

Voltaire, on rebuilding Paris, 31-32, 40

wages, Parisian and provincial compared, 154, 155-56, 160, 162, 163

Walewski, Count Alexandre, 85

walls, fortified walls, 6-7, 169-70, 172-

73; *octroi* wall, 7, 59, 61, 64, 169, 172. *See also* Fortifications

Washington, D.C., influence of Paris on, 4, 220; government of, 43

Water Service, 46, 112, 114, 117, 131

water supply, before Haussmann's time, 13, 21-23, 32, 33, 105; distribution of, 21-23, 111-15 *passim*, 126; Napoleon I's work on, 33; Haussmann's work on, 44, 46, 105-26 *passim*, 221; Belgrand's work on, 46, 107-16 *passim*, 119-22 *passim*; contamination of, 105, 107, 145; private companies' projects for, 105, 106, 125; Napoleon III's interest in, 106, 118-19, 123; costs of, 107, 110-11, 114, 117, 121, 123, 124, 184; opposition to Haussmann's projects, 115-23 *passim*; sewage problem, 130-31; after Haussmann's time, 210. *See also* Dhuis-Surmelin water supply project; Somme-Soude water supply project; Vanne water supply project

water table, under Paris, 134-35

wells, source of water supply, 22, 111, 122; pollution of, 145

Western Railway Station, access to, 60, 216. *See also* Saint-Lazare Station

wine retailers, establishment in Paris, 164

working class districts, location of, 9-10, 12-13

Wren, Christopher, 39

Yonne, Department of, Haussmann Prefect of, 41-42, 43, 46, 107; protests on Vanne aqueduct, 123

Yonne River, 112, 124

Other Titles of Interest
Also Available in Princeton
and Princeton/Bollingen Paperbacks

THE AGE OF THE DEMOCRATIC REVOLUTION, Vol. I: *The Challenge*, by R. R. Palmer (#171), $2.95

THE AGE OF THE DEMOCRATIC REVOLUTION, Vol. II: *The Struggle*, by R. R. Palmer (#192), $2.95

ART AND ILLUSION: *A Study in the Psychology of Pictorial Representation*, by E. H. Gombrich (P/B #156), $5.95

ART FORMS AND CIVIC LIFE IN THE LATE ROMAN EMPIRE, by H. P. L'ORANGE (#269), $3.45

THE BOURGEOISIE IN 18TH CENTURY FRANCE, by Elinor G. Barber (#98), $2.45

CATHOLICS AND UNBELIEVERS IN EIGHTEENTH CENTURY FRANCE, by R. R. Palmer (#35), $2.95

THE COMING OF THE FRENCH REVOLUTION, by Georges Lefebvre, translated by R. R. Palmer (#100), $1.45

THE DOME: *A Study in the History of Ideas*, by E. Baldwin Smith (#245), $4.95

OPPOSITION TO LOUIS XIV, by Lionel Rothkrug (#175), $3.45

THE PALACES OF CRETE, by James Walter Graham (#154), $5.95

TOCQUEVILLE AND THE OLD REGIME, by Richard Herr (#37), $1.95

TOWN PLANNING IN FRONTIER AMERICA, by John W. Reps (#210), $3.95

TRANSFORMATIONS IN LATE EIGHTEENTH CENTURY ART, by Robert Rosenblum (#206), $3.95

TWELVE WHO RULED: *The Year of the Terror in the French Revolution*, by R. R. Palmer (#211), $2.95

Order from your bookstore, or from
Princeton University Press, Princeton, New Jersey 08540

DATE DUE